THE WAR ON HISTORY

THE WAR
ON HISTORY

The Conspiracy to Rewrite America's Past

JARRETT STEPMAN

REGNERY GATEWAY

Regnery Gateway® is a trademark of Salem Communications
Holding Corporation
Regnery® is a registered trademark of Salem Communications
Holding Corporation

Cataloging-in-Publication data on file with the Library of Congress

ISBN 978-1-62157-809-3
ebook ISBN 978-1-62157-907-6

Published in the United States by
Regnery Gateway
an imprint of Regnery Publishing
A Division of Salem Media Group
300 New Jersey Ave NW
Washington, DC 20001
www.RegneryGateway.com

Manufactured in the United States of America

10 9 8 7 6 5 4 3 2 1

Books are available in quantity for promotional or premium use.
For information on discounts and terms, please visit our website:
www.Regnery.com.

To my family, and especially my wife, Inez.

Contents

Introduction

An informed patriotism is what we want. And are we doing a good enough job teaching our children what America is and what she represents in the long history of the world?... If we forget what we did, we won't know who we are. I'm warning of an eradication of the American memory that could result, ultimately, in an erosion of the American spirit.

—*Ronald Reagan*[1]

America is once again at a crossroads. Though this superpower of almost unimaginable wealth is unlikely to be brought low by a disaster, there is an uneasiness about our future that is difficult to explain. An all-important question has opened up a great chasm between Americans: Is the essence of our civilization—our culture, our mores, our history—fundamentally good and worth preserving, or is it rotten at its root?

No policy debate or international crisis quite measures up to this underlying dilemma. As the young Abraham Lincoln asserted in his famed Lyceum Address, no "trans-Atlantic military giant" can crush us at a blow. "At what point then is the approach of danger to be expected?" he asked. "I answer, if it ever reach us, it must spring up amongst us. It cannot come from abroad. If destruction be our lot, we must ourselves be its author and finisher. As a nation of freemen, we must live through all time, or die by suicide."[2]

The gravest threat to the United States in the twenty-first century is not unsustainable debt, inequality, dysfunctional government, foreign enemies, or even radical Islamists. Lincoln's insight that no great power or collection of powers could defeat us is true today, and his warning that our destruction will be our own work is just as urgent as when he uttered it.

When President Barack Obama said that he aimed to "fundamentally transform America," he appealed to a large and growing number of people who believed that there was something deeply wrong with this country that needed transformation.[3] To them, Obama became a kind of prophet who would somehow usher in a new order and wash away all the things they disliked about their country.

The inevitable "march of history," whereby mankind continually improves until some utopia is reached, is an idea with a pedigree reaching back to philosophers like Hegel and Marx. According to this outlook, history does not only advance toward justice. In its relentless drive to perfection, it tramples even the thorny problems and complications of human nature itself.

Obama's supporters hoped that his election as president was a sign that we were well on our way to a society in which America's past—and the people who represent it—were blissfully washed away, clearing the way for a new future. The Americans whom Obama once derided as "clinging" to their religion and their guns[4] were sure to disappear, taking their traditional values with them. We had reached Year Zero of a brave new world, one removed from the nation's old sins.

This narrative suffered a serious blow in the presidential election of 2016 when a "basket of deplorables," as Hillary Clinton labeled them, elected Donald Trump.[5] Suddenly, it appeared that Americans were not yet willing to give up old notions and traditions despite the Left's decade-long effort to erase what they see as the oppressive story of American history. But the shocking 2016 election results only inspired progressives, enraged by their sense of political impotence, to accelerate the movement to obliterate the symbols of our past.

They turned their fury on the source of all their frustrations: the pillars of American identity. They started with the low-hanging fruit of Confederate statues but quickly moved on to more central figures of our nation's past.

A protest by white nationalists and other radical groups at the feet of a statue of Robert E. Lee in Charlottesville, Virginia, sparked a national debate over such monuments. Though the racist extremists in Charlottesville represent a tiny minority of Americans, they provided the leverage progressives needed to take their war on history to a national level, tarring anyone who wishes to preserve it as a moral monster.

President Trump expressed his worries about where the iconoclast movement was headed: "I wonder is it George Washington next week and is it Thomas Jefferson the week after? You know, you really do have to ask yourself, where does it stop?"

The answer is that it doesn't stop. Shortly after Charlottesville, a small but relentless minority of activists went on the march seeking century-old monuments to destroy through legal or illegal means. They called into question memorials of Jefferson, Washington, Andrew Jackson, and Christopher Columbus, among others. Yes, the left-wing activists targeted the author of the Declaration of Independence and even Lewis and Clark. The mayor of Charlottesville called for the removal of a monument depicting the famed explorers of the

West that had been deemed sexist because their Indian guide, Sacagawea, is portrayed crouching.[6] She later called to end the celebration of hometown hero Thomas Jefferson's birthday, wanting to replace it with "Liberation and Freedom Day" despite the fact that Jefferson was the author of the Declaration of Independence, the greatest pro-freedom document in the English language.[7]

It was clear: it wasn't the Confederacy the activists were coming after—it was America. It was everything this country was built on and the people who made it. The attacks became systematic and widespread. If progressives couldn't get local city councils or the proper authorities to take down whatever the Left deemed offensive, the more radical of the activists would gather a mob and smash statues as authorities looked on or show up in the dead of night to vandalize them with red paint or sledgehammers.

This moment should give us pause. Far too few of us lucky inhabitants of the freest, most prosperous country in world history ever bother to ask how we got here and why the United States has succeeded so spectacularly. Far too many of us stand by or even cheer while radicals dismantle the pillars of our nation's greatness on the theory that they are symbols of the oppression, racism, and prejudice that make America an irreparably flawed place.

The war on history did not come out of nowhere. It is not a mere spasm of resentment by a handful of "triggered" snowflakes. In an earlier time, Americans were inoculated by their education against the defamation of their nation. But today, a growing hard-left ideological bloc is preying on a new generation's ignorance to detach them from American ideas, history, and cultural norms.

We were given fair warning of this moment by President Ronald Reagan in his farewell address. The 1980s' resurgence in national pride and prosperity would not be sustainable unless the nation nurtured a deep and genuine patriotism. Reagan feared that a generation of Americans were raising their children to be ambivalent about their country and that popular culture was not interested in filling the gap. "If we forget what we did, we won't know who we are. I'm warning of an eradication of the American memory that could result, ultimately, in an erosion of the American spirit," he said.

Reagan's words went largely unheeded, and what he warned about is coming to pass. The failure of our schools and the indoctrination in our universities has left the Millennial generation, for all its technical savvy, with little appreciation of America's past, which it dismisses as benighted and contemptible.

There is a spreading belief that the men who built this country were oppressive and their values irredeemable. The purveyors of this view argue that we must transcend the ugly ideas, principles, and even people of the past to perfect our society. We must transform America by wiping out what previous generations celebrated as exceptional but we know to be damnable. This is not a matter of honestly recognizing our ancestors' shortcomings (while humbly acknowledging that our own descendants will recognize ours). These militant and self-righteous activists have instilled in their fellow citizens a fear of being labeled bigots and have cowed the silent majority into inaction.

One by one, the great men once universally revered by Americans are becoming reviled or forgotten. Casting aside our heroes is dangerous enough, but we also risk losing something even more essential. The activists' target is not only historical figures but the ideas and values that define America.

Christopher Columbus, for instance, was once a celebrated and uniting figure. The discoverer of the New World represented the spirit of exploration and adventure that is in our national DNA. That is the case no longer. Left-wing historians like Howard Zinn have tied Columbus to the original sins of a wicked American civilization.

Activists are trying to pull down his statues and abolish Columbus Day. This giant of history deserves better. But the anti-Columbus crusade is about more than Columbus the man. It is about undermining what he represents: the world-changing transatlantic migration that brought Western civilization to the Americas and led to the establishment of the United States.

It's not hyperbole to say that the American Revolution was the defining moment not only in American history but in modern world history. Yet it and everything it stands for are under attack. Thomas Jefferson has been singled out as the representative of slavery's evil and the "hypocrisy" that sullied the Founding. Jefferson was a flawed man. But America celebrates him for his role in the founding of the freest nation on Earth, not for his moral failings. There have been many slave owners in world history, but there is only one man who penned the Declaration of Independence. If we Americans abandon that legacy, we abandon our country's soul. This, in some way, is what Jefferson's detractors want.

Columbus and Jefferson are only two of the many men who have been weighed in the progressives' balance and found wanting. Their ranks are growing daily. Many of America's old heroes were far from angels, but if that is the standard, then the pedestals in this country (and every other country) will be empty. The destruction of history will go on until a critical mass of Americans, ones like Reagan, are able to articulate why the pillars of our nation are worth holding up. More of us must be willing to say "Enough!" But to defend our past, we will have to relearn what was once universally known but is now forgotten and neglected.

If the foundational principles of our country are to be put on trial, they at least need a fair representation in the court of public opinion. Human history is brutal and full of tyranny. We lucky few who have been privileged to be born Americans have a great legacy to uphold.

If we wish to pass this legacy to future generations, we must be able to defend the men and ideals that got us here. Fewer and fewer are willing to defend what built this country. Those who want to erase our history will not stop with century-old statues. They want to expunge not only Confederates or Christopher Columbus but the essence of American civilization.

Our history, culture, and institutions have been under assault for generations, and the American elite have failed to defend them. In fact, the elite—the masters of Hollywood, the mainstream media, and our education system—are leading the charge. The number of Americans who still resist speaks to the remarkable appeal of what the United States stands for. But the old values won't last if we stand by as the symbols that represent the best of ourselves are demolished and the great, though imperfect, men and women of our history are systematically erased from our national memory.

Our civilization is at stake. If we recover our history and the traits that have allowed us to succeed so spectacularly in the past, we will rise to the challenges of the twenty-first century as we have in centuries before. If we fail and the country accepts the narrative that America was rotten to the core from the beginning, we will be lost even if we overcome our external foes and rivals.

Those who still care about the principles and historical memory of our nation need to be armed with information so we can teach others about what made America special from the start. We have ignored the invaluable lessons of our parents, grandparents, and great-grandparents. We have dismissed and denigrated the vision that gave us this land of plenty.

The ideas and "mystic chords of memory" that bind the generations are being severed. How do we restore them? As the great historian Arnold Toynbee once said, "Civilizations die by suicide, not murder." This is the profoundest challenge we face, the one that will ultimately decide if we are to remain an exceptional nation or not. If we wish to honor previous generations and do justice to ourselves and our posterity, we must once again try to understand and defend the world-shaking ideas, actions, and men who made America great.

CHAPTER 1

The War on America

Christopher Columbus.... is justly admired as a brilliant navigator, a fearless man of action, a visionary who opened the eyes of an older world to an entirely new one. Above all, he personifies a view of the world that many see as quintessentially American: not merely optimistic, but scornful of the very notion of despair.

—Ronald Reagan, Columbus Day, 1981[1]

A well-crafted bronze statue of Christopher Columbus, hand on the helm, sword at his waist, looks out over Columbus Square in Queens, New York. The statue, next to the Astoria Boulevard subway station, was created by Italian sculptor Angelo Racioppi, funded in part by a local Italian heritage organization interested in preserving the Italian-born Columbus' legacy, and put in place in 1941. It depicts Columbus as a dashing figure with a defiant look in his eyes and a daring zeal in his posture. Curiously, a plaque on the monument says it was dedicated in 1937. It turns out the statue had been hidden in a basement for a few years in the dark days of the World War II scrap metal shortage and during some local political squabbling.[2] But the city unveiled it on Columbus Day, 1941, at an event that was attended by over five thousand people, including New York Mayor Fiorello H. LaGuardia, who shared Columbus's Italian heritage.[3]

Though the Depression-era Italian-American community in New York City was poor, they nevertheless thought it appropriate to sacrifice for the legacy of Columbus, whom they considered a great man. The marker with the misleading "1937" date lays out what this community and so many other Americans believed for centuries: "But for Columbus, there would be no America."

Past Americans found a way to expand their heroic pantheon, to include more heroes instead of tearing down others. This, in fact, is why many Columbus statues were erected in the first place. In the first half of the twentieth century, American citizens were eager to celebrate a man who not only undeniably contributed to the eventual creation of our country but also was a particular source of pride for assimilating Italian-Americans, who had been on the receiving end of discrimination for a generation. Erecting new statues of Christopher Columbus did not necessitate bulldozing statues of, for instance, Samuel B. Morse, whose image still stands in Central Park. Like Columbus, the famed inventor of the telegraph changed the world. Unfortunately, he also wrote angry, nativist screeds against Catholic immigrants. Nobody called for his statue to be removed and replaced with the one of Columbus. America had room for many heroes. It was a more tolerant age.

Much has changed in just over half a century. The city of San Jose, California, recently decided that any public display of pride in Christopher Columbus is simply unacceptable. Egged on by the San Jose Brown Berets, a radical Chicano ethno-nationalist group, the San

Jose City Council voted in early 2018 to remove Columbus's statue from city hall. The statue had been placed there by an Italian heritage organization in 1958. According to a local news report, the statue was set to come down because "activists repeatedly denounced the explorer, whose conquests in the Caribbean led to the deaths of hundreds of thousands of indigenous people, and declared him not statue-worthy."[4]

Like New York in the 1930s, San Jose in 2018 had a mayor of Italian heritage, but this one wasn't keen on the most famous Italian in world history. San Jose Mayor Sam Liccardo, who said that he believed his own grandfather had contributed to the construction of the statue, meekly condoned the decision, saying, "Columbus never landed in the Alviso Marina. So there is no policy basis for keeping a statue of somebody who was not from San Jose in City Hall." Perhaps the state of Washington should abandon its name because George Washington never set foot there. It is particularly sad that a city with a Spanish name, a direct product of the Spanish colonization of the New World, finds its own origins worthy of destruction.

At the time of the city council's decision, not a single local museum would take the statue.[5] To add to the absurdity, a statue to the Aztec god Quetzalcoatl stands nearby in downtown San Jose. The snake-shaped statue, which locals have long complained about as an eyesore, was allegedly placed there for the sake of "cultural balance."[6] Even if one believes that Columbus was a brutal, genocidal monster, there is a bizarre double standard at work in taking down his statue for that reason while keeping a tribute to the religion of the Aztecs, who subjugated local tribes in Central America and used their members as human sacrifices hundreds of years before Columbus and the Spanish arrived in the Americas.

San Jose is just one of many cities that have done their best to erase Columbus and any recognition of his exploits and contributions to our civilization. Even New York, the city that once worked so hard to hand out tributes to Columbus, is now getting rid of its accolades for the explorer.

"Don't honor genocide, take it down." These were the words scrawled across the stone base of the Queens Columbus monument in 2017. What was once a symbol of a community's love and pride had, little more than a half-century later, been marked as a symbol of hate by another mayor of Italian heritage and targeted for unlawful vandalism. The Queens monument was one of numerous Columbus statues defaced and vandalized in the region after New York Mayor Bill de Blasio created a commission to review all "symbols of hate" in the city, including the famed fourteen-foot Columbus statue atop the seventy-six-foot column in his namesake Columbus Circle.[7] The monument's size and public prominence and an around-the-clock armed guard likely saved it serious attacks in 2017, though one vandal was able to splash nail polish on the hands of a Columbus figure at the monument's base.[8] Lesser-known statues weren't so lucky. Numerous other tributes to Columbus around the city have been defaced, and all are facing harsh public criticism.

A two-foot-tall Columbus sculpture in Columbus Memorial Park in Yonkers was beheaded and smashed with a blunt instrument and its shattered remains strewn about the area.[9] A more-than-century-old statue in Central Park was covered in paint. The vandals wrote, "Hate will not be tolerated" and "#Something's coming" and covered the statue's hands with red paint. These incidents were not limited to New York.

Two statues in Connecticut were splashed with red paint on the same night, just before Columbus Day.[10] The oldest Columbus monument in the country and perhaps the world—constructed over two centuries ago—was bludgeoned and damaged at a park in Baltimore, Maryland.[11] The brazen vandals even proudly posted a video of the incident on YouTube.

"Christopher Columbus symbolizes the initial invasion of European capitalism into the Western Hemisphere," said the film's narrator. "Columbus initiated a centuries-old wave of terrorism, murder, genocide, rape, slavery, ecological degradation, and capitalist exploitation of labor in the Americas. That Columbian wave of destruction continues on the backs of Indigenous, African-Americans, and Brown people."[12]

Besides the protest of a few concerned citizens and Italian heritage groups upset with the obliteration of history, there has been little public defense of the explorer, nor widespread calls to restore his reputation. Native American advocacy organizations and left-wing activists, armed with the works of revisionist historians, have been more or less successful in selling their view of Columbus as a genocidal monster to the American public. The narrative that Columbus was an evil monster, worthy only of scorn, has become a mundane truth to many Americans.

It's a stunning fall from grace for a great American hero. Columbus's remarkable westward journey from Europe to the New World is being consigned to the dustbin of history. This all happened within a generation. But why?

Replacing Columbus Day

The first serious modern challenge to the Columbus legacy began in 1970s with the calls to end the observance of Columbus Day, officially established as a national holiday by Congress and President Franklin Roosevelt in 1937, or to replace it with "Indigenous Peoples' Day." The push began in Berkeley, California, a city well known for its radical politics, in the run-up to the five hundredth anniversary of Columbus's voyage. The Christopher Columbus Quincentenary Jubilee Commission was planning for replicas of Columbus-era ships to sail into San Francisco Bay,[13] but local activists and Bay Area leaders flew into a rage and worked to eradicate the Columbus holiday before the ships were set to show up in port. Berkeley Mayor Loni Hancock called celebrations of Columbus "Eurocentric" and claimed that they ignored the "brutal realities of the colonization of indigenous peoples."[14] The ships never arrived, and the Berkeley City Council replaced Columbus Day in 1992. Since then, Berkeley has been joined by Los Angeles, Seattle, Minneapolis, and numerous other cities across the country in avoiding Columbus Day celebrations or commemorations.[15]

At first, the movement to wipe out Columbus seemed to be limited only to small, radically liberal urban enclaves, but it has grown in scope, and, like so many progressive efforts, it was injected with a new vigor after the election of President Donald Trump. Big cities and a number of smaller localities have successfully purged Columbus by official means, but the pace of the war on Columbus has been too slow for some. As we have seen, public declarations against Columbus statues have encouraged radical groups and individuals to take to vandalism in New York and elsewhere.

Still, there have been "54 counties, districts, cities, incorporated towns, boroughs, villages and census designated places" named after Columbus in the United States alone.[16] This list, of course, includes the District of Columbia, the US capital city. While it might seem reasonable to most Americans to celebrate *both* Columbus *and* American Indians, this compromise is entirely unacceptable to the anti-Columbus crusaders. Chrissie Castro, for instance, vice chairwoman of the Los Angeles City-County Native American Indian Commission, said, after her city decided to replace Columbus Day with Indigenous Peoples' Day, that simply celebrating two separate holidays wasn't good enough. It was more important to "dismantle a state-sponsored celebration of genocide of indigenous peoples," and having an Indigenous Peoples' celebration on any other day would be a "further injustice."[17]

What is never explained is why so-called indigenous peoples are worthy of celebration if Columbus is not. Pre-Columbian civilizations from Mexico to Peru were nearly all responsible for brutal violence on a large scale long before Columbus arrived on the shores of the New World—including human sacrifices, even of children, sometimes by tearing out the victim's still-beating heart.[18]

Why is Columbus beyond the pale when the indigenous people who committed such atrocities on a wide scale are worthy of celebration? What crimes did Columbus commit that are so heinous that they justify toppling his statues from our monuments and his heroism from our history?

While there were Columbus detractors almost from the moment he set foot in the Americas, until recently, the misdeeds he was accused of tended to be seen in the broader context of his times. While the Discoverer of America had flaws and while the discovery of America undoubtedly brought terrible suffering to indigenous peoples, Columbus was still a great man, worthy of praise for his enterprise and courage and for his unique role in the spread of Western civilization to the Western hemisphere.

To comprehend the complete reputational reversal, it is important to understand the esteem he once had, not just in the United States, but throughout the Americas. In an earlier time, the life and achievements of Columbus were discussed in almost every classroom, his exploits celebrated all over the world. From the Founding generation onward, Americans paid special tribute to Columbus as the *original* American: a symbol of the transition from Old World to New World. The United States, in its infancy, was searching for heroes distinct from those of Great Britain and Europe. They rediscovered

Columbus and paid homage to the fact that his discoveries made possible the bold new nation that bloomed in 1776.

A Hero for the New World

In 1787, American writer and poet Joel Barlow wrote patriotic verse about Columbus to celebrate his new country's connection to the famed explorer. Barlow eventually expanded his *Vision of Columbus* into the epic—and many say turgid—book of poems titled *The Columbiad*. In the intervening years, Barlow's verse has been written off by literary critics, but in his day, these patriotic poems sold fantastically well and were more or less well received by the American public.

A more impressive accolade than Barlow's was written by Phillis Wheatley, a fourteen-year-old black poet and former slave. In 1775, in a poem addressed to George Washington, she referred to "Columbia's scenes of glorious toils" and Columbia's triumph over the British.

Washington loved the ode and made it public, bringing her work instant fame. The "Columbia" of Wheatley's poem was an allegorical figure representing the United States, guiding Washington and the revolutionary patriots to victory over the British.[19] The subject and Washington's enjoyment of Wheatley's poem created an explosion of interest in Columbus. "Soon Columbia and Columbus were appearing in songs, poems, and essays in newspapers around the colonies...." Edward Burmila, a professor at Bradley University explains. "Columbus went from a minor figure in the history of European exploration to an American hero almost overnight."[20] In Columbus, Americans had found a man who could represent a new nation whose people were trying to draw sharp distinctions between America and the Old World—Europe, and especially Great Britain.

Barlow, Wheatley, and countless others contributed to the widespread embrace of Columbus, but no one did more to cement the

Italian explorer's place in the American hall of heroes than Washington Irving, one of the great American writers in the early days of the Republic. When he traveled to Spain in 1826, Irving was given a chance to translate the newly published journals of Columbus into English.[21] The journals were somewhat technical, but Irving was convinced by a friend that he should write a popular book about the explorer.[22] The result ended up being one of the proudest achievements of Irving's illustrious career.[23] He believed he had faithfully presented a thoroughly American hero to the world in a light never seen before. *The Life and Voyages of Christopher Columbus* deservedly became the definitive account of Columbus for generations.

The Return of Old Prejudice

While most nineteenth-century Americans had warm feelings toward Columbus, he had his critics even then. Criticism of the Discoverer of America sprang primarily from two sources: left-wing ideological movements and ethno-nationalist anti-Italian sentiment. Some of the most savage attacks on Columbus came from Friedrich Engels and Karl Marx, the founders of Communism, whose broadsides against the Italian explorer would be echoed by Marxist historian Howard Zinn a century later.[24] Lamenting Columbus's discovery of America as the birth of capitalism, Engels identified Columbus's colonization of the New World as the point at which "big commerce originated, and the so-called world market was opened." As Engels wrote, "The enormous treasures which the Europeans brought from America, and the gains which trade in general yielded, had as a consequence the ruin of the old aristocracy, and so the bourgeoisie came into being. The discovery of America was connected with the advent of machinery, and with that the struggle became necessary which we are conducting today, the struggle of the propertyless against the

property owners."²⁵ To these Communist thinkers, greed and exploitation were the reasons Columbus and others came to the New
World. Their interpretation was highly reductionist and materialistic.
As we shall see, Columbus made his voyage for a complex web of
reasons. But echoes of these early Communist critiques continue to
resonate today.

Marxist doctrine had little influence in the late nineteenth-century United States. Anti-Italian and anti-Catholic sentiment, on the
other hand, had a great deal.

It is an ironic twist of history that the modern denouncers of
Columbus, who have tried to wrap the white supremacist label
around his defenders, have adopted the language and tactics of white
supremacists who attacked the explorer in earlier times. The Ku Klux
Klan, better known today for being anti-black, was, in the late nineteenth century, just as, if not even more militantly, opposed to Catholics and Italians. Members of the Klan turned their anger on Columbus and statues of him as an Italian "immigrant" whose powerful
influence on American history they wished to deny or bury. The Klan
worked to end Columbus Day celebrations and turn the country
against his legacy in favor of Anglo-Saxon heroes. In the 1920s, a
high watermark for Klan power, they "attempted to remove Columbus Day as a state holiday in Oregon," burned a cross "to disturb a
Columbus Day celebration in Pennsylvania," and successfully
"opposed the erection of a statue of Columbus in Richmond, Virginia, only to see the decision to reject the statue reversed."²⁶

KKK-friendly organizations and publications attempted to generate resistance to state celebrations of Columbus Day—and were
adamant that it should not be celebrated as a national holiday. One
fervently anti-Catholic paper labeled the effort to institute Columbus
Day a "program of propaganda" by the Knights of Columbus—the
Catholic fraternal organization. "In their program of propaganda,

the Knights of Columbus have been stressing Columbus and his alleged discovery of America, and the debt America owes the Catholic Church.... It is time to crush such stuff, sit down on it, smack it to sleep and otherwise put the mark of public discredit upon it."[27]

The anti-Columbus efforts ultimately failed in the face of the widespread American view of the man as a unifying national hero, a symbol of American boldness and, importantly, assimilation. The pivotal year in this debate was 1892, the four hundredth anniversary of Columbus's voyage. Anti-Italian and anti-Catholic prejudices ran deep, but these feelings were outweighed by the widespread willingness to commemorate a true American hero. President Benjamin Harrison proclaimed a day of celebration for Columbus, whom he called a "pioneer of progress and enlightenment," to "express honor to the discoverer and their appreciation of the great achievements of the four completed centuries of American life."[28] There was an explosion of celebrations of Columbus across the nation, and the bitter anti-Columbus groups were simply drowned out by the wave of enthusiasm for this great hero. In 1934, President Franklin Roosevelt made Columbus Day an official federal holiday.

The national embrace of Columbus held more or less unquestioned for the next half-century until the countercultural forces of the 1960s and 1970s reignited a debate over America's role in the world and whether or not this country was "good" or "bad." In those tumultuous times, anti-Columbus attitudes once again found fertile ground in American discourse. They now play a significant role in our culture war.

There are two competing narratives vying for the American soul. In the beginning, there was Christopher Columbus, but the nature of what he began is what is now in question. Columbus was the man who planted the germ of what would become America. For those who value our nation and its history, Columbus is a bold, intrepid explorer to be celebrated for his world-changing discovery of the New World under the banner of the Spanish crown. From his little wooden ships, grand new civilizations would come forth. But the second Columbus narrative, pushed by those who dispute the greatness of our country, goes something like this: The Italian-born navigator set off for what he thought was Asia to find new regions to exploit. Upon arriving in the New World—which he didn't discover, since the Native Americans and Leif Erickson had found it first—Columbus rapaciously plundered the land and abused the native people in a greedy search for gold. He introduced slavery and foreign disease to the Americas, which led to the subjugation and genocide of native peoples. He was the author of a pristine civilization's doom, and he planted a corrupt, murderous, and oppressive one in its place.

Which of the two Columbus narratives holds more truth? While it is tempting to put the great explorer on the right side or the wrong side of history by modern standards and ideological calculations, we should instead appreciate Columbus and his great undertaking in context. His story deserves more appreciation and less castigation from modern audiences. In setting course across the Atlantic, Columbus truly changed the course of human history. Without him, America as we know it wouldn't exist.

The World of Columbus

One cannot understand Christopher Columbus without understanding the world he inhabited when he set sail from Spain in 1492 with three small ships into the unknown waters of the Atlantic. It was a time of great turmoil. Europe was still recovering from the Black Plague, which had stormed through the continent a century before, wiping out approximately a third of the population. The Protestant Reformation was still twenty years in the future, but the Church was already showing the strain that would eventually lead to division. Violent religious wars were taking place between Christianity and Islam in the Middle East and on the fringes of Europe—and the Christians appeared to be losing. Constantinople, a city that had stood as a rock of Christendom for over a millennium—many had deemed the city's defenses impregnable—fell to the Muslim Ottoman Empire in 1453.

It's hard for people in the modern world to understand the profound impact of this event or how it must have shaken the average citizen living in Europe. Constantinople had been a stop for Christian pilgrims headed toward Jerusalem—which was already in the hands of Muslims—and housed countless priceless relics of the Christian religion. It had also been a major trade hub for luxury goods between the East and the West, particularly for Italians.[29] The fall of Constantinople, coming shortly after the Black Plague, seemed to signify to many that the end of all things was near.[30] Few could or would have predicted the reinvigoration of the West that was about to happen—set in motion by Columbus's discovery of the New World.

"Just before the discovery of America, thinking men in western Europe believed that their world, already crumbling, would shortly crash. ..." according to historian Samuel Eliot Morison. "Nevertheless, a new era of hope and glory and enlargement of the human spirit...was about to begin."[31]

Desperation led to innovation. The way to the East through the Middle East was now shut, and the world was suddenly a smaller place. But that fact encouraged European explorers to turn their gaze westward, toward the vast and unconquered Atlantic. The Portuguese were first to go beyond the maps of the ancients. The map as it was known to Europeans had expanded little since Ptolemy had charted out the limits of the Roman Empire in the second century. Early fifteenth-century precursors to Columbus such as Prince Henry the

Navigator began to venture out from the European coast, crawling down the African coastline and discovering uninhabited islands. While the Portuguese got a head start in the burgeoning age of exploration, others were eager to catch up.

Europe's bounded world, with dark and unknown patches on its periphery, was about to expand into something much larger and truly globalized. Out of darkness, a new hope for Christian civilization would emerge as if by Providence. The year 1492 was, in many ways, the first hour of modernity. And the beginning of this transition is marked by the vision of one intrepid explorer.

The Origins of the Voyage

Christopher Columbus was born in 1451, likely in the Italian Republic of Genoa, to a family of no particular high standing. He was named after St. Christopher, the "Christ bearer," who, according to legend, risked death to bring a child, who turned out to be Christ, across a raging river. The name was altogether fitting, for Christopher Columbus would one day carry his Christian beliefs across a great ocean through great peril and change the world.

Little is known about Columbus's early life. His father was a wool merchant and a government official, his family of middling rank and means. No contemporary portraits of Columbus exist, only recreations of what we think he may have looked like.

From descriptions, we know that he was tall and lean. He went gray early in life, something that only added to the striking presence his contemporaries remarked on. He began a career on the seas at a young age, working as a merchant. Most of Columbus's early voyages were along the Mediterranean, but he had ventured as far as Iceland.[32] By the age of thirty, he had turned himself into a first-rate seaman. But he must have known he would never reach the heights of the famed explorers by toiling around the Mediterranean and the African coast in the wake of others. Turning his sights on something far grander in the 1480s, Columbus began to consider a project so ambitious that it would raise him above the great explorers of his age—or any age.

From his youth, Columbus had been acquainted with the stories of Marco Polo, a Venetian traveler to China who pre-dated him by over a century and brought back fantastic tales from the East. Polo was well-known in Genoa. Imprisoned there after the Battle of Curzola in 1298, Polo dictated an account of his journey to fellow prisoner Rustichello da Pisa. This work became known as *The Travels of Marco Polo*. While Columbus likely heard of Polo's travels by word of mouth in his youth—in those days, books were expensive and hard to come by—he eventually acquired a copy and wrote extensive notes in the margins. This book survives today and gives some insight into what sparked Columbus's interest in sailing to the Orient. For instance, his curiosity was piqued by an island named Cipangu, which we now call Japan, because, according to Polo, it was filled with gold.

Much has been made of Columbus's desire for gold. Many have seen it as evidence that he was motivated by little more than greed.[33] But to view Columbus's desires entirely in such crude terms is simply modern folly. Columbus did aggressively seek gold on his voyages, but he did not do so just to enrich himself personally, as many of his detractors have claimed. Instead, it was a means to more high-minded ends. Any voyage he would undertake would be enormously expensive, far too expensive for man of comparatively modest means such as himself to finance. He would have to plead his case to the sovereigns of Europe to back his expeditions. To do so, he would have to convince his investors that the undertaking would pay off in some way. Columbus knew that if he couldn't at least claim to be hoping to find large sums of gold, he would have little success in convincing anyone to put up money for his trip. And if he failed to bring back items of value, it would be difficult to convince his backers to fund further ventures. The earthly reward Columbus would seek from benefactors was not necessarily financial. Instead, he wanted what at that time was worth far more than money—rank and titles for himself and his offspring,[34] something he knew could open doors for success unobtainable by the common man and provide a baseline below which his children could not fall. In the age of kings and lords, it was nearly impossible to be a truly self-made man, and Columbus wanted to raise the station of his family in the rigid hierarchy of Europe.

Marco Polo's book wasn't the only account that influenced Columbus's thinking; he read widely as he developed his idea about a first-of-its-kind trip west to Asia. Another book popular in his time, *The Travels of John Mandeville*, a medieval account of the world beyond Europe, clearly made an impression on his mind.[35] This work, less focused on the potential for commercial success in distant lands, called for Christians not only to retake the Holy Land but to strike out and enlarge Christendom.[36] Being content within the confines of Europe was, in Mandeville's account, little more than indolence and avoidance of the duties of a good Christian to aggressively extend the religion. Mandeville's book was a call for crusade—and to bring back the riches of the East to retake Jerusalem.

Columbus considered searching for riches for this purpose a duty, not greed. Violently expelling Islam from the edges of Europe and the Middle East sounds harsh to modern ears, but the two religions had been locked in a death struggle for centuries. Enlightenment concepts such as religious liberty and religious tolerance were alien to how people saw the world in those days. A civilization would be either one thing or another, and dissent from religious orthodoxy was rarely tolerated. True religious freedom, like many other freedoms, would not be a reality for hundreds of years. Meanwhile, the struggle between the crescent and the cross was a zero-sum game of survival or death, and from the perspective of Christian Europe, it appeared that their side was losing.

Columbus became dead set on being the first explorer to make a journey across the ocean to Asia to take Christianity outward and riches back. He brought his idea to travel to the East by way of westward sailing to courts all over Europe, beginning with Portugal. In a particularly ill-fated pitch, Columbus pled his case to the Portuguese king and explained the technical aspects of how he would conduct his expedition. The crafty King Joao II turned Columbus down—and used the information Columbus had given him to launch a separate voyage with a different captain. It was a nasty double-cross, but Columbus would have the last laugh. The Portuguese king commissioned Fernao de Ulmo for the undertaking, and he only managed to travel a few days before encountering storms and rough seas. Ulmo decided to turn around, deeming the journey impossible.[37]

Columbus pleaded before the Spanish court of Ferdinand II of Aragon and Isabella I of Castile, dual sovereigns of a still un-unified Spain. The dashing and charismatic navigator deftly appealed to Isabella's desire to spread Christendom to the East and Ferdinand's interest in leapfrogging rival nations.[38]

Many legends have been created about Columbus's spirited appeals, some half-truths at best. He certainly never tried to prove that the world was round rather than flat. Unfortunately, Washington Irving created this persistent myth. Irving mistakenly wrote that, in trying to prove the science behind his journey, Columbus had to convince Ferdinand and Isabella's team of experts at the university of Salamanca that their flat-earth theories were incorrect.[39] While Irving's account of the confrontation between the untutored Columbus and the learned men of Salamanca makes for dramatic and inspired reading, Irving was mistaken in thinking that the religious and scientific community of the time contained flat-earthers. Columbus did indeed, rather unsuccessfully, debate a team of what were then considered scientists about his theories on the earth, but most of the debate was on the size of the globe, not its shape.[40] As it turned out, the Spanish experts, who relied on the older—and more accurate—calculations of Ptolemy, were closer to the truth than Columbus was. The world was much larger than Columbus believed. Had the Americas not existed, he would have perished long before reaching Asia.

But neither Columbus nor the scientific community of his day really had an accurate understanding of the world's geography, and both had some silly notions about what Columbus would find at the edge of the map. Yet, unlike the scientists, who could only contemplate their theories, not test them, Columbus was bold enough to sail into the unknown, to stake his life and reputation on what he believed. Columbus could be imperious and difficult, pigheaded and stubborn, but he was also unquestionably brave. And the courage of this untutored man paved the way for the greatest discovery of the last millennium.

Columbus waited years, continually pleading his case, before the Spanish sovereigns were convinced to back his venture. Though the world-changing consequences of Columbus's voyage now make it seem odd that he was rejected so many times, one has to understand how ambitious and absurd many of the claims he was making about his proposed venture sounded. Columbus was looking for a much bigger prize than a few small islands off the European coastline; he wanted to expand the map of the known world into what ancient cartographers had only conceived in theory. It's understandable that European courts would have been wary to expend limited resources on such an improbable venture.

Spain, for example, had been engaged in the final stages of the so-called Reconquista, the expulsion of Muslim powers from the Iberian Peninsula. Ferdinand and Isabella, like most political leaders both then and now, were focused on the immediate threats to their power and interests. But then the sudden resolution of a half-millennium-long war gave Columbus the chance he needed.

Catholic Spain's bloody struggle against the Moorish Caliphate is mostly forgotten in the West, though it is occasionally dredged up as a historical grievance by modern Islamist groups like al-Qaeda.[41] Catholic Spaniards spent nearly five centuries pushing the Moors out of the Iberian Peninsula. Ferdinand and Isabella made the final aggressive drive to rid their homeland of Islamic influence toward the end of the fifteenth century. The so-called Grenada War concluded in January of 1492, opening the door for Spain to set its eyes on grander things. No longer burdened by a costly war on their doorstep, Ferdinand and Isabella could pay more attention to the far-fetched proposal of an eccentric foreigner. The Spanish sovereigns once again considered Columbus's ambitious voyage but still came just short of accepting it. It was still difficult to convince the sovereigns that this expensive venture would be worth it to them. Columbus was ready to leave and plead his case elsewhere, but an influential friend on the court made a last-minute appeal for the king and queen to reconsider the enterprise. That time, it worked, and Columbus was sent off with promises of titles for himself and his posterity.[42]

Columbus then set out on his famed journey, to cross the Atlantic and link East and West, something that had never been done before. He was not looking for an undiscovered continent, nor did he ever conceive its existence while contemplating his venture. Some historians have claimed that Columbus learned of the New World's existence from other explorers before he set out, but these theories have mostly been debunked.[43] He was simply seeking a better path to the "Indies," or Asia, which would have been a notable but more limited accomplishment. Columbus never landed in, nor would he ever see, Asia. Instead, he became the father of the modern world.

Into the Unknown

On August 3, 1492, Columbus set sail into the great "Green Sea of Darkness," as the foreboding Atlantic was sometimes called in those days.[44] He departed from the Spanish mainland with a flotilla that included three Spanish sailing ships that the sailors named the *Nina*, the *Pinta*, and the *Santa Maria*. Unfortunately, we can only guess at what they looked like since no original plans or drawings survive. What is known is that these vessels were tiny by comparison to most ocean-going ships of more modern era. The *Santa Maria*, Columbus's flagship and the largest of the three, was only about sixty feet long.[45] While small, these ships were nevertheless fine examples of the best vessels available at the time. The *Nina*, which was a bit more compact than the *Santa Maria*, was Columbus's favorite and served under his command for three of his four voyages. After one particularly vicious storm on the return from his first journey, Columbus wrote of the *Nina* in his journal, "If she had not been very staunch and well found I should have been afraid of being lost."[46]

With this little flotilla, Columbus set out on a harrowing, two-month voyage. It is particularly difficult for a modern person to understand the challenge that Columbus had before him when he set sail. Navigation tools were incredibly crude by our standards, a far cry from the fully mapped and electronically connected world that we live in today. Instead, Columbus had to rely on simple techniques available at the time and a lot of intuition.

One thing he did not do—this is a common misconception—was travel by stars, or what's called "celestial" navigation. At the time, instruments required for navigating by the location of the stars in the sky either weren't available or were generally inaccurate, so he had to use other means to find his way. Columbus was what is called a "dead reckoning" navigator.[47] This kind of navigation relies on setting course by the precise reading of a compass needle, specialized charts and maps, and calculations based on the speed of the ship. While Columbus used some primitive celestial navigation on his voyage, it was ultimately his dead reckoning skills, which were considerable, that got him where he needed to go. As one historian has noted, "No such dead-reckoning navigators exist today; no man alive, limited to the instruments and means at Columbus's disposal, could obtain anything near the accuracy of his results."[48]

Day after day they sailed, and as the crew became more restless, Columbus must undoubtedly have become more worried. As an Italian foreigner sailing with Spanish crews, sudden discontent could have spelled mutiny, the end of the voyage, and even death for the Admiral of the Ocean Sea. A couple of months into his voyage, Columbus passed the point where he believed Asia would be, yet he continued onward. He was determined to reach his destination despite the simmering discontent among his subordinates. By early October, the journey almost came to what would have been an incredibly unfortunate end. Columbus's underlings were on to the fact that they were far beyond the point at which they should have spotted land, and after a string of false sightings, they were at the end of their patience. Columbus documented this near-mutiny: "Here the people could stand it no longer, complained of the long voyage; but the Admiral cheered them as best he could, holding out good hope of the advantages they might have; and he added that it was useless to complain, since he had come to go to the Indies, and so had to continue until he found them, with the help of our Lord."[49] Columbus promised his crew that they would turn back if they did not spot land within a few days.

In the early hours of October 12, just two days after Columbus had staved off mutiny, a crewman aboard the *Pinta* spotted land and shouted, "Tierra, tierra!" That time, it wasn't a false alarm.

Columbus and select members of his crew came ashore, kissed the ground, and gave thanks to God.[50] According to contemporary historian and critic Bartolome de Las Casas, Columbus "raised the royal standard and the captains carried two banners with the green cross, which were flown by the Admiral on all his ships."[51] Columbus named the island—likely Watling Island in the Bahamas—San Salvador in homage to their salvation and claimed it for the Spanish sovereigns. It was here that the first encounter between the people of the Old World and the New World took place.

Columbus would spend most of the rest of his life making journeys to and from the New World. On his second trip, he brought a flotilla with him and planted colonies on various Caribbean islands. This laid the groundwork for the widespread Spanish settlement in the New World, with thousands of colonists making the journey. Not all was well, though, as the promised gold that some had thought would be covering the ground didn't materialize. Columbus's salesmanship led to exaggeration, disappointment, and ultimately his ruin. In addition, Columbus was a marvelous explorer but perhaps not such a good governor. He quarreled with other colonists, and he was always prone to imperiousness. Doubts that they were in fact in Asia were growing, further undermining Columbus's position.

Columbus's third journey was a disaster. The Spanish colonists resented his rule, became sour when—contra the modern myths about his cruelty to the indigenous peoples—he executed Spaniards for mistreating natives, and plotted to remove him from command.[52] A local

Spanish official had Columbus arrested and sent back to Spain in chains, a mortifying and demeaning blow. In Spain, he was eventually released, but neither his health nor his reputation ever truly recovered. Columbus was to blame for some of his misfortune, but he was always operating with severe limitations as a foreigner from Genoa. And controlling the hotheaded adventurers and rebellious colonists he had to work with would have tested the limits of even the greatest leaders of men.

In 1502, Columbus set out on his fourth and final voyage, which capped off two decades of incredible discoveries never matched in human history. He made landfall on the South American continent, which eroded his stubborn belief that he had been in Asia the whole time. His final years were, sadly, not happy ones. Columbus became embroiled in squabbles about titles and what the crown owed him. He was shunted aside as Spanish conquistadors garnered the credit and adulation for the conquest of the New World. He succumbed to sickness in 1506.

"So died the man who had done more to direct the course of history than any individual since Augustus Caesar...." wrote admiring biographer Samuel Elliot Morison.[53] "One only wishes that the Admiral might have been afforded the sense of fulfillment that would have come from foreseeing all that flowed from his discoveries; that would have turned all the sorrows of his last years to joy. The whole history of the Americas stems from the Four Voyages of Columbus; and as the Greek city-states looked back to the deathless gods as their founders, so today a score of independent nations and dominions unite in homage to Christopher the stout-hearted son of Genoa, who carried Christian civilization across the ocean sea."[54]

Columbus Comes into Question

It wasn't long after Columbus's death that some began to question his legacy. One of his early detractors was the aforementioned

Bartolomé de Las Casas, the first priest ordained in the new world. His father and uncles had been on Columbus's second voyage.[55] Las Casas is both one of the best chroniclers of Columbus's travels and also a ferocious critic of the early Spanish role in the Americas. In *The Devastation of the Indies*, published in 1552, he lays out a damning case against Spanish rule, or what he would say was misrule. It is by far the most citied work by Columbus's detractors up to this time. Many of Las Casas' charges are true. Las Casas highlighted Spanish misdeeds that are serious by the standards our day or any day. Still, one must keep the account in perspective. We must be careful about projecting the perspectives of our time onto debates that took place hundreds of years ago.

Modern people frequently forget or misunderstand the role religion played in the still fundamentally medieval world of Columbus. Columbus, the "Christ bearer," was expected to bring his Christian beliefs to new lands. Everyone with any role in his voyages—from financial backers Ferdinand and Isabella to the lowliest deckhand on the *Pinta*—agreed, at least in theory, that this was a primary objective. And while modern critics slam Columbus, the Spanish, and all the European colonizers for their efforts to spread their faith, the devoutly religious Las Casas heaped scorn on them for their *failure* to do so.

Columbus explained with some excitement in his journal that the natives appeared to have no religion at all.[56] This was considered a good thing. Barriers to conversion were usually found with people who already had a firm and affixed set of religious ideas that were hard to overcome. The less-hardened religious views of the natives in the New World were seen as an exciting opportunity to convert them to the Christian faith. But the results of the efforts to bring these people into the Christian fold in the years that followed were mixed. Cultural misunderstandings, feckless governance, and occasional abuse of natives stymied attempts at universal conversion.

Las Casas was undoubtedly bitter about the roadblocks the colonizers put in the way of his chief goal, which was to proselytize America's native population. But his frustration led him to make at least
one proposal that would not be acceptable to any modern critic of
Columbus. Las Casas denounced the enslavement of the native populations that occurred from time to time, yet his solution to this
problem was to enslave people from Africa and import them to the
New World instead.[57] In Columbus's age, slavery wasn't seen as necessarily reprehensible. It was almost universally sanctioned in both
the Old World and the New. Virtually no one questioned it under the
right circumstances. Las Casas was no different. What upset him was
that souls were being lost because the Spanish policy had alienated
the American natives—and that the Spaniards were prioritizing
material gain over spiritual things.

Howard Zinn and other modern left-wing historians have used
Las Casas writings as a jumping-off point to level their own ideo-
logically oriented accusations to paint "the real Columbus" as a cruel
villain. Certainly the indigenous peoples of America suffered hor-
ribly at the hands of conquistadors and colonists. Those times were,
by almost any measure, harsher times than ours, and the world was
a way off from legal guarantees regarding cruel and unusual punish-
ments. But there is simply no conclusive evidence that Columbus
operated in a particularly cruel manner.

On the contrary, there is good evidence that Columbus did his
utmost to rein in the cruelty of the Spanish colonists. While depriva-
tions and terrible crimes did occur, Columbus was quick to punish
those under his command who committed unjust acts against the
local population. Stanford professor emeritus Carol Delaney explains,
"Columbus strictly told the crew not to do things like maraud, or
rape, and instead to treat the native people with respect. There are
many examples in his writings where he gave instructions to this

effect. Most of the time when injustices occurred, Columbus wasn't even there. There were terrible diseases that got communicated to the natives, but he can't be blamed for that."[58]

Nevertheless, Las Casas' account undoubtedly contains some truth. The Spanish encomienda system, which was comparable to feudalism, was certainly harsh. But it wasn't all that different from practices common throughout the world at that time. And while the Spanish administration of the lands Columbus discovered was flawed and even cruel in many ways, this does not detract from what Columbus accomplished.

Whatever can be said of the colonists who followed him, Columbus was a man who tried to act justly under complicated circumstances. It is fair to say that Columbus was mostly benign in his interaction with native populations. Few men, especially of his time, would have acted better than he did in dealing with the people he met.

Many Spaniards behaved badly in the new world, wantonly killing peaceful natives and committing other crimes and atrocities that embarrassed the Spanish crown, but these acts weren't carried out by Columbus. In a world in which ruthless conquest and enslavement was commonplace, Columbus at least attempted to foster benign relations between European arrivals and native populations.

As Washington Irving judged, Columbus and his benefactor Queen Isabella behaved honorably toward inhabitants in the New World, even when many others did not. Irving wrote that Columbus's "conduct was characterized by the grandeur of his views, and the magnanimity of his spirit. Instead of ravaging the newly found countries like many of his contemporary discoverers, who were intent only on immediate gain, he regarded them with the eyes of a legislator; he sought to colonize and cultivate them, to civilize the natives, to subject every thing to the control of law, order, and religion, and thus to found regular and prosperous empires." Irving was unsparing in his criticism of the unseemly elements of Columbus's crew and those who followed in his wake: "That he failed in this, was the fault of the dissolute rabble which it was misfortune to command, with whom all law was tyranny, and all order oppression."[59]

Irving also lamented the early death of Queen Isabella, who he believed would have contained the abuses of Indians that took place after she had died. "Had she been spared," Irving wrote, "her benignant vigilance would have prevented the scene of horror in the colonization of the New World, and might have softened the lot of its native inhabitants."

In addition, it is important to remember that Columbus didn't break a kind of pacifist seal in the Americas. The New World had been an incredibly violent place long before he arrived. He did break the hermetic biological seal that had protected the peoples of the New World from the diseases of the Old—which, unfortunately, did far, far more devastation to the great New World civilizations than anything else. But, as Delaney asks, how can Columbus be blamed for that? Medical science wasn't really even in its infancy at that point; the nature of communicable disease was unknown. In the end, the diseases introduced to the Americas took more lives than the conquistadors ever could.

Life in the New World before Columbus's arrival could hardly be characterized as one of health, peace, and justice, and it's silly to think that, when Columbus arrived in the Bahamas, he somehow introduced mass violence and slavery to a benign Garden of Eden.

Columbus noted in his journal that when he first encountered natives on San Salvador, virtually none appeared to be above the age of thirty.[60] Tribal life was harsh, and the Spanish were hardly the only threat. The tribe Columbus initially encountered, the so-called Tianos, whose weapons would at best be defined as sharpened sticks, were seemingly living in terror of another tribal group called the Caribs. The Caribs were thought to have practiced cannibalism, but this charge against them has been disputed. It is more likely that the Caribs were simply a warlike tribe that plundered from their neighbors and killed and forced them into bondage rather than eating them. At the very least, their ferocity terrified the other local regional tribes.[61]

The differences between the peaceful tribes that Columbus encountered and liked and the more dangerous Caribs have perhaps been exaggerated. But those differences do explain distinctions in how they were treated. At the time, enslavement of recalcitrant or violent people defeated in war was considered just. Columbus's goal was to show the peaceful people of the region that it would be good to be willing vassals of the Spanish sovereigns. Carol Delaney explains the significance of this distinction between the Caribs and other natives: "vassals cannot be enslaved."

While the Tianos that Columbus initially met were typically gentle and good-natured, they were but a tiny slice of a much larger and more complicated civilizational environment. The nature of Columbus's interactions with the Tianos and the Caribs sheds light on how he viewed the world. He wanted to demonstrate to the Tianos that his aims were benign; to the Caribs, that aggression would be met with overwhelming force.

During his second voyage to the New World, Columbus wrote that defeating and capturing the militant Caribs would set an important early example because other people would "see the good treatment which is meted out to well-doers and the punishment which is inflicted upon those who do evil."[62] According to Delaney, "This is an extraordinarily important statement. It shows Columbus's primary intention was that the natives should be employees of the Crown, not slaves, though he admitted that he didn't know the language well enough to ask them what might be appropriate payment."[63] While the interactions between the natives and early Spanish arrivals did not always go as Columbus hoped, it is clear that his intentions were far from genocidal. And while many who followed Columbus were certainly less enlightened than he was, the notion that he was the sinister author of the destruction of tribal people wildly misses the mark. Columbus, in fact, had chastised his crew and other Spanish settlers in the New World whom he believed had been actually cruelly due to their greed or poor morals. It is a sad twist of fate that Columbus now gets blamed for the very actions he tried to prevent.

Many of the so-called Spanish conquistadors who followed Columbus to the New World undoubtedly came for the purpose of subjugating tribes in the Americas. *Hernán Cortés* famously conquered the Aztec empire in the early sixteenth century—something the Aztecs had been doing to their neighbors for hundreds of years. The Aztecs were accustomed to violence and subjugation of other peoples; *Cortés* simply turned the tables. As one historian has noted, "During the century before Cortes, the Aztecs created their great conquest empire by using a very familiar form of warfare leading eventually to the seizure of land and subjugation of enemy societies as tributaries."[64]

The great Aztec city Tenochtitlan was in many ways sustained by this system of conquest and forced tribute as well as ritualized human sacrifice that almost undoubtedly included cannibalism.[65] While this doesn't excuse all of the Spanish actions in the New World, it does place them in context. Violence and brutality are inherent in the nature of man. Primitive societies are often a far cry from the ideal image of the noble savage famously conjured up by French philosopher Jean Jacques Rousseau.

If the Spaniards and other Europeans who arrived in the New World are guilty of genocide, then so were the natives themselves. It wasn't just one or two militant tribes in the Caribbean and Central America that engaged in the destruction and subjugation of their neighbors. Violence, plundering, and forced bondage on a large scale had been practiced throughout the Americas long before outsiders showed up. If we must condemn Columbus and the Spaniards to the ash heap of history, then we must condemn the natives as well. More sensibly, the savagery that was part of everyday life should be considered before condemning Columbus or any other leader of the time.

Giving Columbus His Due

Christopher Columbus never understood the depth of his discovery, nor did his contemporaries fully appreciate his role in world history. But we should be able to appreciate the magnitude of what he achieved.

It's a true shame that Americans have been so quick to abandon Columbus. His legacy is enormous. He did far more than simply "discover" the New World. Columbus took the first, brave step into the globalized, interconnected world we live in today. He propelled the mass migration of people into the Americas. Most importantly, he planted the seeds of Western civilization in the New World. Unless we believe, which the radical Left clearly does, that these are negative developments in the long scope of human history, we must at least give credit to Columbus as the courageous pioneer who made this transition possible.

Columbus is well worth celebrating. The journey to the New World was an impressive feat of seamanship, and his discovery changed the world. The fact that he didn't get universal recognition in his own time does not detract from what he did. The Founders and early generations of Americans were simply better able to appreciate the full effect of the forces that Columbus's discovery had unleashed. They could see that the seeds that Columbus had, perhaps unwittingly, planted had bloomed with the creation of the United States. From the decrepit and crumbling Old World, whose shores

Columbus left behind, he paved the way for liberty and a revival of the West.

This is why tributes to Columbus sprang forth in the early days of the American nation—why, for example, King's College in New York was renamed Columbia in 1784. America was throwing off the shackles that had bound it to the mother continent and creating its own legacy. Columbus represented the rise of the New World—and America with it.

Certainly others deserve respect and recognition as well. English explorer John Cabot and French explorer Jacques Cartier, among others, quickly followed in Columbus's footsteps; they revealed more about the world Columbus barely knew he had discovered.

They took enormous risks and faced dangers, but they could at least expect and plan for some of the challenges they faced on the journey. Columbus had no such privilege. Historian Samuel Eliot Morison, who reenacted some of the early voyages of discovery, including the those of Columbus, wrote in awe: "There is nothing like a personal visit to newly discovered lands to bring home one the pioneers' dangers and difficulties. My admiration for them increases with time. For years I have been living with the records of heroic navigators and with the ordinary grousing, grumbling, but believing mariner. God bless 'em all! The world will never see their like again."[66]

There is now widespread antipathy toward Columbus in academia—which has been maniacally obsessed with the ideology of oppressors and oppressed for at least a generation—and now in the public mainstream. The barbs thrown at Columbus are part of a larger push to delegitimize Western civilization, to deny its benefits to mankind, and to cast its highest expression—the United States—as somehow ill-conceived, built on a foundation of lies and cruelty.

The modern anti-Columbus movement is an attempt to reverse engineer the narrative created by the Founding Fathers, Phillis Wheatley, Washington Irving, and others. The Founders treated Columbus as a renaissance man who opened the door for the creation of the United States and as the symbol of the rebirth of Western civilization in the New World, which had improved upon the best of European traditions, buried the worst, and ultimately created something unique and grand in its place. They certainly venerated Columbus the man, but they were clearly most interested in what he stood for.

Washington Irving's fable of Columbus standing up to the learned men of Spain and telling them the world was round falls short of the truth, but it does show us something of how early Americans saw Columbus: as fearlessly facing down the myths of the Old World. And it is ultimately that idea—of America as the answer to the stable but brutal hierarchies of Europe's oppressive establishment—that is under attack. In the twenty-first century, we have every reason to celebrate the achievements of this great man of the fifteenth. As a man of his time, he would never fit in with the cultural attitudes of today, but that is no reason to treat him as a pariah, unworthy of praise and recognition.

For almost all of human history, mankind has lived under the crushing weight of tyranny—or, even more perilously, in a state of barbarism, where life was short and typically violent. Columbus opened the door to a future, still centuries away, that would see immeasurable benefits for humanity. The American civilization that ultimately followed in the aftermath of his voyage and discovery would have been impossible without this man, who should be honored for his best qualities: boldness, bravery, and faith.

Without Columbus, there would have been no America, and without America, the blessings of liberty would likely have remained dormant. The Founders understood this, as did the generations of Americans who carried on their legacy.

From Columbus's three little barks crossing the Atlantic, great civilizations arose. Ultimately, it would not be Columbus's Spanish patrons who would build the most prominent among them. Of the waves of colonizers who came to the Americas—Spanish, Portuguese, French, and Dutch—it was the latecomers, the English, who created the greatest of the New World nations and unlocked the awesome potential of the North American continent. Columbus was the unwitting conduit for the creation of a future American Republic, and for that, he deserves our respect and veneration.

CHAPTER 2

The War on Thanksgiving

For we must consider that we shall be a city upon a hill.
The eyes of all people are upon us, so that if we shall deal
falsely with our God in this work we have undertaken,
and so cause Him to withdraw His present help from us,
we shall be made a story and a byword through the world.

—John Winthrop, 1630

I n 2017, far-left writer Belen Fernandez wrote in Al Jazeera that
Americans have no reason to celebrate thankfulness: "A lot of
people in the United States won't have much to be thankful for"
on Thanksgiving due to America's oppressive policies towards Native
Americans," she wrote.[1]

Fernandez concluded her article with this anti-American sentiment: "In the end, you don't need to gorge yourself on turkey and
stuffing to see that the United States itself is positively sick." In this
narrative, the United States is unalterably broken; Americans are either

sustaining a cruel and genocidal cultural heritage or engaging in soul-less materialism. America the beautiful is simply America the damned.

Some go even further, condemning the legacy passed down by Thanksgiving and our Pilgrim forefathers as uniquely evil. "Nobody but Americans celebrates Thanksgiving. (Canadians have a holiday by the same name, but an entirely different history and political import)," wrote Glen Ford, a hard-left commentator. "It is reserved by history and the intent of 'the founders' as the supremely white American holiday, the most ghoulish event on the national calendar. No Halloween of the imagination can rival the exterminationist reality that was the genesis, and remains the legacy, of the American Thanksgiving. It is the most loathsome, humanity-insulting day of the year—a pure glorification of racist barbarity."[2]

Pilgrim-bashing, of course, isn't a sport relegated to the media. On college campuses, the war on history has reached New England's colonists in general.

To get ahead of rampaging iconoclasts, Yale University announced in August 2017 that it would cover up part of a statue depicting an Indian and Puritan pointing their respective weapons at each other. The Puritan points his musket while the Indian responds with his bow, though it's not clear from the work that the two actually intend violence toward each other. Nevertheless, Yale's head librarian called the nearly-century-old statue "not appropriate," and the school placed a covering over the Puritan's rifle.[3]

Amusingly, this cowardice on the part of the administration may have backfired. While the school covered up the depiction of the Puritan's weapon, they failed to cover the Indian's bow pointed in the Puritan's direction. *National Review*'s Kyle Smith mockingly noted the peculiar message the updated statue might be sending: "Now that only one of the two men is armed, does Yale mean to imply that persons of color are irrationally violent or untrustworthy? Troubling, very troubling. A reasonable interpretation of the work now is that an Indian is sneaking up on an unarmed Puritan with intent to do him harm. Why must Yale perpetuate such harmful stereotypes?"[4]

Tellingly, the school acknowledges that the stone tab cover may be removed at a later date. The initial action may simply be the administration's sad attempt to hide the statue from vandals until the war on history has passed.[5]

So is Thanksgiving a celebration of genocide and overconsumption? Were the Pilgrims and the Puritans damnable rather than commendable?

A Puritan Ethos

"The business of the American people is business!"

This misunderstood line from President Calvin Coolidge's speech to a group of newspaper editors in 1925 has frequently been used to malign America as materialistic—and uninspiring as Coolidge himself is portrayed.[6] Both of those contentions are wrong. What Coolidge really said was, "The chief business of the American people is business." Americans were, after all, a notably enterprising people, and Coolidge wasn't afraid to praise them for it. But he highlighted something even more important than America's considerable commercial prowess. He also said, "The chief ideal of the American people is idealism." As he explained, Americans "make no concealment of the fact that we want wealth, but there are many other things that we want very much more. We want peace and honor, and that charity which is so strong an element of all civilization.... I cannot repeat too often that America is a nation of idealists. That is the only motive to which they ever give any strong and lasting reaction."[7]

It is fitting that this paean to America came from the Vermont-born Coolidge, who was both the figurative and literal descendant of the New England Puritans who had arrived on the shores of New England three centuries before. His synthesis of high-minded idealism with the embrace of business as a blessing came straight from his Puritan forbearers.[8] In the Puritans' view, rewards came from hard work, and those rewards could be used to do good that would be impossible without the fruit of labor.

Even today, many come to America for material opportunities. The Puritans, despite their reputation for religious zealotry above material gain, were quite commercial, and they left that legacy to America. But in addition to the raw incentive of economic gain, which drives all men to a certain extent, they also left us the idealistic hope that an as yet unformed America could be transformed into a haven for something better.

From its creation, America has been an idealistic nation, a country set apart, a city on a hill—and, on the elevation of that pedestal, an object of loathing to some. It has also always been a Christian country, despite contentions to the contrary. America's idealism has manifested itself in many different ways, to be sure. America has changed enormously in the past few centuries, yet it still bears ties to its original foundation before the Founding when a few English colonists braved the dangers of the Atlantic crossing and made their home in the New World. What they established outstripped all of the other previous colonial ventures, which had produced only limited success up to that point. As the English trickled into North America, they brought their unique characteristics to the newly discovered continent—a secret sauce of cultural traits and religious doctrines that opened the door for grander things to come.

Of the English who settled in North America, the Pilgrims stand out in the modern imagination. There were other British emigrants who preceded them and became a large part of the development of America; however, it is the image of the Pilgrims, above all others, that is etched our national consciousness. Why?

"They Knew They Were Pilgrims"

The celebration of Thanksgiving has something to do with our long-lasting attachment to the Pilgrims. Days of thanksgiving were common in the early days of the republic, but they weren't necessarily associated with the Pilgrims' "First Thanksgiving." Setting aside a day of thanks to God is hardly an original concept; it exists in cultures, countries, and religions all over the world. But Thanksgiving, one of America's oldest national holidays, is something unique. It was an offshoot of Forefather's Day, a New England—mostly Plymouth—holiday that celebrated the origins of the region, one that, through the efforts of great statesman like Daniel Webster, developed over time into a national tradition.

From the Pilgrim feasts of the early 1600s to the modern development of Thanksgiving in the nineteenth century, this quintessentially American holiday has become a profound expression of our national culture. The Fourth of July is a celebration of American independence, of the creation of the United States, and of the particular ideas on which our American institutions were erected. But Thanksgiving represents something else, something no less important to American civilization. While Independence Day is a celebration of freedom, Thanksgiving is a celebration of the things the Pilgrims stood for: religious faith and the Christian origins of our nation, family, charity, and thankfulness for earthly blessings—the fruits of our labor. Thanksgiving is deeply woven into American culture. And it's what the holiday says about America that makes it problematic to its modern assailants.

Their line of attack is based on a quasi-Marxist reduction of history to the tale of oppressors versus the oppressed. In a narrative remarkably similar to the attacks on Columbus, Pilgrims are portrayed as an oppressor class who came to America, mindlessly butchered and subjugated its native inhabitants, and constructed a wicked city upon the woes of the downtrodden.

The modern celebration of Thanksgiving is written off as a disgusting celebration of capitalism, a crass reveling in material wealth even as oppressed groups suffer.

And the religion of the New England colonists is not admired today. The word "Puritan"—a catch-all description for the radical Protestants who colonized new England, though it more properly describes the founders of the Massachusetts Bay Colony than the Separatist Pilgrims—has negative connotations. The Puritans are caricatured as dour, fun-hating prudes. [9] And worse, they are supposed to be bigoted zealots, full of irrational religious fervor. The Salem Witch Trials, in which several people were unjustly executed for witchcraft, are inevitably dragged up to contrast the New England colonists with our enlightened modern selves. It is forgotten that this sordid affair originated in paranoia over a looming invasion by French Canada—one that never came—and that its abatement came from the intervention of one of the most religious and conservative Puritan leaders, Increase Mather, who was the president of Harvard, a deeply religious institution at the time. It was religion, not science, that stamped out cruel and irrational superstition. [10]

The negative portrayal of the Puritans is nothing new. Even the name "Puritan" derives from the mocking nickname their fellow sixteenth-century Englishmen gave them for trying to purify the Anglican Church in Great Britain. Both the Puritans who founded the Massachusetts Bay Colony and their Separatist brethren, the Pilgrims, were despised and persecuted by the established Church of England—thus their motivation to come to America. And today, the Pilgrims' Thanksgiving feast may be one of the few positive representations we still have of the New England colonists in American life. The zealous Protestants who settled New England may not have had our modern notions of religion, science, and liberty—for good or ill—but we should be thankful that they helped create what would become the dominant culture in the future United States. Without Columbus, the massive exodus across the Atlantic would not have happened, or at least it would have been delayed. But Columbus is the father of the Americas, not of what we would call America—the United States. That nation, different from Europe, and even from the other New World nations, owes a unique debt to this particular band of English colonists.

The Europe of the mid-1500s was a turbulent and fast-changing place. Christopher Columbus opened the New World up to Spanish colonization in the 1490s, but in the century after his death, the great Columbian Exchange flowered into something far greater than he ever conceived. What started as a trickle of swashbuckling Spanish explorers grew into a widespread migration to the Americas by an increasingly diverse assortment of colonists from different European countries, each planting the seeds of its nation's distinct cultural and religious attitudes in new lands. The exodus to the New World was fueled by great changes occurring in the Old. Europe was emerging from its medieval period. When Columbus had sailed in 1492, there was one predominant Christian religion in the West. In 1517, just twenty-five years later, a German priest by the name of Martin Luther questioned the hegemony of the Catholic Church, launching a deep schism that would never be repaired. The Protestant Reformation gained in strength over the next century, causing religious and civil turmoil in and between nations.

England wasn't free from these convulsions. King Henry VIII began the Protestantization of the country when he broke off from the Catholic Church because Rome wouldn't approve of a divorce from his wife, Catherine of Aragon, in 1533. This set off a series of wild religious swings from monarch to monarch as the country flipped from Catholic to Protestant, then back to Catholic and back to Protestant again. Violent purges ensued. As the country finally settled down as a mostly Protestant kingdom under King James I (a monarch of lax morals who nevertheless was responsible for the King James Bible), both fears of a Catholic return to power—which would undoubtedly bring more violence—and discontent that the state-ordained church was failing to uphold the strict doctrines of the Protestant faith continued to fester.

While England was ahead of its peers in developing a modern free market economy and finance capitalism that would soon shatter the feudal order, it was also going through a period of corruption and moral decline. "Enterprising older women stocked bawdy houses with girls, tavern houses hosted crooked gamblers and pickpockets for a share of the take, and the royal monopoly could not keep pace with unlicensed alehouses," explains historian Walter A. McDougal. "Drunkenness and its offspring—crime, fights, and promiscuous sex—seemed out of control. Vagrants accosted travelers, footpads haunted London, gangs of rootless toughs of both sexes lived off the land like brigands."[11]

To the devoutly religious, moral rot seemed to be everywhere.

The turbulent moral climate gave rise to the Puritans, critics of the lax church and what they saw as the increasing depravity of society. Man, they believed, was inherently fallen, doomed to sin and damnation but for the grace of Christ. While a perfect world was never attainable, the world could be improved by those who had dedicated their lives to God. The English Puritans increasingly believed that that project would be impossible in their home country.

They did not lay the blame for declining morals on this growing free market system. While they were some of the strongest critics of the individualism produced by this new development in human relations, they did not believe that either capitalism or wealth was the ultimate problem. Instead, it was the failure of the church to instill the virtues needed to create a good society in accordance with Christian morals. In fact, as we shall see, some of the earliest Puritan settlers in America quickly came around to the idea that a free market was generally in accordance with human nature and that socialist and collectivist economic schemes would only lead to failure—and worse, to vice.

The Protestant colonists who settled New England were from numerous distinct groups of dissenters from the established Church of England. While the Puritans believed it could be corrected from within, others, including the Pilgrims, thought the Anglican Church was hopelessly corrupt and needed to be abandoned entirely. The crown and established church looked at them with unease and occasional outright hostility. Nevertheless, they had reason to fear violence and repression. King James was aggressively asserting "the divine right of kings," a philosophy that had been on the wane in England for centuries.

This philosophy essentially put the king above the law and challenged the limitations that had been placed on his power in English law since the Magna Carta four hundred years before. The rights of Englishmen and the English common law had been cornerstones of the liberty that set Britain apart from the rest of Europe. The established Church of England was also cracking down on dissenters of all stripes.

Violent religious purges were common in that era, as the Puritans were well aware. *Foxe's Book of Martyrs*, a publication popular at the time, described in grisly detail the various ways Protestant martyrs had been killed for their faith, especially under the Catholic Queen Mary I in the 1550s. The practice of executing people by burning them at the stake, though on the decline, was still in use. Persecution of Puritans had calmed down under Queen Mary's successor,

Elizabeth I, who was Protestant, but the looming fear of violent persecution continued, and not without reason. Catholic agitation and the Gunpowder Plot of Guy Fawkes, an attempt to blow up Parliament and overthrow the Protestant king in 1605, fostered a climate of fear.[12]

Today, it is easy to forget how ferocious religious divides could be in earlier times. One may say the Puritans were "bigoted" toward Catholics, but their fear and loathing stemmed from the reality that most of Europe at that time had been convulsed by religious wars. The right of conscience and the freedom to worship were rarely if ever recognized by either side.

In light of growing threats, one group of Protestants, the most well-known to modern Americans, decided to leave England illegally in 1608. The initial destination for these Separatists, as they were sometimes known, was not America but Holland, a familiar Protestant neighbor with a reputation for respecting religious liberty. After several abortive attempts, which led to many arrests, a significant portion of their number were finally able to escape and mostly settled in Leiden, Holland. While the Dutch were mostly welcoming to the newcomers, the English Separatists ultimately found themselves out of place in their new country. Though they no longer feared religious persecution, they struggled to mesh with Dutch society. Many felt that the Dutch lacked morals and feared that their children would be corrupted.[13] Worse, they feared that Catholic Spain, which had once had dominion over Holland, was preparing to invade the small country and make it Catholic once again. A decade after coming to Holland, many of these Separatists decided they needed to move on. As the young William Bradford, who would go on to become one of the greatest of their number, would write, "...they knew they were pilgrims."[14]

Bradford wrote a journal about his experiences. These writings weren't published in his lifetime, but they were eventually turned into the book *Of Plymouth Plantation*, a work widely read in the nine-teenth century. Bradford was an archetype of the best Puritan culture would produce. As one writer said of him, "... all the grandest char-acteristics of the best traditions of puritanism seem to be concen-trated in him."[15] But in 1620, William Bradford was just one of many looking for a new and better life.

These Pilgrims, as we call them today thanks to Bradford's charac-terization, eventually settled on a logical destination for their flock: America. After, perhaps surprisingly, securing a royal charter from King James—mostly by agreeing that the monarchy would have domin-ion over the land but not religious authority—the Separatists set up a joint venture with the Virginia Company to settle in the New World.[16] Thus began the great voyage of the Pilgrims across the Atlantic.

The story of the *Mayflower* is still familiar to most American schoolchildren. A gaggle of about 130 passengers and crew crowded aboard the little wooden ship in 1620, setting sail for the New World on September 6. Shipbuilding had advanced from Columbus's day, but it was nevertheless a tiny ship, only about 100 feet long, and it was battered by storms along the way. Only one man died in the perilous journey to a land in which there would be no welcome, but it was still a difficult crossing. On November 9, they finally made landfall at Cape Cod, which was far away from where they had intended to settle in Virginia. Storms had blown them well off their course. Many of the crew and passengers were ill and desperately needed to get onto dry land. But despite not reaching their original destination, they decided to stay.

"Many of the passengers were no doubt eager to set foot on land once again," historian Nathaniel Philbrick has written. "All were thankful that they had finally arrived safely in America. And yet it was difficult for them to look to the future with anything but dread. There were three thousand miles of ocean between them and home."[17]

William Bradford reflected on the Pilgrims' first day in the New World: "Having thus passed the vast ocean, and the sea of troubles before while they were making their preparations, they had no friends to welcome them, no inns to entertain and refresh their weather-beaten bodies, nor houses—much less towns—to repair to."[18]

After exploring the area for about a month, the Pilgrims decided to settle in at a place they called New Plymouth. It is then that they decided to draw up a plan for a new government for Plymouth Colony. This was necessary in part because they were actually outside the jurisdiction of the Virginia Company. They also had to account for the fact that some of their fellow travelers were not Puritans. So they needed to hash out a document that would set up broad guidelines for the venture's governance. The document they drew up, the Mayflower Compact, is rightly regarded as a triumph of self-government.[19]

In some ways, the Mayflower Compact was decidedly un-revolutionary. The Plymouth Colony would be governed similarly to small towns in England.[20] Nevertheless, it was revolutionary in one key way: it established a society built on consent in the New World. From this firm foundation would sprout the future United States, whose Founders would refine and codify this powerful philosophy of consent into the greatest liberty-protective document ever created: the Constitution of the United States. In addition to creating the Mayflower Compact, the Pilgrims—along with the English colonists in general—brought with them the English common law, which relied on precedent and provided a better bulwark for liberty over other European legal systems at that time.[21]

As important as the creation of the Mayflower Compact would be in American history, the Pilgrims had more immediate practical concerns. They had to survive in the harsh New England wilderness. They had been dropped into an unrelenting world of ferocious winters, foreign terrain, and numerous aggressive Indian tribes. But the

Pilgrims were, in their minds, people on a divinely inspired mission. They were going to make things work. The first year of this attempt was beset by miserable failure, hardship, and death. In just a few months, about half of the Pilgrims had died. They suffered through disease, exacerbated by exposure to harsh elements.[22]

At this moment, they hit a stroke of luck—or Providence. They had met several local Indians in their early days in America, most of whom were aloof or occasionally hostile. Sadly, the local Indian tribes had been utterly devastated by disease, an unfortunate byproduct of being isolated from the larger world for centuries. But one Indian whom they encountered was friendly and healthy and had a strong command of the English language. Tisquantum, or Squanto, came to them at just the right time. A slaver had taken him prisoner over five years earlier, and he had originally been set to be sold into bondage in Spain. But Squanto escaped and ended up in England. In England, he learned English, found employment, and traveled through Europe. He had returned to his homeland in the employ of a British explorer a year before the Pilgrims arrived. When Squanto arrived at his home, he found it desolate; disease had annihilated his village and all his close relations.

As tragic as Squanto's life had been, he used his skills—developed in his experiences on both sides of the Atlantic—to become a serious player in local politics. Regardless of his motivations, Squanto was a godsend to the Pilgrims. Bradford called him a "special instrument sent of God." Squanto helped them make treaties with local tribes, "showed them how to plant corn, where to take fish and other commodities, and guided them to unknown places, and never left [the Pilgrims] till he died."[23] It was the treaty that Squanto brokered between the Pilgrims and the Pokanokets tribe that led to the famous Thanksgiving of American lore. This was a remarkable feat given the way the Pilgrims had bumbled through their initial contacts with

Indian tribes, provoking immediate hostility. It was almost miraculous how Squanto helped patch things up.

After the first year of hardship, the surviving Pilgrims held a day of thanksgiving, the Thanksgiving we have come to celebrate in modern America. Historians have described it as a harvest festival with religious overtones. Of course, nearly everything the Pilgrims did had religious overtones. But although some on the far left have peddled a "National Day of Mourning"—a "holiday" based on racial grievance and animosity—in order to rebuke Thanksgiving as a kind of celebration of white supremacy, the original thanksgiving was actually more of an Indian celebration than an English one.

"Countless Victorian-era engravings notwithstanding, the Pilgrims did not spend the day sitting around a long table draped with a white linen cloth, clasping each other's hands in prayer as a few curious Indians looked on," according to Nathaniel Philbrick. "Instead of an English affair, the First Thanksgiving soon became an overwhelmingly Native celebration when [Indian chief] Massasoit and a hundred Pokanokets (more than twice the entire English population of Plymouth) arrived at the settlement."[24]

The Pilgrims have sometimes been portrayed as charity cases at the original Thanksgiving, being helped along by the good graces of local Indians. This is a misinterpretation. Both sides found that cooperation suited their interests. The Pokanokets saw the Pilgrims as a valuable ally to counterbalance the Narragansetts, a much larger and more powerful local tribe. And the Pilgrims needed local allies and tutors in survival in the New World.

This joint celebration between very different kinds of Americans was appropriate, given the holiday's meaning to our *E Pluribus Unum* nation hundreds of years in the future.

Communism Fails

In this early period of suffering and struggle for the Pilgrims, William Bradford rose to leadership within the colony. After the death of the Plymouth colony's first governor, John Carver, the Pilgrims chose Bradford to be the governor of the colony, a post he held off and on for the rest of his life.

Bradford's writings laid out the tribulations of the early settlers at Plymouth in incredible detail. These mostly middle-class people, used to urban living in England, fared poorly in the harsh climate of their new home. Initially, the Pilgrims attempted to create a communistic economy, counting on altruistic sharing rather than the profit motive in an effort to appease their British investors. Even on this very small scale, and in a tight-knight religious community of true believers, the collectivist economy broke down.[25] Growth was slow, and the people were hardly able to feed themselves. They were suffering the "misery of want," Bradford wrote.[26]

Bradford decided to loosen up the economic restrictions, allowing the settlers to own and cultivate their own crops on their own land. This, as he wrote, "made all hands more industrious, so that much more corn was planted than otherwise."

There has been some debate about whether or not this system was true socialism or a kind of predatory indentured servitude. Historian Samuel Elliot Morison said, "it was not communism" but rather "a very degrading and onerous slavery to the English capitalists."[27] But in practice, it was very similar to a socialized economy, and the sorry results—starvation and misery—exposed precisely why socialism and communism continually fail whenever attempted. Those who worked hard received no additional benefit, and those who worked less did no worse. Without private property, the incentive to work hard dissipated. The unfairness of the system created squabbles and conflict between even religious brethren. Far from a brotherhood of man, the communal economy created enmity and, ultimately, greater scarcity.

Having watched this experiment fail, William Bradford laid out one of the most articulate arguments against socialism long before the modern word even came into use—three centuries before Karl Marx wrote *The Communist Manifesto*. It is worth quoting Bradford at length on his experience with proto-communism and his conclusions about its effects on even a moral people:

> The failure of this experiment in communal service, which was tried for several years, and by good and honest men, proves the emptiness of the theory of Plato and other ancients, applauded by some of later times, —that the taking away of private property, and the possession of it in community, by a commonwealth, would make a state happy and flourishing; as if they were wiser than God.
>
> For in this instance, community of property (so far as it went) was found to breed much confusion and discontent, and retard much employment which would have been to the general benefit and comfort. For the young men who were most able and fit for service objected to being forced to spend their time and strength in working for other men's wives and children, without any recompense. The strong man or the resourceful man had no more share of food, clothes, etc., than the weak man who was not able to do a quarter the other could. This was thought injustice....
>
> This feature would have been worse still if it had been men of an inferior class. If (it was thought) all were to share alike, and all were to do alike, then all were on an equality throughout, and one was as good as another; and so, if it did

not actually abolish those very relations which God himself has set among men, it did at least greatly diminish the respect that is so important should it be preserved amongst them.

Let none argue that this is due to human failing, rather than to this communistic plan of life in itself. I answer, seeing that all men have this failing in them, that God in His wisdom saw another plan of life was fitter for them.[28]

The course "fitter" to man was freedom—what in modern terminology we call the free market—and private property. Having learned this, the Plymouth Colony was able to survive and thrive. The colony moved along the path of privatization, entirely abandoning its brief "communistic" experiment. Over the next decades, Plymouth grew steadily; though not situated to be an economic powerhouse, it survived. The Pilgrims' limited but significant success did not go unnoticed. Others in search of religious freedom began to see the New World as a beacon of hope, a place where they could create a good and great society for themselves.

Alexis de Tocqueville, the famed French observer of American life, attributed the creation of a unique American culture to this Pilgrim experience. As he wrote in *Democracy in America*, "Persecuted by the government of the mother-country, and disgusted by the habits of a society opposed to the rigor of their own principles, the Puritans went forth to seek some rude and unfrequented part of the world, where they could live according to their own opinions, and worship God in freedom."[29]

A Shining City Upon a Hill

Within the next decade, a new king would ascend to the throne, one who was even more unpalatable to the Puritans in England. King

Charles I insisted on enforcing the divine right of kings, began assuming absolute power, laid repressive taxes on the people, and—worst of all from the Puritans' perspective—married a Catholic woman. This encouraged distrust and fear that their way of life was increasingly in peril. John Winthrop, a prominent English lawyer and Puritan leader, began to organize a large migration from England in the footsteps of those early Pilgrims.

Materially, Winthrop had done well for himself in England and was a successful man in his community. To leave for the New World meant he would give up a comfortable existence for a hard life, one that he would likely have to endure for the rest of his days. The Pilgrims may have eked out a meager existence in America, but other colonies had fared worse, being raided by hostile Indians or suffering total collapse. Winthrop thought the risk was worth it. He and other Puritans hatched out a plan to create a more or less autonomous colony in America. They held several meetings, and Winthrop quickly established himself as the lead spokesman of this venture. He was the primary author of a document that laid out the reasons for emigration. In the work, called "General Observations," he explained how, as followers of Christ, they should not turn from the hardships of the New World for the sake of staying in their comfortable homes in England.[30]

Not only were Puritans in danger of religious persecution, Winthrop argued, but in the wake of the economic boom occurring in England, the people had lost their way and were increasingly turning their eyes away from God. While Winthrop personally blamed England's religious authorities for this, he carefully left criticism of them out of his public proposition to emigrate. Criticizing the church directly could have brought his whole project to a screeching halt. Instead, he offered a hopeful vision of a "fresh start" in an as-yet unformed country, separated by thousands of miles from Old World corruption.[31]

The result of Winthrop's efforts was the largest Puritan migration to America. The Winthrop fleet, as it became known, was comprised of eleven ships and over a thousand colonists, dwarfing the Pilgrim venture from a decade earlier. At some point on the journey, Winthrop likely delivered from his flagship, *Arabella*, what became the most important, and certainly the most cited, sermon of the last five hundred years: "A Model of Christian Charity."

The sermon was similar in rhetoric to numerous other Puritan sermons at the time, and it perhaps did not seem so profound to those who first heard it. But like the Declaration of Independence and the Gettysburg Address, "A Model of Christian Charity" perfectly encapsulated something deeply important about America. The broad outline of American exceptionalism and the characteristics that have defined us as a people and have made us unique in the world began to take shape in Winthrop's speech.

Winthrop began:

> GOD ALMIGHTY in his most holy and wise providence, hath so disposed of the condition of' mankind, as in all times some must be rich, some poor, some high and eminent in power and dignity; others mean and in submission.

Material inequality was seen as natural; to fight it would be to fight the laws of God and nature. People were simply different, as God intended. But that some did better or worse materially did not mean that they were better or worse morally; it simply meant that God had different intentions for each. Individuals might have different gifts, but all were sinful and equally guilty in the eyes of God. To be talented and gifted required duty and humility, not the self-worship of innate superiority. Success and wealth were blessings, neither to be envied nor elevated beyond their proper context. As historian

Francis Bremer has written, the Puritans "rejected any perfectionist claims for equality of power or condition," but they were to use the gifts that were given to voluntarily help their fellow man. They sought unity, not conformity; they sought charity, not leveling. This was the basis of a strong community.[32]

Winthrop instructed the Puritan emigrants to create a good and godly society in the New World, to be an example to others:

> For we must consider that we shall be as a city upon a hill.
> The eyes of all people are upon us. So that if we shall deal
> falsely with our God in this work we have undertaken, and
> so cause Him to withdraw His present help from us, we
> shall be made a story and a by-word through the world.

The "city upon a hill" phrase is borrowed from the Bible, specifically Matthew 5:14–16, in which Christ tells his followers, "Ye are the light of the world. A city that is set on a hill cannot be hid." In a fallen world, the Puritans hoped to set an example and be a beacon of light and hope for others.

Winthrop's "city upon a hill" line has echoed down through the centuries, an important element of how Americans view themselves. In his farewell speech to Massachusetts, President-Elect John F. Kennedy—notably, given his Irish-Catholic heritage—paid homage to Winthrop and his state's Puritan forebears.[33]

Winthrop's band of settlers would ultimately form the Massachusetts Bay Colony, including Boston and Salem. In future years, they would merge with others bands of Puritans to form the distinct nature of the New England region.

As others migrated to the New World in future years, Puritan culture spread. A minority faction of people in England became the dominant strain in New England. "In England the stronghold of

Puritanism was in the middle classes, and it was from the middle classes that the majority of the emigrants came," Tocqueville wrote. "The population of New England increased rapidly; and whilst the hierarchy of rank despotically classed the inhabitants of the mother-country, the colony continued to present the novel spectacle of a community homogeneous in all its parts. A democracy, more perfect than any which antiquity had dreamt of, started in full size and pan-oply from the midst of an ancient feudal society."[34]

The Fallen Nature of Man

The relationship between English settlers and Indians was quite complex, just as it was for Columbus and the early Spanish colonists and the natives they encountered. Though treatment of Indians has become a modern reason to rebuke early settlers as uniquely geno-cidal and oppressive, the picture of a pristine continent, untroubled by violence and war like a kind of Garden of Eden until suddenly corrupted by the introduction of Europeans, is not in accordance with reality. While early contact between cultures was often troubled or became violent, the modern narrative—warped by a reduction of all history to endless stories of oppressor against oppressed groups— poorly serves the reality of early-1600s America.

When the Pilgrims arrived at Plymouth, they were surrounded by an interlocking web of local tribes, many of which—despite dwin-dled numbers due to disease—were very powerful in relation to the newcomers.

Though the numbers of Puritans and other English colonists grew substantially while Indian populations shrank or disappeared, it wasn't because the English pursued a policy of annihilation as Communist historian Howard Zinn has framed it. Zinn uses the Pequot War and King Philip's War—which took place in the 1630s and 1670s respectively—as his evidence; in his telling, the Puritan settlers instigated a violent slaughter of local Indians in the first war, then, after years of peace with their Indian neighbors, they initiated another even more genocidal war against them a generation later.[35]

It is true that the Puritan settlers often viewed Indian tribes as mischievous "savages," but this distinction was based less on racial than cultural lines. The Puritans, for instance, saw their Irish cousins, racially indistinct from the English, as "barbarians" as well. In fact, the Puritans had little understanding of racial differences. They thought the people of the New World had darker skin because they had been exposed to the sun.[36]

Fear, misunderstanding, and sometimes prejudice, not deep-seated racism and hatred, defined the Puritan attitude toward native people.

In the Pequot War, which began in 1636, the Puritan settlers were the underdogs. The Pequot were a powerful tribe originally from the area around the modern state of New York. Their name likely meant "destroyer," "destroyer of men," or something to that effect, and they were generally hostile toward their neighbors. They invaded what is now Connecticut and took land from the local Indian inhabitants, which is where they also bumped into the expanding Puritan settlements. The local tribes attempted to ally themselves with the Puritans for security and aid since they had been driven off their land, but the Puritans were initially hesitant to be involved in the conflict at all. Despite attempts to avoid it, they were eventually dragged into this regional struggle. After several English settlers were killed by the Pequot, they decided to wage a desperate war against a numerically superior foe.[37]

The several hundred Puritans that had settled in Connecticut allied with various local tribes and eventually defeated the Pequot, who numbered in the thousands. After this bloody incident, there was about four decades of peace.

Here it is important to note that, as violent as the Puritan battles with the Pequot were, they are in no way outside the norm of violence through human history. Though Zinn and others would pin particular cruelty on the Puritans or the later United States, violence such as this had been committed between peoples, including the native tribes in New England, for a very long time. The Pequot simply saw the Puritans as another local tribe, one that had to be dealt with like any other—often with violence.

Zinn and others on the left tell the story of these conflicts to deceive people into believing that somehow Puritans, Americans, and Westerners are inherently violent and malicious—to convince their audience that somehow the bad things in this world are attributable to Western civilization rather than the fallen nature of man. It's an attempt to prove that our civilization was uniquely built on cruelty and that the Left offers another, better way that is attainable if we reject those Western norms.

What's quite clear is that human societies have generally been violent, especially tribal ones. Yes, modern nations have the technological capacity to kill on a grander scale (and let us note that nations governed from the left—namely Stalin's Soviet Union and Mao's China—are the most guilty on this count, outdoing even the Nazis in murder on a mass scale), but the life of the average citizen in these modern societies is notably longer and less subject to violence. In fact, modern Western nations are some of the least violent places in all of human history.[38]

Tribal societies fought over land, they fought over food—they fought over everything just as frequently—if not far more frequently—than modern nations.[39] It is only our removal from the brutality of these primitive societies that has allowed the fanciful notion of the "noble savage" to gain a foothold on our imaginations. And this mythical notion has created the perception that civilization is somehow worse than tribal society and somehow against our nature.[40]

Peddlers of the myth of the noble savage, like Zinn, play a shell game to deceive people, most of whom live in the very comfortable world created by Western civilization—which was not, despite Zinn's dishonest rhetoric, built on a foundation of unique violence and plunder.[41] The truth is quite the opposite.

The rule of law, respect for private property rights, and strict limitations on the power of government made it so Englishmen, Puritans, and eventually Americans could live in a society of less violence, not more. The technology created by this uniquely successful culture also gave it unique advantages in winning wars, if it had to wage them. Thus, the Puritans defeated their neighbors when conflict arose. That the Puritans fought and defeated the Pequot proves nothing more sinister than that they were human beings trying to cope in a fallen world in which only the dead have seen the end of war. Those who believe in the perfectibility of man can't accept this—something that helps explain their apparently unquenchable rage at our history.

The unique characteristics of the British settlers—not just the Puritans, but the other groups that settled in the New World as well—set the course for American civilization in the centuries to come. But it was not just their Britishness that made them unique. It was also the enterprising attitude of those who dared to cross an ocean to build a new life in a strange land, those who struck out to form a new society. As Winston Churchill wrote, these people were outsiders, and "out of sympathy with the Government at home. The creation of towns and settlements from the wilderness, warfare with the Indians, and remoteness and novelty of the scene widened the gulf with the Old World."[42]

Diverse Backgrounds, Same Forefathers

These early American settlers laid the foundation for a self-reliant, self-sufficient, and Christian society in the New World. Though they would have never seen themselves as anything other than British, they were creating the basis for a new civilization that would emerge in coming centuries—and chart a distinct course away from Great Britain and Europe as a whole. They did not seek liberty in the same sense that their descendants would in 1776, but they established the rudiments of self-government that would allow the American Revolution to succeed where other revolutions failed. The cultural norms for a free and independent society were being molded long before the United States existed.

The Thanksgiving we have today isn't exactly like the one Pilgrims and Indians shared in 1621. Thanksgiving, as we know it today, is mostly a creation of the eighteenth and nineteenth centuries rather than the seventeenth. It was George Washington who issued the first proclamation declaring a national day of thanksgiving in 1789 to mark the beginning of a new nation under the Constitution.

Washington said that Congress had recommended "a day of public thanksgiving and prayer to be observed by acknowledging with grateful hearts the many signal favors of Almighty God especially by affording them an opportunity peaceably to establish a form of government for their safety and happiness."[43]

Many other presidents would issue proclamations of thanksgiving after the initial one, but Thanksgiving didn't become an annual holiday until the days of Abraham Lincoln. And it might have never become a national holiday if not for two important people: Daniel Webster and Sarah Josepha Hale.

Thanksgivings, plural, were haphazardly commemorated throughout the country, especially in New England, but we have

Daniel Webster, a New Hampshire-born politician who became a leading Massachusetts statesman and one of America's most famous men, to thank for laying the groundwork for the national holiday. It was Webster who merged Thanksgiving proclamations with tributes to Pilgrim and Puritan forefathers, who became forefathers for us all. In his profoundly important early nineteenth-century tribute, Webster explained why we must keep the flame of the Pilgrims alive and why it was important to foster and pass on the cultural inheritance that New Englanders—and in some sense all Americans—had received from them.

What was this great inheritance? It was the Puritan ethos: the values of hardy folk who braved incredible hardship so that future generations could enjoy a new and better world than the one their ancestors lived in. When we think of "American exceptionalism," a concept more fully fleshed out by Tocqueville in the nineteenth century, we are thinking in part of the ideals of the Puritan forbearers from two centuries before. These settlers were looking for nothing less than a promised land across the ocean, as John Winthrop ably articulated for posterity.

It was American cultural mores, not just abstract ideals, that made America's experiment in liberty uniquely successful. As one political scientist summarizes Tocqueville's analysis: "the Puritans taught their descendants that freedom was given by God for moral and religious purposes and that those who ignored these purposes did so at their souls' peril."[44] Even as the country secularized in the late eighteenth and early nineteenth centuries, many of the cultural habits of the original colonists stuck. This culture endured at the bedrock of American life, and Daniel Webster cemented its importance in the minds of Americans for his generation and those that followed.

On a mild winter day in 1820, a large crowd gathered at the First Parish Church in Massachusetts to celebrate Forefather's Day. The regional New England holiday would be particularly special that year, the two hundredth anniversary of the Pilgrims landing at Plymouth Rock. Daniel Webster, a prominent orator and a budding American statesman, was set to address the crowd. Webster had been preoccupied with his role in amending his state's constitution, but he couldn't pass up the opportunity to speak at this special event. As historian Robert Remini explains, "Here in Plymouth, Massachusetts, in 1820 he was asked, in effect, to speak to the origins of the nation, its basic foundations. Nothing short of an effort worthy of Edmund Burke would suffice."[45]

For an hour and a half, and mostly without notes, Webster delivered one of the greatest patriotic speeches in American history. He began by noting that the "Pilgrim Fathers" had left their descendants an incredible legacy, then called for his own generation to offer future ones "some proof that we have endeavored to transmit the great inheritance unimpaired; that in our estimate of public principles and private virtue, in our veneration of religion and piety, in our devotion to civil and religion's liberty, in our regard for whatever advances human knowledge or improves human happiness, we are not altogether unworthy of our origin."[46]

Webster made the case for commemorating history: "Human and mortal although we are, we are nevertheless not mere insulated beings, without relation to the past or the future. We live in the past by a knowledge of its history; and in the future, by hope and anticipation."

This was not a call to venerate history for its own sake or simply to tell an engaging story; instead, it was a call to grapple with the past in order to better ourselves and our future. Webster explained how the unique traits of the Puritans had ultimately contributed to the creation of the United States. Their most important values—self-government, private property, Christian morals, industry, and even, to a certain extent, religious liberty—lived on in his country centuries later. These ideas, he argued, had deepened with time. And he called on these moral underpinnings to oppose a great evil of his age, one with which Americans were becoming ever more consumed: the institution of slavery. Webster denounced the slave trade in particular as the ultimate offense against the nation's Puritan heritage. Webster said, "It is not fit that the land of the Pilgrims should bear the shame longer."

A Noble Tradition of Giving Thanks

Webster's speech elevated the Puritans in the eyes of Americans and defined them for his generation. He helped expand their heritage beyond New England: Americans of all regions and all backgrounds were the sons and daughters of the Puritan forefathers. But it wasn't until the mid-nineteenth century that the modern Thanksgiving, with the Pilgrims as central characters, took real shape. For that, we must thank Sarah Josepha Hale, a famed New England author—born in New Hampshire, like Webster—who wrote books and children's poems, including "Mary Had a Little Lamb."

Sarah Hale was a fierce advocate of education and the preservation of American history. She was involved in efforts to create the Bunker Hill Memorial in Boston and in the preservation of Mount Vernon, George Washington's Virginia estate.[47]

Hale was among the greatest of a proud tradition of American female educators. Starting in the 1830s, Hale began a campaign to solidify Thanksgiving as a national tradition along with the celebration of Independence Day. If the Fourth of July was a celebration of American ideas, then Thanksgiving would be a celebration of American culture, family, and religion.

Hale wrote in 1837 that such a celebration "might, without inconvenience, be observed on the same day of November, say the last

Thursday in the month, throughout all New England; and also in our sister states, who have engrafted it upon their social system. It would then have a national character, which would, eventually, induce all the states to join in the commemoration of 'Ingathering,' which it celebrates. It is a festival which will never become obsolete, for it cherishes the best affections of the heart—the social and domestic ties. It calls together the dispersed members of the family circle, and brings plenty, joy and gladness to the dwellings of the poor and lowly."[48]

By the 1850s, most states had a thanksgiving celebration of some type on the books, but Hale wanted to make it a national celebration. In 1852, a decade before Thanksgiving became a nationally recognized holiday, she wrote, "The Fourth of July is the exponent of independence and civil freedom. Thanksgiving Day is the national pledge of Christian faith in God, acknowledging him as the dispenser of blessings. These two festivals should be joyfully and universally observed throughout our whole country, and thus incorporated in our habits of thought as inseparable from American life."

It was during the Civil War that Hale had a breakthrough. She had called for Secretary of State William H. Seward and President Abraham Lincoln to create a day of national thanksgiving. Lincoln had made several calls for thanksgiving during the war, but he eventually came around to Hale's idea of codifying it into a standing holiday. Lincoln issued a proclamation on October 3, 1863. After describing the state of the Civil War as it stood at that time, he said, "I do therefore invite my fellow citizens in every part of the United States, and also those who are at sea and those who are sojourning in foreign lands, to set apart and observe the last Thursday of November next, as a day of Thanksgiving and Praise to our beneficent Father who dwelleth in the Heavens."[49]

And so began the celebration of Thanksgiving, tied both to what America was and to what it became. It is a celebration of family and material prosperity; two things the Puritans would have undoubtedly appreciated. The underlying message of the holiday is that America is a promised land of plenty and that we should be grateful to be blessed with such abundance. Nothing captures this better than the 1943 Norman Rockwell painting *Freedom from Want*, which depicts a happy extended family about to eat turkey at table full of food. It's notable that this idyllic painting was released in the dark days of World War II. Even amid the most devastating war in human history, Americans had an expectation of material satisfaction and a belief that they would soon return to the good life. The fascists and communists may have promised struggle and the forward march of man, but America offered hearth and home and plenty.

Our Puritan Heritage: A Blessing, Not a Curse

Though the United States may be far removed from the world of the Puritan forefathers, elements of Puritanism remain in our culture. Americans consistently rate as the most charitable people on earth, surpassing most others countries by wide margins.[50] We outpace Europeans in charitable giving and donate more than any developed nation in terms of the share of GDP, which far exceeds that of other countries.[51] And religious Americans, who see a much larger role for private charity and a smaller one for government agencies, are the most giving among us.[52] In this, Americans today uphold what Winthrop commanded in his speech on Christian charity.

The Puritans and the other early English colonists established the cultural norms that would lead to a successful Revolution and American independence. Religious liberty—expounded upon by philosopher John Locke and embraced by the Founding Fathers—was still several generations away when the Puritans came to America. Yet they gave American the concept of ordered liberty, of men constrained by moral law rather than the divine right of kings. The United States did not turn out precisely as the Puritans had envisioned; we nonetheless owe them a great debt. While America's has undoubtedly expanded from its narrower Protestant origins and become more pluralistic, it is undeniable that America and Christianity are intertwined.

It is often debated whether the United States was founded as a Christian country. In the sense of an established religion, as in many nations throughout world history, the answer is no. But having no established national religion is a very different thing from being anti-religious. America certainly wasn't founded as an atheist country or even as a non-religious country. Nor would the Founders, regardless of their personal views, have encouraged us to go down that path.

More important for the sake of our current debates, it is impossible to separate America from its profoundly religious, mostly Protestant Christian origin as some modern, mostly left-wing historians have tried to do.[53] Efforts to purge Christianity and religion from American public life are not true to our nation's heritage.

The history of America from the time of the Puritans to the Founding and through the eighteenth- and nineteenth-century Great Awakenings, to the debates over slavery and to the religious references in the speeches of prominent American figures across the political spectrum up to our own day shows that America is unquestionably imbued with a Christian culture. Christianity was baked into American DNA, in large part thanks to Puritans and other early English settlers.

Before the Founding Fathers created the United States in 1776, rupturing with England forever, American culture had had almost two centuries to develop apart from the Old World. While the Puritans were subsumed into general New England and then into a wider American culture, there were undoubtedly traits that survived—beliefs, traditions, and a general outlook that made Americans particularly fit for liberty and ready to transition to life under free, republican institutions that could only be dreamed about in Europe and around the globe. These traits poured out from America's deeply religious origin. The Founders, who had various religious views whether orthodox Christians or deists, drew from this cultural well even as they sometimes questioned religious establishments.

Even Thomas Paine, one of the least religious of the Founders, used biblical arguments in his wildly popular book *Common Sense*, which helped galvanize the country to declare independence and reject monarchy forever.

It is common today to say that America is the only country based on an idea. That is only partly true. The United States, when it was formed as a political unit in 1776, was based on ideas, but so was the First French Republic in 1792. Why did the one succeed while the other degenerated into bloody chaos? American culture preceded American ideas. Notions of liberty fit the new nation like a glove.[54]

Tocqueville admired America's successful blend of religious and secular elements.[55] This was a great strength for the newly founded country—a critical element in producing a virtuous citizenry able to pursue happiness within a system of ordered liberty.

America has been blessed to be a Christian nation from its inception. Though it has gone through periods of spiritual decline and revival, religious faith has always been the frame of reference for how we see the world. Many see this as a threat and an impediment to their ambitions for transforming America—something that explains the ferocity of their attacks on the Christian history of our nation. Americans shouldn't buy into the silly suggestion that Christianity and Puritanism are sources of intolerance and authoritarianism. If anything, they have been the vital check on the worst impulses in human nature and the vicious ideologies—such as fascism and communism—that have plagued modernity.

"Puritanism" is far too often used by Americans as an epithet to malign their political opponents. Despising our Puritan forefathers is an easy trap to fall into. But Puritanism, rightly understood, has meant liberty, prosperity, and a culture of self-restraint balanced with the desire for and celebration of plenty. Today, we must consider the consequences of rejecting these values, disdaining the—fortunately still widely practiced—holiday that celebrates them, and abandoning the strength that America's religious history has given to our nation. Today, Thanksgiving is a holiday largely embraced by immigrants. Though they may not be Christians, they are joining the larger American cultural tradition. It's a tradition that welcomes all Americans to the table, and it is a tribute to the hard work, generosity, and thankfulness inherent in our culture—in contrast with the selfishness and greed with which angry leftists falsely charge America.

The chief ideal of the Thanksgiving holiday is gratitude: gratitude for the blessings of life and labor. It is with this healthy attitude that Americans have viewed their nation's past, even as times have not always been good; the fact is they have often been far, far worse elsewhere. Rare has it been in our history that large swaths of Americans, even those who suffered or were treated poorly by fellow citizens or their government, fled to other lands. Instead of the ethos of gratitude embraced by Thanksgiving, the war on history offers resentment, narrow-mindedness, and ingratitude. It is easy for students or faculty at Yale to demand the removal of a statue or plaque because their institution was built on "racism" and "slavery," but it is much harder to turn down a scholarship or tenure. Would they really pledge their "lives, fortunes, and sacred honor," as the "first" generation of Americans did, to that cause if they knew that their blessings might be stripped from them?

CHAPTER 3

The War on the Founding

To Americans and all peoples who fight that tyranny against which he swore eternal hostility, Thomas Jefferson is an ever-living and ever-inspiring champion of man's inalienable rights.

—*Bernard Mayo, 1942*[1]

Weighing in on the debate over Confederate statues in 2017, President Donald Trump said to reporters, "George Washington was a slave owner...are we going to take down statues to George Washington? How about Thomas Jefferson? What do you think of Thomas Jefferson? You like him?...Are we going to take down the statue? Because he was a major slave owner."

Trump's insinuation that activists would turn their attention to the Founders after they were done with Confederates was mocked by many in the media and even some historians on the premise that the difference between the Founders and the Confederates would be obvious to Americans. "It's the difference between a monument to the founder of our nation, and a monument to a key figure in an effort to break apart the nation," said Douglas Blackmon, an author and senior fellow at the University of Virginia's Miller Center in an interview with the *Washington Post*. "The most kind explanation of that can only be ignorance, and I don't say that to insult the president."[2]

Unfortunately, the president was right. First, they came for the Confederates, and then they very quickly came for everyone else, the Founders included. This was always the real goal: to uproot and demolish traditional America, to attack the men, institutions, and ideas that set this nation's course over the centuries. For them, America was never great. And to sell the rest of us on that proposition, they need to tear down everything that represents American greatness. The Founders, the American Revolution they made, and the Declaration of Independence are at the top of their list. The Declaration and its author, Thomas Jefferson, are special targets of their calumny. If they can persuade America to despise and reject our Founding, they will be well on their way to their ultimate goal of "fundamentally transforming" the United States.

What made our Revolution one of the very few successful revolutions—arguably the only one—in the history of mankind? Progressive thinkers in the early twentieth century attributed the American Revolution to economic factors, using quasi-Marxist historical interpretations to claim that the Founders were just wealthy men trying to protect their interests.[3] These leftists promoted their vision of the Founders as anti-Democratic to justify upending the institutions the Founders created, and they had some success in doing so.

But historians in the later twentieth century, like Gordon Wood and Forrest McDonald, reexamined the progressives' history and

found it wanting. Reducing the Founders' motivations to mere economics was wildly off base. Ideas, not base interests, motivated the
men who founded the United States. A simplistic economic narrative
was inadequate to the complicated history of the American rupture
with England.

While the causes of America's Revolution remain hotly contested,
historian Walter McDougal has succinctly summed up the multiple
factors in play: "The whole experience of the colonists dating back
to 1607 . . . made self-government, religious freedom, economic
opportunity, and territorial growth inseparable. Almost everyone
from Massachusetts to Georgia could agree that civil and religious
liberty went hand in hand, liberty could not long survive without
virtue, an exploding population could not survive without virtue,
and an exploding population could aspire to no liberty at all if its
territorial and commercial expansion were artificially choked."[4]

The foundation for an independent and unique experiment in
self-government in the United States had already been established
over generations, from the time Columbus arrived in the New World,
through the English migrations and settlement in the thirteen colonies, and up to the moment when the British Parliament and King
George III foolishly tried to put the genie back in the bottle and chain
this burgeoning nation to their will.

And perhaps no man represented the soul of that new nation
yearning for liberty better than Thomas Jefferson.

For much of American history, the Founders were untouchable.
Even as many powerful men, including Woodrow Wilson and Franklin Roosevelt, worked to undermine their legacy, few would have
dared attack them openly. Members of the Progressive Movement in
the early twentieth century may have opposed the principles of constitutional government that the founding generation created, but they
carefully avoided publicly denouncing them. President Franklin

Roosevelt's "Second Bill of Rights," harkening back to the original Bill of Rights, was a clever sleight of hand, a successful attempt to convince the American people that ideas in fundamental opposition to those of the Founders were somehow what the Founders would have wanted.[5] It was Roosevelt who had the Thomas Jefferson Memorial constructed in Washington, D.C., in the 1930s. This is somewhat ironic given the fact that Jefferson's strict constructionist constitutional principles would have prevented him from carrying out such a federal project. Roosevelt's New Deal economics would also likely have horrified Jefferson.

Today, attacks on the Founders typically start with Jefferson. With the emphasis now on what the Founders didn't do (abolish slavery) rather than what they did (build the foundations for the freest country in human history), the contrast between Jefferson's eloquent denunciations of slavery and his failure to put his principles into action make him an easy target for those want to paint the Founders as rank hypocrites. The self-contradictions of the author of the Declaration of Independence on what is increasingly the only issue modern audiences care about has made Jefferson ripe for destruction.

That's not to say that other Founders haven't found themselves on the wrong side of the war on history.

Even George Washington, the "indispensable man"[6] of the Revolution, has had a few salvos thrown his way. The famed Christ Church in Alexandria, Virginia, which Washington attended for years, decided to take down a plaque in Washington's honor in the name of inclusivity. The church, which has displayed a banner outside saying "All are welcome—no exceptions," made an exception for the Father of Our Country.[7] Perhaps even more pathetically, the San Francisco school board voted unanimously to destroy a mural with George Washington at a public school because it also depicted slaves and a dead American Indian.[8] The school board deemed the mural too offensive for modern sensitivities. The mural was painted in 1936 by artist Victor Arnautoff, who was, ironically enough, a man of the Left in his time and was trying to present a less flattering portrayal of Washington.[9] No matter—staying sufficiently "woke" typically prevails over reason or thoughtfulness.

If Jefferson falls to this crusade, there will be no stopping the eventual takedown of Washington. That Washington freed his slaves upon his death will be seen as insufficient—just as Jefferson's writing the greatest anti-slavery document of the modern age fails to save him from scathing attacks.

Jefferson's perceived hypocrisy in regard to the institution of slavery has made him the chief target of modern attacks on the Founders. In fact, this isn't the first time Jefferson's legacy has come under siege. In the nineteenth century, one radical abolitionist wrote of Jefferson's failure on the slavery issue, "Never did a man achieve more fame for what he did not do."[10] That statement may have been true at the time, but Americans today are starting to forget what he did do. They have lost touch with the immense accomplishments of this venerated American whose greatest fault is that he dared criticize an institution as old as mankind while failing to extinguish it within a single generation. This is no reason to abandon Jefferson, who may be one of the most influential men of the last millennium. Jefferson and the Founders delivered to posterity a timeless model for man's liberty and flourishing that has never been matched.

Americans of the past generally revered the Founding Fathers and what they accomplished for good reason. Though the Founders were fallible, like anyone else, unlike anyone else, they built a uniquely successful system for ordering society upon great truths about human nature.

But if they are regarded at all in modern times, the Founding Fathers are increasingly dismissed for their failings, large or small, while the transformative nature of what they accomplished is down-played or simply neglected. Americans would be foolish to abandon this inheritance.

At the critical moment of our nation's conception, the American colonies contained a deep roster of talent. And the Revolution was a fortuitous moment for these talented men. Few of the great statesmen and philosophers through history ever had anything like the oppor-tunity they had: to create enduring institutions for a new civilization at the moment of its birth. Thomas Jefferson, among the greatest of that illustrious group, was a key figure in the early debates over what America could and would be. Though his archnemesis Alexander Hamilton—who has had a bit of a revival of late—certainly had his victories and did much to set the course of our burgeoning country, Jefferson's ideas have had a unique impact on America for two and a half centuries—from Independence to the Civil War and Emancipa-tion to the Civil Rights Movement. Mid-twentieth-century historian James Thurlow Adams surmised that, without Hamilton, our coun-try "would assuredly have been killed in body," yet, "without Jefferson the new nation might have lost its soul."[11]

That the United States in the twentieth century is an unrivaled superpower of vast economic and military strength is a tribute to Hamilton, who foresaw our fate as a commercial and military power. But in times of turmoil and uncertainty over who we are, generations of Americans have turned to Jefferson as a source of inspiration. America is at its best when it is strong in body *and* soul. When our civic traditions are under threat, it is to Jefferson, the original articu-lator of our liberties, that we look for renewal.

Americans through the generations have fought over the mean-ing of the Founding—but always reclaimed its legacy. The Founders have been criticized in every era, but that criticism used to be made within the framework of understanding that their accomplishments were enormous and worth studying. Now a pernicious dogmatism about the Founders' failures is obscuring the most important aspects of their legacy. We no longer embrace what made them great while occasionally being disappointed by their all-too-human shortcomings. Instead, their flaws are magnified out of proportion and out of the context of the time they lived in. And, perhaps because of the loftiness of rhetoric, no Founder has suffered more from this way of thinking than Thomas Jefferson. His reputation has undergone a dramatic reversal—nowhere more than at the university he created and was so proud of.

From Champion of Freedom to Deplorable

Thomas Jefferson's face appears alongside those of George Washington, Abraham Lincoln, and Theodore Roosevelt on Mount Rushmore for good reason. He has been one of America's most celebrated men and presidents. But the famous Virginian never cared much for touting his presidential legacy. Jefferson's tomb, located near his Charlottesville home, is adorned by an impressive granite obelisk with an inscription representing what he believed were his greatest accomplishments. Jefferson specially designed the gravestone with meticulous care.

The obelisk reads:

> Here was buried
> Thomas Jefferson
> Author of the Declaration of American Independence
> of the Statute of Virginia for religious freedom
> & Father of the University of Virginia

"By these, as testimonials that I have lived, I wish most to be remembered," Jefferson wrote.[12]

If Americans entirely forget everything about Jefferson or turn on him as a monstrous hypocrite, they will still enjoy the fruits of these three indelible marks of his legacy: a nation founded on the timeless principles of liberty and the natural equality of men laid out in the Declaration, religious liberty enshrined in our laws, and a commitment to education that has produced a population capable of sustaining freedom.[13] All of these things are under attack in America, but at least they exist in our national DNA, waiting to be rediscovered.

Noticeably missing from Jefferson's list of accomplishments was his service as president of the United States or in any other public office that he held in his long political career. Jefferson, the man of ideas, wished for future generations to know him by the "self-evident truths" that he would pass down to them, not by the practical compromises of his political career. He hoped these ideas would be transmitted through his beloved school, the University of Virginia, which he founded in 1819.

The university went through some tumultuous early years, and many thought it was doomed to fail. Charlottesville was seen as a backwater; the early students were often substandard. What's more, the school was created as a radical experiment. It wasn't attached to a religious denomination—though religion itself wasn't discouraged—and students were expected to abide by an honor code rather than the strict rules that governed other universities, a tradition that continues today.[14]

The early struggles of the school took a huge toll on Jefferson. A near-rebellion by professors and students in 1825, just a year before Jefferson's death, brought the distraught and ailing Founder to tears.[15] But thanks to his care and enormous personal sacrifice, the school ultimately found its footing, becoming one of the most prestigious universities in the country. Students at UVA have more or less venerated Mr. Jefferson, as they reverently call him, ever since. It would be unthinkable to denounce him. Until now.

The traditional Grounds of UVA have played host to many tributes to Jefferson, but one act in the late nineteenth century was perhaps the school's greatest demonstration of devotion to its founder.

The Rotunda, which Jefferson designed, caught fire in 1895. Through the fearsome inferno, in a daring deed of bravery, students dragged Jefferson's statue out of the Rotunda, allegedly on a mattress.[16] The life-sized marble statue, created by sculptor Alexander Galt in 1860, took a few bumps in the dramatic rescue, but it survives to this day. Students managed to save many of the books in the Rotunda too, something that would undoubtedly have made the legendary bibliophile happy.

UVA wouldn't exist without Mr. Jefferson, but that hasn't stopped some of today's students and professors from trying to erase the institution's connection to its founder. A group of UVA students and outside community activists gathered in front of the restored Rotunda in 2017 to protest Jefferson and "white supremacy" after a group of white supremacists had gathered in the city to protest the removal of Confederate statues. Any distinction between Confederates and the Founders seemed to make little difference to those assembled on the Grounds. The university had already gone out of its way to acknowledge Jefferson's legacy as a slaveholder—and even planned to erect a memorial to the enslaved laborers who helped build the school—but this clearly wasn't enough for the aggrieved.[17] Protesters besieged the Jefferson statue that stands in front of the Rotunda and placed signs on it calling the Founding Father a "rapist" and a "racist." Then, in a defiant and illegal act, they covered the statue with a giant shroud. One would think this act would have provoked a harsh and defiant rebuke from school authorities in defense of the man to whom they owe so much. Instead, UVA President Teresa Sullivan offered only mild condemnation of the attack on the school's founder and seemed to accept the behavior as a reasonable protest.

"I strongly disagree with the protestors' decision to cover the Jefferson statue," Sullivan said. "I also recognize the rights of those present at the protest to express their emotions and opinions regarding the recent horrific events that occurred on our Grounds and in Charlottesville," Sullivan wrote. "Our community continues to heal, and we must remain respectful of one another."[18] Apparently "one another" did not include the school's founder.

This wasn't the first time that Jefferson had come under attack at the school. Sullivan had been embroiled in another controversy the year before when students and faculty publicly lambasted her for quoting Jefferson in messages to the student body. "For many of us, the inclusion of Jefferson quotations in these emails undermines the message of unity, equality, and civility that you are attempting to convey," read a statement to Sullivan from the angry students and teachers.[19] "I think that Jefferson is often celebrated for his accomplishments with little or no acknowledgement of the atrocities he committed against hundreds of human beings," wrote a UVA psychology professor.[20]

Thomas Jefferson is now politically incorrect at the school he founded. While he still has defenders and admirers at the university, the attacks on his legacy and the lack of an effective rebuttal would have been almost unthinkable a century ago.

The collapse of Jefferson's reputation has spread far beyond the college campus. All around the country, state Democratic Party chapters are changing the name of Jefferson-Jackson Day dinners, which were named after Jefferson and Andrew Jackson, two figures they used to celebrate as their party's founders. But no more.

Even the Jefferson Memorial in Washington, D.C., the cherished project of Franklin Roosevelt, has come under fire. In the wake of the Charlottesville controversy, the Reverend Al Sharpton absurdly suggested that public financial support of the monument cease and that the statue of Jefferson be moved to a private museum.[21] "When you look at the fact that public monuments are supported by public funds you're asking me to subsidize the insult of my family," Sharpton said. "I would repeat that the public should not be paying to uphold somebody who has had that kind of background. You have private museums, you have other things that you may want to do there."

This is a shabby way to treat the legacy of a man who contributed in so many ways, great and small, to who we are today. The attacks on Jefferson are emblematic of the overall assault on the Founding, an attempt to eject from our institutions, culture, and people the philosophy that underpins the American Republic and has left a permanent stamp on the American character. From the perspective of the modern Left, that philosophy, that Republic, and that American character are all problematic—in dire need of being "fundamentally transform[ed]."

The Founding of the United States was a pivotal moment not just in American history but in all of human history. What the Founders achieved was the creation not just of a new nation but of a "*novus ordo seclorum*"—a new order of the ages. The thirteen colonies, with a population of only about three million people—roughly equivalent to the population of Arkansas today—produced one of the most extraordinary generations ever to grace the earth. Gaining Independence from Great Britain, the preeminent world power at the time, was itself impressive. But even more important, the Founders, drawing on the wisdom of millennia of philosophy and history, defined what it meant to be a free country.[22]

They transformed their collection of colonies, at the time little more than a New World backwater, into the focus of Western civilization. In a few short centuries, this fledgling republic, once a rare outlier in a sea of monarchies and other tyrannical governments, bloomed into the most powerful nation on earth. But it has always drawn sustenance from its original dedication to freedom. Expanding on that tradition, America became the "Empire of Liberty" Jefferson once dreamed about.[23]

Author of Liberty

At a White House gathering of Nobel Prize winners, President John F. Kennedy famously said, "I think this is the most extraordinary collection of talent, of human knowledge, that has ever been gathered together at the White House, with the possible exception of when Thomas Jefferson dined alone."[24] Even among the great thinkers who founded the United States, few matched the sheer breadth of what Jefferson was capable of intellectually—he was a great architect, inventor, and scientist. He even popularized American culinary habits that have persevered to our day, such as eating ice cream.[25] He played a large role in the design of America's most famous buildings and battled with European students of natural history to demonstrate that New World flora and fauna were in no way inferior to those of the old world.[26] He was a true Renaissance man. But his greatest achievements lay in the realm of politics.

Jefferson, the greatest dreamer of the Founders, sometimes let his flights of nearly utopian fancy lead him to absurd, naïve, or simply wrong conclusions. He loved France and believed in the French Revolution, and he certainly overestimated its positive effects, clinging to faith in it far longer than more hard-headed Founders like John Adams or Alexander Hamilton. In some of his private notes, particularly to James Madison, Jefferson proposed wild ideas that have unfortunately been taken by those unfamiliar with his eclectic mind as fundamental elements of his political philosophy. Jefferson's more eccentric flights of fancy were usually deftly shot down by his friend

Madison, who—even Jefferson would likely have admitted—was the better constitutional thinker. Like many brilliant men, Jefferson had a significant number of bad ideas for every great one. But for all of Jefferson's ideological excesses and contradictions, no Founder better expressed the highest ideals of the Founding.

The first gift that Jefferson bequeathed to America was independence, which he and the Founding generation secured through great risk and sacrifice. But the Declaration of Independence laid claim to more than separation from Great Britain. Jefferson gave expression to the American mind in its formative moments. In one sense, the Declaration of Independence merely formalized a separation that had been long in the making, after repeated abuses from parliament and the king. While there were obvious practical urgencies to prioritize at the moment of declaring independence, looking back in 1825, just a year before his death, Jefferson explained to his friend Henry Lee that in writing the Declaration, his goal had been "Not to find out new principles, or new arguments, never before thought of, not merely to say things which had never been said before; but to place before mankind the common sense of the subject, in terms so plain and firm as to command their assent, and to justify ourselves in the independent stand we are compelled to take. Neither aiming at originality of principle or sentiment, nor yet copied from any particular and previous writing, it was intended to be an expression of the American mind, and to give to that expression the proper tone and spirit called for by the occasion."[27]

The beautiful language and "self-evident" truths that flowed from the pen of Jefferson left a lasting mark on the country. Jefferson's words articulated the goal of the American Revolution: not to overthrow just one hated king but to overthrow tyranny itself. Jefferson's America would be great because it was committed to liberty from the moment of its birth.

The Declaration of Independence distinguishes the United States not only from its mother country of Great Britain but also from revolutionary France. The Declaration is quite different from the English Bill of Rights, created in 1689 after the Glorious Revolution, which makes no mention of God-given rights and instead refers to the traditional "ancient rights and liberties" of Englishmen. It was born of the long English Civil War and makes no universal claims about humanity.

There is also, as political theorist Charles Kesler explained, a wide philosophical gap between the Declaration of Independence and the French Declaration of the Rights of Man. A critical distinction between them is that they rely on different philosophical traditions within the Enlightenment. Americans were committed to the moderate version of the natural rights philosophy articulated by John Locke (Jefferson once described Locke as one of the three greatest men who ever lived). The French relied more heavily on the doctrines of Jean-Jacques Rousseau, which ultimately place the power of the state and the "general will" over the rights of man and put less importance on "the consent of the governed."[28] It is also notable that the Declaration of Independence is exceedingly cautious about revolution for a revolutionary document. Jefferson took care to cite a "long chain of abuses"—rather than a more limited injury, even to fundamental rights—to justify political separation from Britain.

Americans did not demand that government be perfect, and they did not revolt after even serious grievances. They turned to revolution only when it had become clear that submission to these continual abuses would lead to absolute tyranny. The Declaration was radical for the time in the universality of its claims of right but prudent in its implementation of those principles. The Founders recognized that even the greatest people are still subject to the temptations of human nature and that the best governments can make grievous mistakes, which are better resolved through deliberation than revolution. This understanding of human nature also informed the Founders when they later designed the Constitution, which they created with the intention of checking power with power, ambition with ambition, rather than empowering a "general will." The American Founding gave birth to a nation with the liberty of the Roman Republic and the power of the Roman Empire.

America's unique path after the American Revolution cannot be attributed merely to our British cultural inheritance, nor can it be chalked up to abstractions—like the *"liberté, égalité, fraternité"* that fueled the French Revolution. The United States charted its own course, in large part thanks directly to the Declaration of Independence, the greatest accomplishment of Jefferson's life and one that should always keep him in the pantheon of greatest Americans.

The Scourge of Slavery

The issue that most threatens to destroy Jefferson's legacy is his failure on the issue of slavery, in part because this failure seems to run entirely counter to the claims of the Declaration of Independence. Because of the cavernous gap between Jefferson's words in the Declaration—"all men are created equal"—and the reality of slavery in early America and specifically in his own life, Jefferson is charged with being a charlatan. This is simply not true.

While Jefferson had personal and intellectual failings when it came to slavery, it is absurd to single him out as the man to blame for it. Jefferson's greatest accomplishment, the Declaration of Independence, was, as Martin Luther King would say, a "promissory note"—"a promise that all men would be guaranteed the inalienable rights of life, liberty, and the pursuit of happiness."[29] And America would eventually make good on that promise. The Declaration ultimately made it impossible for slavery to continue into America's future.

Americans today have a distorted view of slavery. Too commonly, it is seen as a uniquely American problem, one of the prime reasons to doubt America was ever a good or great country to begin with.

But in fact, in the four hundred years of the trans-Atlantic slave trade, only about four percent of imported slaves came to the British North American colonies and the United States. Most were initially brought to Brazil, the West Indies, and the Caribbean, though many of these eventually ended up in the US.[30] The United States was far from the only place that had slavery in the eighteenth and nineteenth centuries—an incontrovertible fact that many Americans, even those attending our elite schools, would be shocked to hear.

After passing out short quizzes to test the general knowledge of his students for over a decade, college professor Duke Pesta of the University of Wisconsin—Oshkosh has observed a worrying trend. A growing majority of his students now believe that America invented slavery and that the institution had no history outside the United States. Worse, slave ownership seems to be just about the only thing students know about the Founders. "On one quiz, 29 out of 32 students responding knew that Jefferson owned slaves, but only three out of the 32 correctly identified him as president," according to a College Fix article about Pesta's quizzes. "Interestingly, more students—six of 32—actually believed Ben Franklin had been president."[31]

Today's students have turned the way we see slavery's history in the United States on its head. Its existence here was astonishing not because it was a uniquely American institution but because it was so deeply out of step with a country founded on the concepts of liberty and the natural equality of man. That a nation that had allowed, by far, the greatest freedom to ordinary citizens also allowed an institution so removed from that ideal was what was shocking.

At the time of America's creation, most of mankind was in one form of bondage or another. Grinding poverty and repressive governments were the norm; they were accepted as the simple reality of human existence. That the "peculiar institution," as slavery was once called, lingered and festered for the nearly ninety years it took from the Founding of the United States to Emancipation is certainly lamentable. But it was the exceptional creed of America, written into its DNA from infancy, that allowed slavery to be wiped out in the Civil War.

That exceptional creed was enshrined in the Declaration of Independence, which Abraham Lincoln called the "apple of gold" to the Constitution's "frame of silver."[32]

Some today argue that Jefferson meant his assertion that "all men are created equal" to apply to white men only. But this slander is false.

As historian Dumas Malone has written, "If Jefferson had been present and had been questioned on this point he would have said that the general statement did apply to slaves, and that these unfortunate creatures had lost their freedom and all semblance of equality through the operation of human law, which in this respect was in conflict with the higher law of Nature."[33]

Does the fact that Jefferson could write stirringly of equality while owning other human beings make him, and the rest of the Founders, contemptible hypocrites? One particularly uncharitable historian has called Jefferson's inability to end slavery both personally and for the nation a "treason against the hopes of the world."[34]

It is easy to condemn Jefferson and the Founders for not doing enough to extinguish a social system now universally reviled when we don't have to deal with the complex consequences of abolition. Slavery was woven into the cultural and economic fabric of American society, and it could not be so easily removed even by those who deeply hated it. Given this reality, it is perhaps less remarkable that they failed to immediately rid themselves of it, and more remarkable that their efforts put it on the inevitable path to extinction.

Historian Bernard Bailyn has written of the wrongheaded modern inversion in the way of looking at the slavery issue: "To note only that certain leaders of the Revolution continued to enjoy the profits of so savage an institution and in their reforms failed to obliterate it inverts the proportions of the story. What is significant in the historical context of the time is not that the liberty-loving Revolutionaries allowed slavery to survive, but that they—even those who profited directly from the institution—went so far in condemning it, confining it, and setting in motion the forces that would ultimately destroy it."[35]

The personal reasons for Jefferson's failure to release his slaves will perhaps never be known to anyone but him. In Jefferson's day, there were many obstacles to and few avenues for personal or general emancipation. Despite these barriers, in the years immediately after the War of Independence, many slaveholders, even in the South, released their slaves in order to stay true to the principles of the American Revolution. For a while, slavery was seen as the unfortunate legacy of British colonial policy—in fact, it was an abuse that an early draft of the Declaration of Independence had laid at their feet.[36] But that window was short-lived, as Virginia and other states, increasingly paranoid about slave rebellions, created laws that made it difficult to free slaves within the state, especially for slaveholders with considerable debts, which Jefferson certainly had.

Jefferson, like many planters, and especially public men of his time, lived with high expenses and debt, due in part to the nature of farming and in part to the high cost of public life. At times, Jefferson lived beyond his means, but decades of time in public life would have taken a toll on anyone's finances. In sharp contrast to today, there were few ways for politicians in those days to enrich themselves, and they mostly had to finance their own careers in public service, as Jefferson did.[37]

Even the best businessmen among the Founders, like George Washington, struggled to maintain their income while serving their country in office. And debt made it difficult for slaveholders who wished to emancipate their slaves to do so, even at the time of their deaths. A Virginia law passed in 1792 gave creditors the ability to seize even freed slaves to recoup what was owed them. Not only would this mean that emancipation could be temporary, but it could also lead to the sudden breakup of families as people were re-enslaved by creditors.[38]

Jefferson nearly had a financially plausible avenue to release his slaves in 1817 when his great Polish friend, Thaddeus Kosciuszko, who had fought in the American Revolution, bequeathed part of his own wealth to Jefferson so that Jefferson's slaves could be freed, cared for, and educated.[39] Tragically, because of legal complications over this will, Jefferson never received the money.[40]

Even if Jefferson had been able to free his slaves after death, as George Washington famously did, those so emancipated would not necessarily have remained free. Many former slaves were put back in bondage, unable to care for themselves in a society that greatly restricted their ability to make a living and a new life for themselves.

Jefferson was aware of these complications, and the problem tortured him. As he aged, he became gloomy at the prospects for general emancipation and worried that insurrection and ugly race wars would result. But even with these doubts, Jefferson still believed a day would come, the sooner the better, when an institution he saw as a blight on society would be ended.

The Hemings Affair

One particularly common attack on Jefferson as a slaveowner is that he engaged in an illicit relationship with one of his slaves, Sally

Hemings, and sired several children by her. Some have gone as far as to call Jefferson a rapist. At one time, these accusations were entirely dismissed by historians as the baseless ramblings of a few hyperpartisan journalists, in particular James Callender, a disgruntled former Jefferson supporter who was angry that he didn't get a government job.[41] But recent scholars have been more willing to accept the idea that the liaison is possibly true, historian Annette Gordon-Reed having made the best case in its favor.[42] In fact, it has now become common to accept the story as an unquestionable fact rather than the conjecture it is. In 2018, Monticello, which is run by the Thomas Jefferson Foundation, decided to "end" the debate and officially declare that Jefferson indeed had children by Sally Hemings. But while it is indeed possible that Thomas Jefferson had children by her, it is far from the settled fact.

A 1998 DNA test showed that at least one of Sally Hemings' children, Eston, shared genetic heritage with the Jefferson family. What is harder to determine is which Jefferson is the father of Hemings' children. There are over two dozen potential candidates for paternity.[43]

Nevertheless, many have taken this DNA evidence as proof that Thomas Jefferson indeed had children with Sally. But there are many reasons to doubt that conclusion. A report from the Thomas Jefferson Heritage Society, composed of twelve serious scholars—including some of the best Founding-era historians—concluded that, based on the historical and DNA evidence, it is unlikely that Jefferson was Eston's father. All but one of the scholars leaned toward identifying Jefferson's younger brother Randolph as the more likely candidate for paternity. The one scholar who dissented, saying that Thomas Jefferson was the more likely candidate, also acknowledged that, "On the available evidence, it is impossible to be certain which Jefferson fathered Eston Hemings."[44] On top of uncertainty about the facts, we don't know the nature of Jefferson's relationship with Sally Hemings, if it existed at all. Though relationships between slaves and slave owners always had an immoral element due to the intrinsic power dynamic, it seems highly unlikely that Jefferson "raped" Hemings in the traditional sense of the word. Though her thoughts and opinions are lost to history, her actions demonstrate that she had as friendly a relationship with Jefferson as possible given her servitude.

Jefferson brought Hemings and another slave, James, with him to Paris while he served as a diplomat to France. Given that slavery was actually illegal in the city, Hemings had the opportunity to appeal to the courts for her freedom after she had stayed there for a period of time, but she never did. There are many ways to interpret this fact. She could have been romantically involved with Jefferson, or she could have simply wanted to return to Virginia to the only home she had ever known—as did other slaves who accompanied Jefferson on the trip.[45] Human relationships are complex in every era, and projecting modern sensibilities back to Jefferson's day is too blunt a tool to explain the actions of the men and women of the time.

We simply cannot know, and the evidence doesn't show us, the full truth of what happened between Thomas Jefferson and Sally Hemings centuries ago.[46] But that hasn't stopped the allegation of their relationship from being used as a club against Jefferson. Though so much attention has been given to this topic one way or another, it doesn't diminish the magnitude of what Jefferson has given our civilization. Though his life, like many of those in his generation, was deeply intertwined with the institution of slavery, it was the philosophy that he expounded upon in the seminal moment of our nation's creation that put us on the path to its eradication.

A Rebuke to Tyrants

Jefferson's legacy with regard to slavery is complicated, as contradictory as the institution itself, interwoven into the social fabric of a nation dedicated to liberty. While Jefferson's failed attempts to eradicate it personally and publicly in his lifetime will always stand out as a disappointment to future generations, they don't relieve us of the obligation to understand how his legacy administered a poison pill to this loathsome social arrangement.

The biggest blow to slavery, of course, came from the Declaration of Independence, which made slavery in a country founded on natural human equality an absurdity. This created an inescapable conundrum for slaveowners as well as non-slaveowning Americans. In the final years before the Civil War, many of the most pro-slavery radicals in the South entirely rejected Jefferson's ideas on account of his dedication to equality and natural rights. But Jefferson's contribution to ending slavery in America was not merely rhetorical or philosophical. He was a key driver in passing the Northwest Ordinance under the Articles of Confederation in 1787, before the creation of the Constitution. The Northwest Ordinance prohibited slavery in new territories that would become the states of Ohio, Indiana, Illinois, Michigan, Wisconsin, and Minnesota—all free states. These states, which grew rapidly in population and wealth in large part because they were free of slavery, would supply essential manpower for a Union victory in the Civil War a generation later.

This remarkable piece of legislation, a tribute to the anti-slavery and freedom-loving impulses of the early republic, may have even been overshadowed by a 1784 law that would have prohibited slavery in any new state formed after the year 1800. Sadly, the anti-slavery measure was defeated by a single vote. In a letter to James Madison, Jefferson blamed a single Virginia legislator, his unnamed protégé James Monroe, for being sick in bed and not coming to cast his vote. "The voice of a single individual of the state [of Virginia] which was divided, or one of those which of the negative, would have prevented this abominable crime from spreading itself over the new country.

Thus we see the fate of millions unborn hanging on the tongue of one man, and heaven was silent in that awful moment! But it is hoped it will not always be silent, and that the friends to the rights of human nature will in the end prevail."[47]

Jefferson was perhaps exaggerating the likelihood of this anti-slavery legislation passing, but there is no doubt that it would have substantially altered the future of the growing United States. It is difficult to prognosticate how different things might have been, but if the institution of slavery had been contained to the states in which it had initially existed, it might have withered on the vine without the need for the bloodiest war in American history.

Jefferson lamented his inability to end the scourge of slavery, and even as he became less hopeful in old age, he never wavered from his belief that America would in the end do away with it forever. At the twilight of his life, he said, "At the age of eighty-two, with one foot in the grave and the other uplifted to follow it, I do not permit myself to take part in any new enterprises...not even the great one [of emancipating the slaves] which has been through life that of my greatest anxieties. The march of events has not been such as to render its completion practicable within the limits of time allotted to me; and I leave its accomplishment as the work of another generation.... The abolishment of the evil is not impossible; it ought never therefore to be despaired of. Every plan should be adopted, every experiment tried, which may do something towards the ultimate object."[48]

There can be no doubt from the historical record that the Founders as a whole were strongly against the institution of slavery even as they compromised with its existence. And Jefferson provided some of the most potent explanations of why it was an evil to be eradicated from the new republic. Though his most fervent denunciations came in private letters and correspondence, his public works were littered with arguments against slavery as incompatible with a free country. In his only book, *Notes on the State of Virginia*, Jefferson wrote some of the most incredible denunciations of slavery ever penned by man, including the dire warning, "I tremble for my country when I reflect that God is just: that his justice cannot sleep forever."

It is easy for a man to condemn a sin he knows he will never commit, easy for modern Americans to chastise the slaveowners of our nation's past. But it is far harder to condemn a sin we ourselves are guilty of, one pervasive and common among our neighbors. And yet Jefferson did that because he believed that, as deeply entrenched as slavery was, it could not survive forever in a country dedicated to the principles he had expressed in the Declaration.

In the end, despite Jefferson's failure to personally ensure that slavery would be abolished, perhaps no single man in the history of the United States besides Abraham Lincoln did more contribute to its extinction.

And though Lincoln, a generation later, was privately critical of Jefferson and according to one historian had doubts about his "moral character," he nevertheless gave enormous credit to the Sage of Monticello for cementing universal notions of liberty in the American mind.[49]

Lincoln made clear what the opponents of slavery owed to the author of the Declaration of Independence in a famous 1859 letter regarding a birthday celebration for Jefferson in Boston. "The principles of Jefferson are the definitions and axioms of free society," Lincoln wrote. While the zealous defenders of slavery had called Jefferson's "self-evident truths" nothing but "self-evident lies," Lincoln gave "[a]ll honor to Jefferson—to the man who, in the concrete pressure of a struggle for national independence by a single people, had the coolness, forecast, and capacity to introduce into a merely revolutionary document, an abstract truth, applicable to all men and all times, and so to embalm it there, that today, and in all coming days, it shall be a rebuke and a stumbling-block to the very harbingers of re-appearing tyranny and oppression."[50]

This is Jefferson's ultimate legacy.

Lincoln understood that Jefferson's words served as a powerful refutation of those who claimed that some were born to rule and others to serve in bondage. The Declaration asserts that we were all born free—despite the power of positive law to deny us that God-given right. And when it was not just America but the whole world that was threatened with subjugation and bondage, at the zenith of fascism and communism in World War II, Jefferson's words reverberated to freedom-loving people everywhere. The great Jefferson historian Dumas Malone wrote just after World War II, "In the very recent past, when totalitarianism threatened to engulf the world, men's minds inevitably turned back to this foe of every kind of tyranny.... the doctrines of the Declaration stand in complete antithesis to those which the totalitarians of the twentieth century proclaimed. Jefferson's words should make tyranny tremble in any age."[51]

Jefferson's contribution to America's founding was both radical and conservative. It was radical in that he embedded potent abstract ideas in our nation's creation and purpose. It was conservative because Americans of every generation can look back to the very moment of our creation as a people and point to the most eloquent defense of the natural rights and freedom of man in human history.

Whether the abstractions of the Declaration of Independence are, in fact, self-evident truths is still debated today. Regardless, Jefferson's effort to etch a love of liberty onto the hearts of his countrymen succeeded.

The reason Jefferson's ideas still reverberate is that the Founders weren't great merely because they were around when the United

States was created, nor merely because they were learned and led fascinating lives. They were great because they were right, because they hit upon universal truths about humanity and the correct way to organize political institutions. This is what the hard-left statue-topplers deny and oppose. They have turned on the monuments to Jefferson's legacy in their as-yet-futile attempt to crush his timeless ideas out of existence. Unable to convince their fellow citizens of the justice of their very different understanding of human rights, human nature, and human happiness, they turn to cowardly acts of vandalism for validation and catharsis.

We should also keep in mind, for those who at least still nominally embrace the abstract principles that the Founding generation brought into focus, that it was these flesh and blood men who brought them into being for untold numbers of people thereafter. If we believe, as Jefferson did, that all men are created equal and endowed with unalienable rights, then we do a disservice to ourselves by simply casting aside the very real men who conceived and brought those ideas to fruition, regardless of their faults.

It was Jefferson, together with the American people—with slavery still a part of their heritage—who were at the forefront of making self-government and preservation of natural rights a reality. It should not be difficult to honor them while acknowledging when they were wrong, mistaken, or simply fell short of their goals.

For those across the political spectrum who still wish to preserve the philosophy on which our nation was founded, Jefferson's great achievements remain to teach and inspire. These lessons will be ignored or reviled by those who are gleefully taking an ax (or a can of red paint) to his legacy, but they should be embraced by an America that is still the chief champion of liberty in the world.

Jefferson's assertion of universal God-given rights was a necessary—if not sufficient—cause of the eventual abolition of slavery in the United States. Slavery was wrong, in part, because it violated the notion that all men are created equal. In the end, America could not escape the logical conclusions of the philosophy articulated in the Declaration.

And that same philosophy also has implications for Americans today. If it is wrong to deny the rights and the personhood of individuals of certain races and put them into bondage, thus depriving them of liberty, isn't it just as bad to deny life to innocent human beings because they have not yet been born? As science has given us a better understanding that life begins long before birth, can we so harshly judge men of Jefferson's time for failing in the moral cause of abolishing slavery when we today deny life and personhood to the unborn?[52]

Abortion is a complicated issue, to be sure, but the question is not above our pay grade, as President Barack Obama once suggested.[53] It is a matter of life and death, right and wrong, and to hide from such questions is every bit as self-serving as the choices of slave owners who couldn't free their slaves because the institutions paid too well. Should we not, like Jefferson, shudder at the idea that God is just and that his justice cannot sleep forever?

Legal abortion is not the only thing in America today that flies in the face of the bedrock principles articulated by Jefferson. As the reader will recall, one of Jefferson's proudest moments that he put on his tombstone was a law protecting religious liberty in the Commonwealth of Virginia. Jefferson has sometimes been claimed as a hero by militant secularists who resent religion and wish to purge it from American public life. But that was not the agenda of the Sage of Monticello.

Jefferson was certainly no orthodox Christian; his cutting up the Bible to create a version that suited his beliefs certainly demonstrates that fact. But he had no desire to remove religion from public life. If anything, he encouraged robust debate about religious doctrines, by which he thought we would better be able to discover the truth.

Jefferson financially supported churches of all types in his hometown of Charlottesville. What he feared was religious establishments—in the same way he feared all powerful institutions that could compel a man to act against his will and his conscience by force.

In the 1770s, established mainline churches often suppressed various Evangelical churches and other dissenters, such as Jews and Catholics. But today, religious believers are under siege from a new force in American life. It's not religious establishments forcing people to accept and financially support doctrines that violate their consciences; it's so-called social justice warriors who are attempting to establish their own belief systems as a kind of established national secular religion—and requiring religious people to kowtow to those beliefs in violation of their consciences. They are ruthlessly turning the force of government coercion on Americans of faith who don't accept their social philosophy.

Jefferson poignantly wrote in his 1777 Bill for Establishing Religious Freedom in Virginia that "to compel a man to furnish contributions of money for the propagation of opinions he disbelieves and abhors is sinful and tyrannical." To use the power of government to force an individual to embrace principles he does not believe or to reject beliefs that he holds to be true is nothing short of tyranny. And this is precisely the battleground on which we're fighting over religious liberty in modern America. The case of Jack Phillips, a Christian baker who refused to create a cake specifically for a gay wedding, which was against his religious convictions, is the exactly the sort of thing that horrified Jefferson. In regard to religious liberty, Jefferson has much to teach us.

An Ungrateful Posterity

Thomas Jefferson did not get everything about America's future right. The nation embraced finance capitalism and became an industrial powerhouse, abandoning its reliance on agriculture. Despite this Hamiltonian transformation, we have maintained some connection to one of the things Jefferson most admired about agricultural society: widespread property ownership.

The property-holding ethos was dominant when Jefferson became president in 1800. Remarkably, there were more property owners in America at that time than in all of Europe, even though Europeans outnumbered Americans by about thirty to one. This incredible statistic is simply early evidence of the existence of the great property-holding middle class that would make the United States not only an economic powerhouse but a desirable place to live. Jefferson furthered promoted land ownership through the Louisiana Purchase, which opened up the West to development and settlement.[54]

In one of his most consequential acts as president, Jefferson took advantage of Napoleon's need for money in his European wars to purchase just over eight hundred thousand square miles of territory in the American West. The Louisiana Purchase nearly doubled the size of the US. This masterstroke has paid dividends for over two centuries. By pushing out Old World empires and creating a haven for a multitude of self-governing people, America could truly claim to be the land of opportunity for the common man.

Jefferson's accomplishment is somehow lost on modern-day Louisiana Democrats, who said that they needed to end their traditional yearly dinner honoring Jefferson and Andrew Jackson to "reflect the progress of the party and the changing times." It is an incredibly sad rebuke to a man who did so much to ensure that their state would be American rather than part of the French or Spanish empire. One need only look slightly southward, to the sad state of modern Mexico, to understand how this might have turned out. But Louisiana and the West were added to Jefferson's "Empire of Liberty." All who live under this system today should be thankful.

Jefferson said that the Louisiana Purchase would be "replete with blessings to unborn millions of men." And so it has been.[55]

But as great as the Louisiana Purchase was for this country, it pales in comparison to the gift of a culture of liberty, now and forever buttressed by the timeless ideas of Jefferson in the Declaration of Independence.

This, above all things, was his gift to Americans. While activists comb through Jefferson's life to find faults and hypocrisy—largely to discredit the American Founding as a whole—it is instructive to step back and consider how few great men would survive such scrutiny.

Martin Luther King, Jr., is one of the most admired men in America. King, like Lincoln before him, channeled Jefferson's words and philosophy to fight against the injustice of unequal treatment under the law on the basis of race. He spoke in a language that Americans of all backgrounds understood; he appealed to their Christian values and to the nation's founding ideals. King offered reconciliation and redemption and dreamed of an America free from racial strife, one where individuals could be judged based on the content of their character.

There are some interesting similarities between King and Jefferson, who both dreamed of an America that did not quite exist in their time—but would be brought into existence in part by their own words. Both were Southerners, of course. Both embraced failed economic ideas—agrarianism in the case of Jefferson and a mild form of socialism in the case of King. Both have been accused of gross sexual impropriety. Given his serial affairs and alleged abetment of a rape, MLK would likely not have survived the scrutiny of the modern "#Me Too" movement.[56]

In the end, these failings do not outweigh the gifts that both men gave our civilization. We must return to that statement by Lincoln: "all honor" must be given to Jefferson, who injected into the American DNA a creed that would serve as a standing rebuke to injustice.

As Peter C. Meyers has written, "What Lincoln said of Jefferson is, in its essential spirit, also properly said of Lincoln and King. All three shared the convictions that just government must be dedicated to the universal principles of natural human equality and natural rights. All three agreed that when tyranny and oppression reappear, as in the course of human events they inevitably will, it is the highest duty of statesmanship to rededicate society to those guiding principles."[57]

Today's Left is out of step with these ideas. But the alternative they offer amounts to nothing more than unrealistic utopianism and cynicism and hate aimed at the actually successful American experiment in liberty that was launched by Thomas Jefferson and the other Founders. The ideas of Jefferson, Lincoln, and King are under attack. Something called "colorblind racism" is now an object of scorn as increasing numbers of Americans reject Jefferson's equal rights and King's "content of their character" for the victimhood mentality of "intersectionality." Collective guilt and collective retribution are substituted for justice and the spirit of reconciliation.

But Jefferson's legacy cannot be expunged by damning his name or turning his statues to dust. It lives on in the liberty-loving culture that makes America an exceptional nation. Exceptionally equal, just, and free—because of the world-changing Declaration of Independence. Because of Jefferson's Declaration, America, despite all its flaws, always has the potential for a new birth of freedom.

Chapter 4

The War on the Common Man

Andrew Jackson.... was the man who had his way. He was the American whose simple virtues his countrymen most clearly understood, whose trespasses they most readily forgave; and until Americans are altogether changed, many, like the Democrats of the Twenties and Thirties, will still "vote for Jackson,"—for the poor boy who fought his way, step by step, to the highest station; for the soldier who always went to meet the enemy at the gate; for the president who never shirked a responsibility....

—William Garrot Brown, 1900[1]

When the Obama administration announced in 2015 that Andrew Jackson might be removed from the $20 bill, few rushed to his defense in the way that people around the country had clamored to save Alexander Hamilton on the $10 bill. In fact, a flood of detractors piled on to condemn the old hero. In one particularly vicious article on the left-wing website Vox, Dylan Matthews laid out a smorgasbord of accusations against Jackson that portrayed him as the Adolf Hitler of the nineteenth century.[2]

According to Matthews, Jackson was "perhaps America's worst president and the only one guilty of perpetrating a mass act of ethnic cleansing.... Andrew Jackson was an executioner, a slaver, an ethnic cleanser, and an economic illiterate. He deserves no place on our currency, and nothing but contempt from modern America."

Even Jackson's contemporary arch-nemesis Henry Clay would likely have blanched at this farfetched description.

For the most part, the modern Democratic Party has followed the direction of progressive ideologues like Matthews. As we have seen, chapters of the Democrat Party are renaming their annual Jefferson-Jackson Day dinners, state by state.[3] And for some Jackson opponents, getting rid of the dinners and stripping him off the currency isn't enough. Activist group Take 'Em Down NOLA has called for the removal of a prominent statue of Jackson along with the Confederate statues in New Orleans, the city Jackson famously saved in the War of 1812.[4] Some anti-Jackson activists have even chosen to take their contempt directly to the dead. Vandals attacked and defaced Andrew and Rachel Jackson's tombs at his historic home in Nashville, Tennessee, spray-painting profanities and the word "killer" across the broken tomb.[5]

Was Jackson as bloodthirsty as portrayed by activists? Few today know much beyond his involvement with the legitimately tragic Trail of Tears, but statues and towns across the country bear his visage and name. An entire era took his name. Who was he?

As the Founding generation of Jefferson, Hamilton, and Washington faded, a new one rose to take its place. The Founders had fought to ensure the blessings of liberty to posterity, and posterity had arrived. With the doctrines of the Declaration of Independence in their hearts and the robust institutions created by the Constitution binding them together, this next generation of Americans cemented the United States as an enduring republic. The country would be no temporary experiment in self-government.

No man better represented that generation than Andrew Jackson. Thomas Jefferson used his pen to write the Declaration of Independence and secure western territory through the Louisiana Purchase, but Andrew Jackson secured our independence and made the West unquestionably American.

Andrew Jackson has always been controversial. From the moment he burst on the American political scene, he began to attract devoted admirers and militant opponents. In his own time, Jackson made his share of enemies, and his finest moments took place when he was locked in combat with an opponent, whether it was the British at the Battle of New Orleans or his political rivals when he was president. Jackson was born fighting: if you were on his side, you loved him; if he was against you, you hated him. From the time he became nationally renowned for his stunning victory at New Orleans, which brought down a glorious curtain on the mostly inglorious War of 1812, nearly until the day he died, Jackson found himself at the heart of American events. Controversy usually followed.

Jackson's detractors could be harsh. His opponents believed him to be imperious, lawless, and ignorant. James Parton, one of his early biographers, wrote, "His ignorance was as a wall round about him— high, impenetrable. He was imprisoned in his ignorance, and sometimes raged round his little dim inclosure [sic] like a tiger in his den."[6]

Jackson certainly had his faults, as do most great leaders, but few of his contemporaneous political opponents questioned his bravery, patriotism, and vital contribution to the strength and survival of the country. Parton may have criticized Jackson's alleged ignorance, but he also wrote, "Most citizens of the United States will concur in the wish, that when next European army lands upon American soil, there may be a Jackson to meet them at the landing place." Fortunately, because of men like Jackson, no invading army has landed in America since, and likely never will.

As much antipathy as there was to Jackson in his own day—and even through the partisan cloud of politics—there was still a universal understanding that Jackson, whatever his shortcomings, had rendered a vital service to his country. But the common perception of Jackson today has managed to sink lower than the estimation of even his most uncharitable adversaries in his own time. Gone is the recognition of his accomplishments, and in its place is a distorted and magnified roster of his flaws.

It may seem strange today, but there was once a time when the American Left embraced Andrew Jackson as one of their own—the first "man of the people," who did battle with "conservative" plutocrats. Democrats celebrated Jackson as the father of their party, and many liberal historians of the mid-twentieth century lauded him as a progressive hero. Arthur Schlesinger Jr.'s *Age of Jackson*, a marvelously engaging but flawed account of Jackson's time, portrayed him as a precursor to President Franklin Roosevelt and a kind of proto-New Deal'er. It was a tenuous thesis, given that Jackson and much of the Democrat Party in the 1820s and 1830s believed that virtually any federal involvement in the economy and state politics was tyrannical. Schlesinger and other progressives carefully skirted around these Jacksonian beliefs, usually by claiming that they were pursuing Jacksonian ends through Hamiltonian (by which they meant big government) means. Jackson, who had followed politically in the steps of Jefferson, was portrayed as a critical step from the "elitist" worldview of the Founders to modern "democracy." In this somewhat fanciful historical narrative, Jackson was a useful symbol for the Democratic Party.

He was quickly abandoned when that usefulness came to an end.

As the race, class, and gender "intersectionality" of the New Left eclipsed the views of the Old Left, Jackson suddenly found himself on "the wrong side of history." No longer were men like Jefferson and Jackson figures of democracy and progress; they were reactionary symbols of all that was wrong with America. Andrew Jackson is a character almost tailor-made to be demonized for the modern Left. He has become a caricatured redneck, a gun-toting white Southerner who owned slaves and fought Indians. It's no surprise that Jackson has been dumped into the rapidly filling dustbin of past American "deplorables."

While Americans in Jackson's time made him a symbol of all that was good about their country, today many project onto him all of the perceived sins of our past. Modern antipathy toward Jackson, unlike that toward many other figures of the country's history discussed in this book, is not coming only from hard-left progressives. Even conservatives have piled on or merely shrugged at the attacks. Conservative columnist Dan McLaughlin wrote that replacing Jackson on the $20 bill with Harriet Tubman, a well-regarded abolitionist who nevertheless never affected the country nearly as much as Jackson, would be a good thing. "Do not weep for Andrew Jackson. He had a good run on the money," McLaughlin concluded.[7]

Other conservatives weren't so ambivalent. Conservative author Dinesh D'Souza wrote this in *Hillary's America: The Secret History of the Democratic Party*: "I support the debunking of Jackson, but not because he was a bad American—rather, because he was a typical crooked Democrat. . . . He mastered the art of stealing land from the Indians and then selling it at giveaway prices to white settlers. . . . Jackson was indeed a 'man of the people,' but his popularity was that of a gang leader who distributes his spoils in exchange for loyalty on the part of those who benefit from his crimes."[8] Jackson, in D'Souza's account, isn't quite a devil, but he is a dishonest crook—which is not much better.

Americans of all political stripes have accepted the idea that Jackson was at best not particularly praiseworthy, and at worst an evil, pro-slavery racist who committed genocide against Indians—a cartoon villain.

It seemed that this once-venerated American would slide into irrelevancy; Andrew Jackson would be abandoned and forgotten by the country he spent a lifetime fighting for. But as on so many other issues, President Donald Trump has bucked the increasing bipartisan consensus on Jackson.

President Trump put Jackson's portrait in the Oval Office in 2016 and doubled down later that year with a visit to Jackson's historic home in Nashville, Tennessee—the first such visit by a president since Ronald Reagan in 1982.

"Andrew Jackson was called many names, accused of many things, and by fighting for change, earned many, many enemies," Trump said in his speech at Jackson's home. "Today, the portrait of this orphan son who rose to the presidency hangs proudly in the Oval Office, opposite the portrait of another great American, Thomas Jefferson."

The similarities between Trump and Jackson may be more superficial than real, but there is no doubt that "Jacksonian" politics are currently seeing a revival on the American Right. Burying Jackson's legacy just as it becomes more relevant is a missed opportunity.[9]

And the truth is that Jackson deserves to be defended.

When the Founders created the American Republic, it was an untested experiment in liberty. They made it work despite ferocious battles. But the first real test was not getting it to work for themselves; men have briefly stitched dysfunctional governing systems together plenty of times in history. No, the real measure of the Founders' success would be whether the system they had created would work for their children and the generations that followed. Napoleon's genius in battle and expansion of the French Empire will never quite measure up to the far grander accomplishment of George Washington, who played a key role in creating an enduring political system. In the two centuries that followed both men's deaths, France has gone through five republics, two empires, and four monarchies, while America has been blessed with one grand republic under a single Constitution.

The first great test for the American Republic began as the Founders faded from public life and a new generation took their place. It was at that moment that Jackson, a common man with uncommon gifts—a born leader whose formative experiences mirrored that of his countrymen—rose to meet the challenge.

The Old Hero

Andrew Jackson was born in 1767, the child of relatively poor Scots-Irish immigrants. His father died shortly before he was born, but he had strong ties to his mother, siblings, and extended relations. The deteriorating relationship between the American colonies and the mother country upended the world of Jackson's youth in the South Carolina backcountry. As leaders gathered in makeshift assemblies and finally in Philadelphia to discuss separation from Great Britain, Jackson and his kin were fighting an increasingly bloody civil war with their neighbors.

Jackson's experience was like that of many Americans of his generation. As a young man in a family of no particular reputation, he was thrown into the dangerous and disorienting world of the American Revolution. This war was not just between Americans and a professional army of redcoats. It pitted neighbor against neighbor, and the South Carolina backcountry was a particularly fractured and violent place. Jackson and his close relations were firmly in the Patriot camp. Jackson was too young to serve in the regular militia, but he did act as a courier and a scout. One incident demonstrated what kind of man he would become.

When British soldiers captured the thirteen-year-old Jackson and his brother in 1781, a British officer demanded that Jackson clean his boots. But Jackson said to the officer, "Sir, I am a prisoner of war and deserve to be treated as such"—a clever line, given that the treatment of American prisoners of war was a sore spot for the British.[10] For the insolent remark, the British officer slashed at Jackson with his sword. Jackson blocked the blow, but received a deep gash on his hand and head. Jackson's brother died in captivity, and his mother, who nursed sick American soldiers, fell ill and died as well. Jackson was an orphan in a perilous world; however, tragedy and misery toughened him up and molded him into a leader.

British soldiers and frontier violence destroyed the world of Jackson's youth. At a young age, he had already sacrificed much for the infant United States, but through these experiences, he learned the value of independence and the consequences of being at the mercy of tyrants. Jackson's early experience gave him a lifelong and absolute belief in his new country as well as a healthy distrust of Old World meddling in American affairs. As historian James Parton wrote, Jackson was "the most American of Americans—an embodied Declaration of Independence—the Fourth-of-July incarnate!"[11]

Jackson was brash and brave and grew into a natural leader. Whatever dire situation he was in, whether a political fight or a literal fight to the death, he was always at his best when embroiled in conflict. "I was born for the storm. Calm does not suit me. I try to live my life as if death may come at any moment," Jackson once said. The consequence of his youthful experiences, one historian wrote, was "something he shared with many young backcountry men who survived the war: a total fearlessness, a sort of fatalistic feeling that the worst had already happened and that there was nothing left to be terrified of."

In the decades following the Revolution, Jackson strove to become a successful gentleman of means. Ultimately, he would leave the Carolinas for frontier Tennessee, where he became a lawyer, judge, and notable member of his community. Through hard work, risk-taking, and a substantial dose of violence, Jackson made himself a prominent leader in the state, even briefly becoming a senator. Jackson was a self-made man in an era that came to idolize the self-made man.

For the most part, though, Jackson's early fame extended little beyond the borders of Tennessee, and he might have been a mere footnote in American history if not for his role in the War of 1812, which thrust him into the international spotlight.

Don't Tread on Me

It is hard to understand how Americans could have thought it was a good idea to go to war with Great Britain in 1812. Certainly, some American leaders at the time vociferously railed against the folly of this war of choice.[12] The impressment of American sailors by Britain and other nations, which was occurring in large part because of the wars taking place in Europe, had a relatively small effect on American commerce (which actually suffered more from the misguided embargos of the Thomas Jefferson and James Madison administrations). Great Britain, like most other major European powers, paid little attention to the affairs of the United States and certainly wasn't inclined to wage a massive transatlantic war at a time of so many other concerns and immediate threats.

Were Americans simply thick-headed warmongers? Hardly. British treatment of Americans in the lead-up to the conflict struck at the very heart of American independence. The egregious molestation of Americans on the high seas and the flagrant violation of treaty terms were reminders that Europe still didn't see the United States as an independent country. America was still viewed as a rabble of upstart colonies, disrespected and not considered an equal nation. That Americans were willing to fight a costly war to ensure that their liberty and independence would not be violated was a crucial factor in the nation's future success. The Revolutionary War might have divided the United States from Britain, but in the War of 1812, Andrew Jackson secured her independent future.

The late-nineteenth-century American statesman and historian Carl Schurz explained that "if war is ever justified, there was ample provocation for it" in the actions of the British toward Americans on the world's oceans. "The legitimate interests of the United States had been trampled on by the belligerent powers, as if entitled to no respect. The American flag had been treated with a contempt scarcely conceivable now." Americans had to ask themselves whether they should simply allow themselves to be wantonly abused by Old World superpowers—not only "robbed, and maltreated, and insulted," but also "despised." All this "for the privilege of picking up the poor crumbs of trade which the great powers of Europe would still let them have." Ultimately, Schurz wrote, "When a nation knowingly and willingly accepts the contempt of others, it is in danger of losing also its respect for itself."[13]

The United States had to go to war for the sake of its own dignity. Inconsequential nations lay down to take the abuse, but while America was outmatched by any objective assessment, it was not created to be an inconsequential nation. Failure on the battlefield would be far less destructive than the crisis that the fragile nation would face if it allowed transgressions to continue with no military response. Young patriotic Americans were having none of it. They would fight regardless of the disparity in power between Great Britain and the United States. They would take their lumps and defeats, for sure, but they would show that abusing the rights of their countrymen would come at a price. And no man personified the "Don't tread on me," belligerent underdog ethos better than Andrew Jackson.

Jackson's service in the War of 1812 culminated in America's greatest battlefield victory since George Washington's world-changing triumph at the Battle of Yorktown. After a series of successful wars against a violent faction of Creek Indians, Jackson, who had quickly risen to the rank of brigadier general, turned his military talents against the British, who planned to strike New Orleans, the most important city in the West and the lynchpin of trade in North America. Jackson was pitted against British General Edward Packenham, a veteran of the Peninsular War against France and the brother-in-law of the Duke of Wellington—the famed British general who would to defeat Napoleon at Waterloo. Jackson, the untutored frontier lawyer, and his polyglot group of army regulars, state militia, pirates, and freed black slaves annihilated the professional British army, ending the war on a spectacular note. The British suffered over two thousand casualties and the American forces just a handful. Jackson's defense of the city was a masterful performance, effectively using a defensive position and superior artillery—much of it borrowed from the local pirates he had added to his ranks—to obliterate the invader. It was a monumental victory, one still worthy of celebration today.

Many elements of this battle have been overlooked, but one is Jackson's use of free black volunteers. He addressed these men several times on the eve of the battle. In his call for volunteers, Jackson said that it was a "mistaken policy" to deprive black Americans of the right to serve their country in combat. He insisted that these men, whom he called "sons of freedom," would be paid as much as white soldiers and expressed full confidence in their abilities.[14]

This moment is notable not just because Jackson, a slaveowner, was making a fairly radical argument of racial equality for the time but also because it set an important precedent for the future. Abolitionists and anti-slavery advocates such as Frederick Douglass would use Jackson's words to urge the Union to use freed black soldiers in the Civil War. Interestingly, some of the "free men of color" who served under Jackson at the Battle of New Orleans volunteered to fight as a unit for the Confederacy at the beginning of the Civil War. Though Louisianans were eager to have them deployed into battle, the Confederate government did not grant their request to serve. When the Union Army took New Orleans, this unit joined its ranks.[15]

Though memory of Jackson's great victory has faded in the minds of modern Americans, there is no doubt that the Battle of New Orleans holds a significant place in the history of the United States. In many ways, it was the final act in America's struggle for independence. The War of 1812 went poorly for the outmatched US military outside a few dramatic ship-to-ship engagements, and it culminated in the burning of the nation's capital. But this was not the war's legacy. The resounding lesson Jackson dealt to European powers at New Orleans was that Americans would not relinquish their rights without violent protest.

Some historical revisionists have tried to write off the significance of this battle by claiming that, because it took place weeks after a peace treaty had been brokered in Ghent between the United States and Great Britain, it was a meaningless victory. But news traveled slowly in those days. This is the wrong way to look at the battle for several reasons.

First, just because diplomats had brokered a treaty did not mean the war was really over. The treaty had still not been approved by either Congress or Parliament, meaning that either side could have reneged on the agreement. While neither side was interested in continuing the fight, British capture of New Orleans, an indispensable city for control of the American west, could have encouraged the British to fight on. On top of that, even if the British decided to stick with the peace treaty, there was no guarantee that they would relinquish their hold on the city. The British had never accepted the legality of the Louisiana Purchase, and they could have easily refused to give up New Orleans once it was under their military power. The British might have held onto this economic hub in the same way that they held onto the rock of Gibraltar at the tip of Spain, gaining a chokehold over American commerce and neutering the nation's push west.

The victory also came at a crucial time, when national unity had unquestionably corroded. A sizable number of New England Federalists were so opposed to fighting Great Britain that they considered seceding from the union—culminating in the infamous Hartford Convention, at which some delegates considered secession unless a list of demands was met. The victory at New Orleans embarrassed the convention attendees, whose representatives appeared in Washington, D.C., just as word got out about the great victory. The whiff of treason wafting from the Hartford Convention wrecked the Federalist Party and buried talk of secession for a generation.

Most important of all, the triumph gave Americans a surge of confidence in themselves. The nation could hold its head high, having matched and defeated one of the great armies of the Old World.

The incredible triumph was a sort of cathartic moment for the young country, and the sometimes exaggerated claims about its magnificence and place in history can be explained by the passionate feelings Americans of all backgrounds experienced at that moment. And their national pride centered on Andrew Jackson, who became a hero. Following the Battle of New Orleans, neither the British nor any other any European power would ever again land an invading army on America's shores, and the nation gained respect on the international stage. For that, the American people thanked Jackson by making him president of the United States.

Jackson and the Indians

Much is now made of how Western expansion came at the expense of American Indians, and there is some truth to that charge. But North America was not a bubble in which the only sides were the American oppressors and the Indian oppressed. In fact, the Western lands were a mosaic of competing powers and rivalries. There was conflict not just between the United States and the Indians but between and within tribes. In addition, there was the ever-looming threat of European nations eager to pluck off parcels of territory to add to their empires.

A few other things about American interaction with tribal people must be noted in order to put in context the conflicts between settlers and Indians for which America is so widely condemned today.

First, the United States is almost unique in the world—particularly for such a large country—in how much land it has acquired through purchase rather than conquest. There was, of course, the Louisiana Purchase of 827,000 square miles of land. But there were other purchases too: the Alaska Purchase, the purchase of Florida in the Adams-Onis Treaty, the Gadsden Purchase of what became part of several Southwestern states, and a few smaller deals for islands. Even our most notable addition of land through conquest, following the Mexican-American War, ended with the United States paying a hefty sum for the land it had taken at the end of that conflict.

Jackson's plan to move Americans *en masse* to lands out West has been attacked by historians on the Left and Right. But he was not acting chiefly from financial motives, as some suggest.[16] Any desire for personal enrichment took a back seat to his political philosophy, which dictated that Americans of all backgrounds should move to uncultivated lands in the West and settle them. This would serve the multi-part purpose of developing the national economy, establishing a bulwark of landowners who would bolster national defense in the sparsely populated border lands, and making financial prosperity possible for enterprising men and families who wished to risk a life in the rougher parts of the country. If Jackson's policy was crooked, as Dinesh D'Souza and others have charged, then so was Abraham Lincoln's Homestead Act in the 1860s. Jackson, like Jefferson before him, wanted to create a nation of property holders.

But as Americans pushed West, they came into direct conflict with the peoples already living in those lands. The citizens of other nations such as France, Spain, or Mexico became citizens of the United States or simply left. But the situation of the Indian tribes was much more complicated. While the United States often purchased land from these people too, those purchases were made more convoluted by the fact that tribes typically had no central authority to hold their people to the terms of the treaty and often little concept of property rights. In addition, squatters, immigrants, and ruffians often barged in without government permission and took over.

To deal with these problems, the United States created a series of protected "nations" within a nation—what eventually would become the modern Indian reservation system. This seemed to many to be the best and most ethical way to deal with the situation. It was an imperfect resolution, but it was a far cry from what had happened through most of history, when stronger peoples simply marched in and annihilated natives and other weaker peoples at worst or enslaved them at best. Yet there have always been difficulties with having one state within another state, and these became acute following the War of 1812. Although the US had acquired the Louisiana territory from the French a decade earlier, the purchase wasn't set in stone; the land had to be populated and won on the ground.

Jackson's first taste of battlefield leadership had come in a series of wars with the Creek in the Southwest on the eve of the War of

1812. The wars were sparked by the tense situation of the frontier, where there was a confluence of rival powers and factions vying for control. Tension between the United States and the tribes in the region was exacerbated by the presence of rival European nations, such as England and Spain, which posed a real and existential threat to the United States. The relationships among all these groups were often muddled. When the Creek went on the warpath and committed what Jackson saw as atrocities on American citizens (as well as their fellow Creeks), he became enraged and resolved to smash their power in the American Southwest.

One incident in which Creek warriors—likely egged on by the British—slaughtered a family and carried off the mother particularly outraged Jackson, who wrote to a friend, "My heart bleeds within me on the recep[tion] of the news of the horrid cruelty and murders committed by a party of Creeks, on our innocent wives and little babes.... They must be punished—and our frontier protected—and I have no doubt but the[y] are urged on by British agents and tools, and the sooner the[y] can be attacked, the less will be their resistance, and the fewer will be the nations or tribes that we will have to war with."[17] Jackson, always the man of action, would not sit by when he believed his community and his country were under mortal threat.

The violence that this aggressive Creek faction, called the "Red Sticks," orchestrated against their neighbors allowed Jackson and his allies to form a coalition in opposition, including members of other Indian tribes. Andrew Jackson, his collection of militia, and his Cherokee allies warred with the Red Sticks in a series of engagements that culminated in Jackson's overwhelming victory in the Battle of Horseshoe Bend.

Though Jackson's critics point to his Southwest Indian wars to portray him as an Indian hater, it is absurd to think that Jackson's military campaigns against a violent opponent of the United States demonstrates any special antipathy toward native peoples. Jackson's experience growing up in the war-torn South Carolina backcountry undoubtedly inured him to some harsh realities. He was always prone to fight if he believed his community was in danger, whether from a European power or a tribal war band. In the complex and dangerous environment of the early nineteenth-century frontier, one had to be willing and able to do violence. He fought Indian enemies in these wars, yes, but he also fought beside Indian allies. Even more telling is the fact that it was during the war against the Red Sticks that Jackson adopted his son, Lyncoya, a Creek Indian abandoned by his family on a battlefield.

Following a particularly bloody battle, Creek women and children who had been captured by the Americans were brought to Jackson. He singled out one child whose mother had been killed in the battle and asked the Creek to care for the boy, but they answered that since all of his relations were dead, he should just be killed. According to Jackson biographer Robert Remini, the situation struck Jackson, who three decades earlier had seen his own family wiped out in war. Jackson adopted the child and sent him home to be raised as family. Some have dismissed Jackson's adoption of a Creek child as a cynical and cruel abduction to provide a "pet" for his other adopted white son. To modern progressives, of course, the actions of all white Americans in our country's past are cynical ploys and examples of white supremacy.[18] The simpler and more plausible explanation is that Jackson genuinely felt compassion for the child and wished to bring him into his expanding family. His actions after the adoption certainly seem to suggest that.

Jackson gave very explicit instructions to his wife Rachel about how he wanted Lyncoya to be treated: "I therefore want him well taken care of.... when I reflect that he as to his relations is so much like myself I feel an unusual sympathy for him." It is clear that, as

Remini explains, Jackson "wanted the boy kept in the house and not treated like a servant—or an orphan."[19]

Jackson had no biological children of his own, but he reared many adopted sons and daughters on his plantation. Lyncoya was a wild young man who, much like his adoptive father, loved the outdoors and caring for horses. Jackson made personal appeals to get him into West Point, America's premier military college, but he was rejected, likely because of political opposition from the incoming John Quincy Adams presidential administration, or perhaps even out of racial prejudice. Sadly, as was common in those days, Lyncoya contracted tuberculosis as a teenager and died. He was "mourned as a favored son" according to one newspaper account, which said that Lyncoya had "expired under the roof of the hero who had conquered his nation but who followed his remains to a decent grave, and shed a tear as the earth closed over him forever."[20]

Jackson and the Cherokee

The primary charge against Andrew Jackson, the deed that is inevitably brought up in refutation of the "genocide" against the "Five Civilized Tribes"—the Cherokee, Chickasaw, Choctaw, Creek, and Seminole Indians—is the infamous "Trail of Tears." Thousands of Indians, expelled from the Southeastern states, died as they trudged from the Southeastern states through wild lands to their new home in modern Oklahoma. Jackson is portrayed as an irredeemable butcher and a heartless racist for his role in this dark chapter in American history.

This is where the story usually begins and ends. But this simplistic picture is wildly distorted. Though earlier generations often glossed over the troubling elements of Jackson's dealings with Indians, including the Trail of Tears, in recent times, there has been an absurd overreaction and mischaracterization of his attitude and actions in the affair.

Jackson tended to hate tribal governments but not tribal people. He dealt with Indians as he dealt with anyone else, on a case-by-case basis, seeing some as villains and others as friends. Unlike many of his modern detractors, Jackson never viewed Indians as an undifferentiated mass; instead, he saw them as individuals. But he never trusted tribal governments, whether Creek, Cherokee, or otherwise. "In his direct dealings with the Indians, Jackson insisted on justice toward both hostile and peaceful Indians," as historian Francis Paul Prucha wrote in the 1960s. "Those who committed outrages against the whites were to be summarily punished, but the rights of friendly Indians were to be protected. Too much of Jackson's reputation in Indian matters has been based on the first of these positions. Forthright and hard-hitting, he adopted a no-nonsense policy toward hostile Indians that endeared him to the frontiersmen."[21]

Jackson thought the American way of life was simply better than that of the tribes, just as he thought it was better than the British or European way of life. He grew to distrust the tribal authorities, often made up of mixed-race "half-breeds," as they were called, who, Jackson said, used their relative wealth and education to gain power and enrich themselves at the expense of other Indians.[22] These leaders, Jackson wrote in a letter, "are like some of our bawling politicians, who loudly exclaim we are the friends of the people, but who, when the[y] obtain their views care no more for the happiness or wellfare [sic] of the people than the Devil does- but each procure[s] influence through the same channell [sic] and for the same base purpose, self-*agrandisement* [sic]."[23]

Add to that the inherent threat that the tribes posed to American settlers, and it's easy to see why the ferociously patriotic and nationalistic Jackson would be skeptical about the wisdom of their existence within the borders of settled states or the United States in general. "No country, said Jackson, can long survive such an arrangement— a sovereign nation within a sovereign nation," wrote historian Robert Remini. "It would prevent the United States from developing into a strong, independent country. The presence of the Indians jeopardized the ability of the nation to defend itself. Since the Indians wished to preserve their culture, language, and tribal identity Jackson saw only one solution to the problem: removal. Otherwise they faced certain annihilation."[24]

Though Andrew Jackson spearheaded the final removal of the Cherokee people to the West, he was by no means the originator of the idea. Removal was used by President Thomas Jefferson and every administration thereafter. This policy wasn't created out of pure malice toward native people as is now often believed. To American leaders, Indian removal was a practical solution to a vexing long-term issue, the difficulty of dealing with generally autonomous Indian societies operating within the fast-growing American states that were developing around them, creating uncertain boundaries we still struggle with today.[25]

Indian removal was not just an idea that came from the United States government. Many tribal people worried about maintaining some level of self-determination in the society that was surrounding and engulfing them. For most American leaders, the ultimate goal was assimilation. But they acknowledged that that outcome wasn't immediately attainable—or even desired by the tribes.[26]

The reality for the Americans of Jackson's day is difficult for modern Americans to comprehend. Americans were confronting the result of a clash of civilizations. And in the end, they did manage to preserve remaining Native tribes as self-governing and independent entities, despite the on-the-ground reality of the American push to the West. Many, including Jackson, thought that the best solution might be to grant Indians American citizenship, but tribes, including the Cherokee, often rejected that idea as antithetical to their traditional way of life. The second-best solution was therefore adopted: separate the tribes from the frontiersmen with whom they had sometimes openly bloody relations and hope that Indian settlements in the West might remain peaceful, and perhaps eventually join the Union on equal footing through statehood.

American leaders had additional and even more pressing concerns besides tension between the tribes and the settlers. The existence of Indian nations within the states posed a threat to national security hard for Americans of our time to fathom. It is easy to forget how perilous the country's position was in the initial years of its existence. In the early nineteenth century, it was quite possible that a transatlantic giant could deal America a tremendous blow and end its existence. Having Native tribes nestled throughout the United States raised the constant specter of their forming alliances with European powers. This was not an idle fear; in the Revolutionary War and the War of 1812, the British had effectively worked with various tribes, such as the Creeks, to attack Americans. The British had no qualms about inciting Indians to attack the United States, nor did other European powers with interests in the New World.

Conflict with the Cherokee came to a head in the 1820s. Georgia's population was swelling and beginning to crowd out the Cherokee tribe, which at the time numbered less than twenty thousand yet which owned a chunk of land roughly the size of New Jersey.[27] Georgian authorities resented that an enormous part of the state was outside their jurisdiction and under Cherokee control. Many Georgians skirted the law and trespassed onto Cherokee land, and there were numerous border disputes. But it became clear that the situation could no longer be contained when gold was discovered on Cherokee territory, setting off a prospecting mania that no government could stop. The Cherokee government was overwhelmed by the stream of immigrants into their territory, and their only real recourse was to turn to the increasingly hostile state of Georgia or the federal government for help.

In an 1831 letter to then-President Andrew Jackson, Georgia Governor George R. Gilmer explained the situation and demanded a resolution: "... the Indians have neither been compelled to pay taxes nor perform any civic duties. The only operation of the laws since the extension of the jurisdiction of the State over them has been to protect them from injury by the punishment of crimes, & the removal of the whites who had been tempted into their Country by the attraction of the Gold Mines.... If the Cherokees are to continue inhabitants of this State, they must be rendered subject to the ordinary operation of the laws with less expense and trouble and more effectually than heretofore."

Whether Jackson intervened or not, this crisis was coming to a head.

In his 1828 inaugural address, Jackson had pledged to find some kind of solution for the tribal problem, saying, "It will be my sincere and constant desire to observe toward the Indian tribes within our limits a just and liberal policy, and to give that humane and considerate attention to their rights and their wants which is consistent with the habits of our Government and the feelings of our people."[28] While previous presidents had often chosen inaction on this complicated issue, Jackson was always willing to confront a challenge head on.

Jackson believed that the only way the Cherokee could survive was if the tribe was quickly moved out West, beyond the Mississippi River. Before one concludes that the just action would have been to simply deploy troops to Georgia to protect the Indians' lands from incursion by their neighbors, it's necessary to understand the crisis that such an action could have triggered. The nation was already on edge over confrontation between South Carolina and the federal government over tariffs. Secession and the breakup of the Union were ever-present possibilities in the period preceding the Civil War. At a time when Americans were fearful of standing armies, and in which the trust between the regions was disintegrating, marching an army southward could easily have provoked rebellion.

It was also far from certain that even federal troops could have actually stopped the Georgians from moving in and taking Cherokee land regardless.

The issue landed in the Supreme Court. In the famous case *Worcester v. Georgia*, which dealt with missionaries arrested for going onto Cherokee land in defiance of Georgia law, Chief Justice John Marshall ruled that Georgia's laws dealing with the Cherokee were null and void and that all legal interactions with Indian tribes must be exclusively under federal jurisdiction.

Another modern attack on Jackson is that he was lawless and defied the court ruling. This simply isn't true. "John Marshall has made his decision, now let him enforce it"—the oft-repeated and infamous quote from Jackson—is likely fake news, nineteenth-century style. It actually came from a member of the opposition press, Horace Greeley, in an attack on Jackson. What Jackson really said was "The decision of the Supreme Court has fell still born, and they find that they cannot coerce Georgia to yield to its mandate."

In other words, the Supreme Court ruling had no power of enforcement because the language of the Judiciary Act of 1789[29] meant that the court couldn't force the state to release the trespassing missionaries at the center of the case. It was Jackson himself who eventually worked out a deal with Georgia to have them released.

Historians mostly agree that Jackson followed the letter of the law. As law professor Gerard Magliocca has written, "Notwithstanding the myth that Jackson said, 'John Marshall has made his decision;

now let him enforce it,' in reality there was nothing to enforce. One could say the president had a moral obligation to persuade Georgia to obey.... But the president had no legal duty to act."[30]

In fact, Marshall's decision actually gave *more* authority to the Removal Act by ruling that the federal government had the sole jurisdiction to deal with tribal matters.[31]

Jackson's actions may not be acceptable to modern Americans, who don't have to face the specter of civil war, but given the bloodbath of the 1860s, it seems quite reasonable for a president to go to great lengths to avoid one.[32]

Numerous other eastern tribes had been obliterated in the previous centuries, and the Cherokee were now veering close to that same fate. By placing them beyond the reach of rapacious states, Jackson and many others believed the Indians might be able to build themselves up—turn to agriculture over nomadic hunting—and join the Union on more solid footing.[33]

Of course, the final negotiations with the Cherokee were highly complicated. Their self-appointed leader, John Ross, a man about one-eighth Cherokee—he was mostly Scots-Irish, like Jackson—was adamant about staying in Georgia. He was a wealthy plantation owner with many slaves and deep roots in Cherokee territory. Ross had little desire to pull up stakes, and he convinced many Cherokee that they needed to hold out. But Ross wasn't the only Cherokee leader. Another faction, led by Major Ridge, who was ethnically half Cherokee and had earned his adopted name "Major" from a rank he held fighting *with* Andrew Jackson against the Creek, believed the key to Cherokee survival was to move West. Ridge, a celebrated warrior, thought so highly of Old Hickory that he named one of his sons "Andrew Jackson Ridge." Ridge was only one of many Cherokee who believed that, by staying in Georgia, completely surrounded by often hostile people, the tribe risked destruction, both morally and physically.[34]

Ridge and others in the so-called "Treaty Party" worked out a deal with the Jackson administration to move into lands in the West and accept a hefty payment from the federal government that was to be distributed to the tribe. They did this knowing full well that it would make them hunted men within their own community. Ridge said at the signing, "I have signed my own death warrant."[35] He wasn't wrong.

Members of the Treaty Party and their followers actually conducted a successful and mostly uneventful move to their new land in the West while many other Cherokee stayed behind. Those who stayed behind held out for years until, under the Martin Van Buren administration, the federal government insisted they abide by the treaty. What followed was an utter catastrophe as thousands of Cherokee were forcibly removed from their property. The Trail of Tears was one of America's greatest humanitarian tragedies: Cherokee and members of several other tribes were set on a death march into the West. Thousands died as a result of the harsh conditions, exacerbated by corruption and greed among those tasked with implementing the removal.

The situation barely improved for the Cherokee once they reached their new home. Ross's allies conspired and targeted the leaders of the Treaty Party for assassination. Ridge and other members of the Treaty Party plead their case to Jackson, who had retired from office, believing him to be the one American who might be able to help. Jackson flew into a rage and wrote a letter to President Van Buren calling Ross's behavior "outrageous and tyrannical."[36] But there was little Jackson, Van Buren, or the federal government could do for them. In the final act of this sad fiasco, most Treaty Party leaders, including Major Ridge, were murdered by assassins.

It is reasonable to criticize Jackson's removal decision, and even to charge him with callousness to the Cherokee. His misguided and often condescending paternalism—a consistent character trait of Jackson's that on one hand was a source of his impressive leadership but on the other sometimes generated a kind of clueless cruelty—undoubtedly played out in his actions. Perhaps a more cautious or enlightened president could have untangled the situation in Georgia in a better way. What is not reasonable is to portray Jackson's actions as those of a murderous tyrant blinded by animosity and bigotry. This assessment fails to recognize any of the complexity of the situation on the ground or the possible consequences of any of the other options on the table.

Some of the blame for the ultimate outcome must fall on Jackson. He was the commander in chief, and he made the call that directly led to Cherokee misery. But it's also fair to blame some Cherokee leaders, like John Ross, who led their people to believe falsely that the federal government wouldn't hold them to a negotiated treaty. The whole tragedy was a mess, with plenty of blame to go around. At the end of it all, the Cherokee endure today as the largest tribe in the United States. Despite their tribulations, they survived and continue to contribute to the great patchwork that is the United States.

What is clear from both his public and private statements is that Jackson didn't seek to wipe out the Cherokee and other tribes. Jackson said in a letter to his friend, Captain James Gadsden, "You may rest assured that I shall adhere to the just and humane policy towards the Indians which I have commenced. In this spirit I have recommended them to quit their possessions on this side of the Mississippi, and go to a country to the west where there is every probability that they will always be free from the mercenary influence of White men, and undisturbed by the local authority of the states: Under such circumstances the General Government can exercise a parental control over their interests and possibly perpetuate their race."[37]

Again, Jackson's view was closer to paternalism than bloodthirsty genocide.

If Jackson had had his druthers, he would have had Indians live under American rather than tribal law.[38] True, many Indians had been treated as second-class citizens by their fellow Americans, but looking forward to a time in which they could live side by side with their countrymen, having equal rights under the Constitution, is hardly the philosophy of a would-be Hitler.

Historian Robert Remini perfectly summed up Jackson's outlook:

> It has been asserted that Andrew Jackson hated the Indians and that racial annihilation was his real objective. Nothing could be further from the truth. Jackson neither hated the Indians nor intended genocide. For a slaveowner and Indian fighter he was singularly free of racial bigotry. He killed Indians in battle, but he had no particular appetite for it. He simply performed his duty. Moreover, Jackson befriended many Indians; dozens of chiefs visited him regularly at the Hermitage. He adopted an Indian orphan boy (Lyncoya) and raised him as a son. He sanctioned marriages between whites and Indians. He believed citizenship inevitable for the more civilized Indians, and he argued that Indian life and heritage might be preserved (and should be preserved) through removal.[39]

Jackson hardly had modern racial views, yet his overall philosophy couldn't be more fundamentally opposed to the modern ethno-nationalists of all stripes. He wanted to offer the Indians American citizenship and assimilation or, alternatively, to allow them to preserve their tribal way of life away from the bloody territory battles that had become inevitable in the Southeastern states. While he hated the idea of having states within states, there is little evidence that his hatred of tribal governments extended to individuals. While critiques of his Indian policies, which were inherently paternalistic, are fair, it must be stressed that Jackson was no twentieth-century-style genocidal dictator.

Jackson's complicated role in Indian affairs is hardly his greatest legacy—though it is now, increasingly, the only thing young Americans know about our seventh president. However, before we get too high on our horses about Jackson's treatment of Indians in his time, it should also be noted that few today concern themselves with the plight of numerous Indian reservations, which suffer with ineffective and obnoxious government paternalism, crippling poverty, and shamefully terrible schools.

As Naomi Schaefer Riley, author of *The New Trail of Tears: How Washington Is Destroying American Indians*, wrote, according the *Washington Examiner*, the unacceptable failure on modern Indian reservations stems from "lack of economic opportunity, lack of education, and lack of equal protection under the law." Further, she wrote that it wasn't "the history of forced assimilation, war, and mass murder that have left American Indians in a deplorable state; it's the federal government's policies today [that are] a microcosm of everything that has gone wrong with modern liberalism."[40]

It's easy to condemn the people of the nineteenth century while ignoring our problems in the twenty-first century.

If Jackson had done nothing but fight in the War of 1812 and win his monumental victory at the Battle of New Orleans, he would be worthy of respect and admiration today. But an entire epoch in American history, the Jacksonian Era, was named for this man—and not just because of his battlefield exploits, as great as they were. It was the ethos that Jackson represented that established his reputation as one of the most consequential Americans who ever lived.

The Rise of the Common Man

Following his great victories in the War of 1812, Andrew Jackson became a symbol for everything Americans admired and wanted to be. Though Jackson himself felt he had no talent for politics, his fame made him an instant contender for president. This was at the time of an important political transition for the United States. States were becoming more "democratic," expanding the franchise to the common man. Voting rights, which before had generally been restricted to men of wealth and property, were being extended to white males of every socioeconomic class.

This expansion of the franchise became nearly complete after the contentious presidential election of 1824. None of the candidates for president received a majority of the Electoral College vote that year, so the presidential election was thrown to the House of Representatives. Even though Jackson had won the popular vote, the House chose John Quincy Adams, son of Founding Father John Adams. Henry Clay, the Speaker of the House, who had been one of the presidential candidates that year but just missed the cutoff for eligibility in the House Election, cast his vote for Adams. Clay was a representative for Kentucky, a state that had backed Jackson over Adams. This already seemed suspicious to voters. But when Clay was made Adams's secretary of state, it provoked cries of a "corrupt bargain."

The corrupt bargain charges were probably untrue, but an enraged Jackson, convinced he had been robbed of the presidency, was not a man to be trifled with. During the next four years, Jackson and his growing list of backers became furious at what they saw as growing elitism and malfeasance from Washington insiders. When a popular wave catapulted Jackson into power in 1828, it was a dramatic moment in the history of the Republic, the first truly popular election in our history. Washington, D.C., was appalled.[41]

How had an ignorant backwoods buffoon become president? Something must be deeply wrong with the country. The American people saw things differently.

Jackson may not have been a philosopher, an intellectual, or an Ivy League graduate, but he had qualities that average Americans respected. Despite being rough around the edges, Jackson had leadership qualities that few men of any time possess, along with a profound personal courage and conviction that made many flock to support him.

The late nineteenth-century American statesman and historian Carl Schurz wrote a profile of Jackson that perfectly captured the moment of his election. Though Schurz said that Jackson could be "very ignorant" and lacked a deep understanding of many policy issues, he also said that it would be a foolish mistake to dismiss him: "His was in the highest degree the instinct of a superior will, the genius of command. If he had been on board a vessel in extreme danger, he would have thundered out his orders without knowing anything of seamanship, and been indignantly surprised if captain and crew had not obeyed him. At a fire, his voice would have made bystanders as well as firemen promptly do his will. In war, he was of course made general, and without any knowledge of military science he went out to meet the enemy, made raw militia fight like veterans, and won the most brilliant victory in the War of 1812. He was not only brave himself; his mere presence infused bravery into others."[42]

In short, Jackson was a natural leader who possessed the rare gift of command. Born to hardship, fiercely patriotic, and with an absolute belief in the American experiment in liberty, Jackson was the quintessential representative of an America that was coming into its strong youth. His countrymen elevated him to the highest office in the land because they saw in him an idealized reflection of themselves—a tough, honest, and confident individual who believed that

America would always be the greatest country as long as it held tight to its Founding principles. The American people saw him as one of themselves, not above them. Though he had fervent detractors, especially among the nation's intellectual class, he garnered a kind of universal begrudging respect.

Jackson was fighter at a time when a rough man in office seemed the logical choice for an America still under existential threat from enemies that included the greatest power then on Earth—the British Empire. In an America whose recently forged political institutions were still fragile, he was an important symbol for a people who refused to be trampled underfoot. One childhood classmate of Jackson's said he could "throw him three times out of four, but he would never stay throwed."[43] It was the perfect description—not only of the youthful Jackson, but also of the youthful nation.

When Jackson was swept into office in 1828, he stunned the American political establishment, which had dismissed him as an unserious ruffian at best, a dangerous proto-Caesar at worst, and likely some combination of the two. But they had been blind to some very serious problems that had taken root in Washington, D.C. Following the collapse of the Federalist Party after the War of 1812, one-party rule had developed into a cushy, back-scratching affair among those in power. This era has sometimes been called the "Era of Good Feelings," but, as historian Robert Remini pointed out, it really deserves to be called the "first Era of Corruption."[44]

When a serious financial panic in 1819 sent the economy into a tailspin and a series of scandals at the federal, state, and local level broke out, many began to doubt their elected officials. That the Bank of the United States, a public-private hybrid and a bit of a precursor to the modern Federal Reserve, appeared to have a significant role in the downturn was enough to make many Americans move beyond questioning their political leadership and toward serious examination of their nation's elite institutions.[45]

Some demanded debt relief and government intervention, but the wide swath of Americans who would ultimately put Andrew Jackson in the White House weren't asking for a government handout in the wake of the downturn. Instead, they demanded that government be strictly contained and held to its proper role. They believed that their representatives were using government institutions for self-interested ends. The elite was not wise or beneficent, just better at staying in power than the average American. This was an unacceptable violation of the most cherished principles that the country was founded upon—or so the Jacksonian populists claimed, in a narrative that should sound familiar from our own time.

Principled Populism

What Jackson and his followers of the 1820s and 1830s left us was the "democratic" creed in the American bloodstream. It was populist but principled, as oxymoronic as that may sound. Jackson had surrounded himself with thinking men—like Martin Van Buren, Francis Preston Blair, Amos Kendall, a few eccentric "Locofocos" (precursors to modern libertarians), and other leading lights of his day—who gave political and policy form to his Jeffersonian instincts. Jackson embraced the Jeffersonian notion that the government needed to get out of people's way, but he abandoned Jefferson's more utopian ideas. Jackson once said of Jefferson that he was "the best Republican in theory and the worst in practice."[46]

While Jackson was not the political theorist and wordsmith that Jefferson was, he did offer a coherent worldview to the American people. And in many ways, he was a far greater leader of men. The basic outline of the Jacksonian creed was simple, but it had a lasting impact on the course of the nation.

The first plank of Jackson's political philosophy was that entrenched interests in places of power can become dangerous to the liberties of the American people. This was something Jackson stressed when he ran for president, and it remained an important theme throughout his two terms in office. In modern times, people think of issues like term limits—which Jackson would have certainly been amenable to—for members of Congress. But Jackson took it a bit further. As small as the federal bureaucracy was at the time, Jackson believed that civil servants, who tended to see their office as their own private property, had wiggled their way into comfy positions in Washington, D.C., and had become slothful, incompetent, and in many cases corrupt. He intended to drain the swamp.

In his first annual message to Congress, Jackson explained his philosophy: "In a country where offices are created solely for the benefit of the people no one man has any more intrinsic right to official station than another. Offices were not established to give support to particular men at the public expense," Jackson continued. "No individual wrong is, therefore, done by removal, since neither appointment to nor continuance in office is a matter of right. The incumbent became an officer with a view to public benefits, and when these require his removal they are not to be sacrificed to private interests. It is the people, and they alone, who have a right to complain when a bad officer is substituted for a good one."[47]

During Jackson's presidency, there was actually a law on the books that limited a civil servant's time in office to four years, after which he had to apply for the position again.[48] Though many have blamed Jackson for instituting the "spoils system"—by which political parties reward their political friends with jobs and punish their enemies by booting them out—Jackson's role in perpetuating this problem has been vastly overstated. So has its pernicious effect on our politics. That system had marked advantages over the modern one in which, of the nearly three million federal government employees today, virtually none can lose their jobs for any reason, including criminal activity.[49] And the disadvantages of the "spoils system" pale in comparison to the dangers of "the Deep State"—a massive and powerful unelected bureaucracy whose staff appears to feel justified in interfering in our elections. Andrew Jackson would have been horrified at the total lack of democratic accountability over these bureaucrats, and we should be too.

The second major plank of Jacksonianism was an intense opposition to crony capitalism, the symbiotic relationship between big government and big business, in which the government interferes with the free market to pick winners and losers. The forgotten men under this system are the average Americans without influence in the halls of power, those who work hard and play by the rules. Jackson's solution was not to give away handouts nor to have the government control business—which he would have seen as economic folly and un-American—but instead to sever the corrupt ties between business and government whenever possible.

Jackson gave one of his most eloquent denunciations of crony capitalism in his message to the nation on his veto of the Second Bank of the United States Charter. Though the national bank did provide financial stability for the economy, Jackson worried that it had become too powerful and unaccountable. Indeed, many politicians were on the bank's payroll. "It is to be regretted that the rich and powerful too often bend the acts of government to their selfish purpose.... When the laws undertake to add to these natural and just advantages artificial distinctions...the humble members of society—the farmers, mechanics, and laborers—who have neither the time nor the means of securing like favors to themselves, have a right to complain of the injustice of their government."[50]

Jackson's position is often mischaracterized as anti-capitalist. The reality is that his hostility to the Bank was of a piece with his overall economic philosophy of opportunity for all, favoritism to none.[51] Jackson did not seek to control business by regulatory fiat or high taxation. Instead, his philosophy revolved around opposing crony kickbacks to the well-connected at the expense of the average American, seeking to ensure a level playing field upon which all could compete in a free society.

The third essential plank of the Jacksonian agenda was an aggressive military and foreign posture in the world—something that differentiated Jackson from earlier members of his Jeffersonian Democrat party.

It's important not to overstate Thomas Jefferson's rejection of military force as an essential element of American foreign policy. He did launch a major naval attack against North African pirates, after all, and signed legislation creating West Point, America's premier military school. But Jackson relied even more heavily on the concept of "peace through strength," to quote a favorite phrase of Ronald Reagan's. Jackson invested heavily in the Navy as a prime weapon for preventing the abuse of American citizens around the globe and called for a major naval buildup in his farewell address, in which he paraphrased an ancient Latin saying that expresses a similar sentiment: "We shall more certainly preserve the peace when it is well understood that we are prepared for war." His foreign policy maxim was "ask nothing but what is right, permit nothing that is wrong."[52]

Jackson was willing to threaten to unleash American military force, even against superior foes, in order to get diplomatic concessions out of other countries that he felt were treating the United States unfairly. For example, when France failed to pay America the agreed-upon spoliation claims from the undeclared "Quasi War" at the end of the eighteenth century, Jackson's brinksmanship ultimately convinced the French to pay up. As powerful as France was compared with the United States of the time, Jackson's threats and unwillingness to apologize for them had a powerful result. "The effect of Jackson's attitude was not lost upon European governments," wrote early twentieth-century political scientist John Fiske. "At home the hurrahs for Old Hickory were louder than ever. The days when foreign powers could safely insult us were evidently gone by."[53]

Jackson's militant persona allowed America to punch above its weight in foreign policy and to establish its claims as more than an afterthought in European power struggles. Jacksonian militancy in demanding respect for the rights of American citizens and asserting America's national interests abroad was effective in persuading foreign powers not to molest America and to respond favorably to America's demands in trade and other deals.

Despite Jackson's belligerence—more likely because of it—the United States was not embroiled in any major wars during Jackson's presidency, and the country secured more trade agreements than under any previous administration. The man America's political establishment had called a reckless incompetent was getting things done, and his supporters cheered him on.

Perhaps the most overlooked aspect of Jackson's presidency was among the most important issues for the future of the United States: the delicate balance between state power and federal union, which was in jeopardy from Jackson's time until after the Civil War.

Jackson was a nationalist, but he was also a federalist: he thought that most policies should be left to the states and individuals but that the union itself was necessary and indivisible. For America to be strong, the federal government had to be circumscribed to important but limited functions such as foreign policy and projects of truly national scope. Jackson vetoed state-level infrastructure projects as a waste of federal dollars—and more properly the responsibility of the states. He loathed the idea of federal funds being used as a slush fund for local interests and politicians. Jackson issued what was at the time a record number of vetoes, many of which were used to stop these sort of schemes. The Jacksonian creed was, as emblazoned on the letterhead of a popular newspaper, "The World is governed too much."[54]

This cussed independence has been a part of the American soul since the beginning, but it was solidified in the Age of Jackson, the age of the self-made man. And from time to time, it surges back to life in a wave of populist, anti-elite discontent. In the 1820s, it brought Jackson to power; in 1980, it put Ronald Reagan in the White House; in the 2010s, it fueled the Tea Party movement, which took to the streets motivated by the notion that the American taxpayer should not bail out major banks that had acted irresponsibly in the financial crisis, nor should they have to pay for their neighbor's house. Like the Jacksonians of earlier times, the Tea Party feared that the government was working against the average American who had acted responsibly—and was now being punished for it.

In a campaign promise that would have undoubtedly thrilled Tea Party supporters, Jackson promised to pay off the national debt, which he thought was a "national curse." Remarkably, his administration did just that in 1835—the only time in history that an advanced modern nation has pulled off such a feat. This, along with his general opposition to crony capitalism, left an important mark on American culture thereafter. "The conviction that the government ought not involve itself in the marketplace remains alive and well in the United States today and constitutes a bequest from the Jackson era to our own," historian Carl Lane has written. "Indeed the nature of American capitalism today owes much to Jackson's elimination of the national debt in 1835."[55]

Jackson's insistence on constraining the power of the federal government and eliminating debt, curiously enough, led him to a

confrontation to defend the Union itself. Though Jackson's supporters, especially in the South, were generally proponents of free trade,
Jackson was willing to use tariffs to serve specific ends, namely to
generate revenue to pay off the national debt. A Southern faction
within the Democratic Party led by John C. Calhoun, Jackson's one-
time vice president, with whom he had had a falling out, led a resistance movement to the tariffs. Calhoun and his partisans argued that
states could "nullify"—essentially, ignore—federal laws. Many of the
nullifiers were becoming openly secessionist, willing to break up the
Union over the issue.

Because Jackson was a South Carolinian by birth and culture and
a strong proponent of federalism by creed, many assumed that he
would support South Carolina's proto-secessionist position. But Jackson was militantly opposed to lawbreaking—and to the idea of shat-
tering the Union. At a gathering of prominent Democrats for Thomas
Jefferson's birthday, Jackson gave a toast in a crowd full of nullifiers:
"Our federal Union. It must be preserved." His unequivocal support
for the Union shocked the crowd and roused the nation. Jackson would
eventually issue his famed "Proclamation Regarding Nullification,"
which countered the arguments of the nullifiers and declared their
doctrines unconstitutional. He even threatened to march federal troops
into his home state to rein in what he considered close to treason.

Jackson was ready to do violence to preserve his country if that's
what it took. He wrote in a letter, "I thought I w. have to hang some
of them [the nullifiers] & wd. Have done it."[56] Jackson's fervent pro-
Union stance may have saved the nation in the 1830s. And yet President Donald Trump was aggressively mocked by the media for
claiming that Jackson might have prevented the Civil War in the
1860s had he been president at that time.

"Had Andrew Jackson been a little later you wouldn't have had
the Civil War. He was a very tough person, but he had a big heart. He

was really angry that he saw what was happening with regard to the Civil War, he said, 'There's no reason for this,'" Trump said in an interview with journalist Salena Zito for the *Washington Examiner*. "People don't realize, you know, the Civil War, if you think about it, why? People don't ask that question, but why was there the Civil War? Why could that one not have been worked out?"[57]

Of course, it is difficult to say how history would have played out with Jackson at the helm in the run-up to the Civil War. But one thing is for certain: he would have taken a harder line than the mealy-mouthed James Buchanan, who signaled to the nation that while secession was wrong, there was nothing he could do about it. Jackson, in his day, had made it clear that he was ready to do battle at a moment's notice if that was necessary to save the Union.

Men like Jackson and Daniel Webster, his occasional political opponent, united in the 1830s to save the nation from immolation. Eventually, Congress hashed out a compromise on the tariff and the controversy subsided. But the deep divisions between the North and South survived to fracture the Union a mere three decades later.

This was a stunningly important moment in American history. Jackson perceived, accurately, that the nullification crisis was precipitated not just for the sake of tariffs but by Southern radicals who were concocting arguments to sever the nation if the institution of slavery came under attack. To be sure, Jackson, a slaveholding plantation owner, disliked abolitionist "fanatics," but he saw them as less of a threat than the nullifiers. While on the question of slavery Jackson held a different view from Abraham Lincoln, he, like Lincoln, elevated the Union over slavery.

"The nullifiers in the south intend to blow up a storm on the slave question," Jackson wrote prophetically. "This ought to be met, for be assured these men would do any act to destroy this union and form a southern confederacy bounded, north, by the Potomac river."[58]

While Jackson was dead by the time the Civil War broke out, its successful conclusion and the salvation of the Union can fairly be said to be in part his legacy. Though Abraham Lincoln had been a Whig for most of his life and had often opposed Jackson's party on domestic matters, he embraced Jackson's defense of the Union in the run-up to the Civil War, citing Jackson's nullification proclamation in his arguments against secession. Lincoln rallied many Jacksonians to the banner of his new Republican Party, including some of Jackson's closest advisers. Jackson adviser Francis Preston Blair, for example, one of the founders of the Democratic Party, ended up also being among the founders of the Republican Party decades later. Lincoln, like Trump today, kept a portrait of Jackson at his office in the White House, a fitting homage from one great American president to another.

But Lincoln's view is no longer good enough for Jackson's modern detractors, who think his faults outweigh his contributions and wish to see him stripped from our currency, his statues brought down, and his name cursed and maligned in our classrooms. This is an insult to a man who helped America get to its feet in a savage world.

The Founders created the American Republic. But the second generation of Americans left a powerful impression of its own, an indelible cultural mark on the country for the generations that followed.

"Populism" is a bit of a loaded term. It conjures up images of an unthinking rabble egged on by self-interested demagogues, or worse, of French Revolution-style mobs murdering innocents. Undoubtedly, going back to ancient times, many populist revolutions have ended badly. The Founders understood this, which is why they placed brakes on pure democracy when they created our Constitutional system of government. Yet they also opened the door for genuine democracy to play a serious role in our system.

The Jacksonians of the early nineteenth century represented a distinct kind of American populism. At its best, Jacksonian democracy was a genuine and principled restoration movement that drew upon the best influences of the Founding to rein in a corrupt ruling class. Both Andrew Jackson and the movement he represented were ultimately more conservative than radical.

America has never since matched the elite talent of the Founding generation, never again produced men like Thomas Jefferson, James Madison, George Washington, Benjamin Franklin, and so many other great leaders, thinkers, and statesman at once. But fortunately, America's greatness does not stem only from its great men; it also comes from the timeless greatness of the system they created. That system of self-governance relies on the often unheralded "middling men," the generally unknown common folk of America, who may not be as learned as the great elite that once guided the country in its infancy but who nevertheless maintained and improved the Republic created by those who came before. Jackson always believed unwaveringly in such men, and that faith is the key to his enduring legacy, which resonates through the generations.

Jacksonian populism did not destroy America; it reinvigorated it. While Jackson had his contemporary detractors, the country was stronger when he left the presidency than it had been before his ascent to the office. It had achieved enormous successes. And perhaps just as important, he staved off worrying trends that endangered the Republic. Jackson was no crooked gangster masquerading as president, gleefully committing genocide against vulnerable people. He was an honest, dedicated son of the Founding who used his presidency to restore what he saw as the original republican vision for the country, while acting as the great protector from both internal and external threats to the Union.

The Jacksonian creed, which resides in the American political bloodstream still, serves as a vital counterweight to the long progressive trend of the last century, whereby America's sovereign power has been transferred from We the People to unaccountable "experts" in Washington, D.C. It is the often unacknowledged and generally maligned Jacksonian instinct that still stands in direct opposition to the centralization of power in the hands of unelected elites.

In an age when a bloated government, an unbridled administrative state staffed by an arrogant bureaucracy, and a corrupt—and increasingly anti-American—elite hold enormous power, the lessons of the Jacksonian era are more relevant than ever. We have every reason to want another Jackson, or series of Jacksons, to step in, drain the swamp, and restore the Republic.

CHAPTER 5

The War on the Union

*Madam, don't bring up your sons to detest the United
States government. Recollect that we form one country
now. Abandon all these local animosities, and make your
sons Americans.*

—*Robert E. Lee to a Confederate widow*[1]

I n 1861, Robert E. Lee took up arms against the United States. A
century and a half later, it is Lee's attackers who are fighting to
rend the Union into hostile factions, to divide us from our fellow
citizens, and to make it impossible for the American Republic to
continue whole and entire into the future.

Ironically, today's attack on Confederate monuments is an
attempt to destroy the same Union that Abraham Lincoln defended
against the Confederate heroes. The Great Emancipator and the
Northern soldiers who fought to save the Union were willing to

reconcile with their fellow Americans in the South after the war. And America went forward from that point in history free of shameful race-based slavery—but also honoring the men who fought on both sides of the conflict that abolished it. But today, Robert E. Lee's detractors are committed to ripping up the reconciliation that bound the United States together after the Civil War. They deplore racial harmony. They are doing all they can to increase hostility between Americans, black and white. And they betray their true agenda by tearing down not only the heroes of the Confederacy but those of the Union as well.

When President Gerald R. Ford reinstated Robert E. Lee's citizenship on July 24, 1975, the president said that he was correcting a historical oversight.[2]

"As a soldier, Gen. Lee left his mark on military strategy," Ford wrote. "As a man, he stood as the symbol of valor and of duty. As an educator, he appealed to reason and learning to achieve understanding and to build a stronger nation. The course he chose after the war became a symbol to all those who had marched with him in the bitter years towards Appomattox."

Ford signed the House resolution at the Arlington House, Lee's former Virginia home, which was captured during the initial stages of the Civil War and turned into what became Arlington National Cemetery, America's most hallowed ground. The house stands not as a tribute to slavery but as a monument to freedom and valor. It stands silent among the greatest men the United States has ever produced.

The National Parks Service website once said, "The Robert E. Lee Memorial honors Lee's military and public leadership in pre- and post-Civil War America. Congress designated the memorial to recognize that 'the desire and hope of Robert E. Lee for peace and unity within our Nation has come to pass.' From the portico you can contemplate our nation's fate as you gaze across the river that once divided us."

On August 14, 2017, that description was changed to language less complimentary of the Confederate general.[3] It could have been worse; Robert E. Lee was in the news—and he needed to be erased.

After the infamous fringe white supremacist rally in Charlottesville at the feet of a statue of Lee, demands to remove every symbol associated with the Confederacy, already strong on far-left college campuses, became widespread. There were even calls to remove a picture of the Arlington House from the official logo of the northern Virginia county of Arlington because, according to a Virginia attorney leading the effort, it was a house owned by a slaveowner, and "maintaining the current brand/logo... will do damage to the county's image."[4] Regrettably, the absurdity was not limited to Arlington.

Even many conservatives joined the Left's calls to bring down Confederate statues after the Charlottesville rally, leaving Lee with few defenders. Rich Lowry, the editor of the conservative *National Review*, wrote a lengthy column calling for the banishment of Confederate monuments to cemeteries and museums.[5] "The monuments should go," Lowry wrote. "Some of them simply should be trashed; others transmitted to museums, battlefields, and cemeteries. The heroism and losses of Confederate soldiers should be commemorated, but not in everyday public spaces where the monuments are flashpoints in poisonous racial contention, with white nationalists often mustering in their defense."

Because a Robert E. Lee statue had become a rallying point for white supremacists, according to Lowry and others, Americans should generally bow to the demands of the activists and tear down similar Confederate statues nationwide. This position, though well-intentioned, was ultimately short-sighted. It wasn't the statues that created poisonous racial contention, as Lowry called it. Appeasement did nothing to stop increasingly aggressive calls by activists to further erase history; in fact, it accelerated them. In addition, the position was out of line with the views American people held. Immediately after the Charlottesville incident, polls indicated that a significant majority of Americans supported keeping the Confederate statues, with a majority also indicating that they saw the statues as symbols of Southern pride rather than racism.[6] Even a plurality of black Americans favored keeping the Confederate statues—something that highlighted a huge gap between elite and popular opinion.[7]

Predictably, instead of a surge of white supremacist rallies after Charlottesville—in most cases, barely more than a few dozen people were willing to demonstrate for that cause—there was a mad dash by left-wing agitators to tear down monuments and statues around the nation.

The Southern Poverty Law Center, a left-wing activist organization, created a map of Confederate "statues" around the country, many of which were simple plaques to bring attention to historical battles across the country, and called for them to be removed. "The effort to remove [the monuments] is about more than symbolism," the SPLC website said. "It's about starting a conversation about the values and beliefs shared by a community. It's about understanding our history as a nation. And it's about acknowledging the injustices of the past as we address those of today."[8] It's difficult to have a "conversation" about history that has been consigned to a literal trash heap. This is what the movement became as activists wantonly attacked statues and monuments around the country.

A "Confederate" monument that was dedicated to post-war peace was torn down by an angry mob in Atlanta. In Durham, North Carolina, a crowd assembled in front of a bronze statue dedicated to the young men who had fought for the Confederacy, tied a rope to it, and pulled it down as police looked on. Once the statue had been brought down, the protesters kicked and spat on it. Perhaps unsurprisingly, many of the groups that organized these attacks on statues have Marxist leanings—an ideology which arguably has contributed at least equally to human misery as that of the Confederacy.[9]

A visage of Robert E. Lee carved into limestone at Duke University was badly mauled. The statue, above the entryway of Duke Chapel, was carved up and had a chunk of its nose removed. The school didn't bother to restore or replace it. An attack on a statue in Houston was fortunately thwarted by police. A twenty-five-year-old man allegedly carrying materials that could be turned into explosives was arrested near the statue of a Confederate soldier. The statue, dedicated to Irish immigrant Richard W. Dowling, was "erected in 1905 to honor rebel soldiers who died at the Battle of Sabine Pass." The militant push to erase Lee from memory got so absurd that the sports network ESPN pulled an announcer of Asian descent from a broadcast of a University of Virginia football game because his name was Robert Lee.[10] These were just a handful of the incidents that took place in the months after Charlottesville.[11]

Anti-Confederate activists somehow missed Abraham Lincoln's address warning of the danger of mob rule.[12] If cities and states wouldn't willingly pull the statues down, then to hell with democracy. Lawless vengeance would suffice. It's an ironic tactic for so-called "anti-fascists."

To defend Lee—or even fail to denounce him with utmost vigor—was suddenly tantamount to being pro-slavery, or at least certainly racist. President Donald Trump's chief of staff, John Kelly, learned this the hard way. Following the decision by Christ Church in Alexandria to remove plaques dedicated to George Washington and Lee, Kelly defended the Confederate commander on Laura Ingraham's show on Fox News.[13] The church's decision was absurd. Church leaders said of the removal, "The plaques in our sanctuary make some in our presence feel unsafe or unwelcome."

Kelly stepped into the debate, warning that it was a lack of compromise that had led to the Civil War—a fairly uncontroversial opinion not long ago. He said, "I would tell you that Robert E. Lee was an honorable man. He was a man that gave up his country to fight for his state, which 150 years ago was more important than country. It was always loyalty to state first back in those days. Now it's different today. But the lack of an ability to compromise led to the Civil War, and men and women of good faith on both sides made their stand where their conscience had them make their stand."[14]

Kelly's comment—which may have been incomplete or lacking in nuance—was nevertheless nearly identical to the opinion of Civil War historian Shelby Foote, who appeared on a Civil War documentary by the renowned left-wing documentarian Ken Burns in the 1990s.[15] But just two decades later, a similar statement made Kelly a neo-Confederate propagandist and a slavery apologist.[16] A day after Kelly made his comments, CNN contributor April Ryan actually asked White House Press Secretary Sarah Huckabee Sanders whether the administration thought "slavery is wrong."[17]

The Confederacy Must Be Destroyed…and the Union Too

Attacks on Confederates were only the tip of the iceberg; any figure condemned as politically incorrect was ripe for targeting. Christopher Columbus, the Founders, and Andrew Jackson came under fire, but still the PC gods were not appeased. Perhaps even more tellingly, Unionist heroes who directly contributed to defeating the Confederacy have also come under siege. Men who had actually bled and died to eradicate slavery were tossed aside for their failure to conform to modern sensibilities—by people who had never sacrificed a thing to rid the world of any great injustice. This turn of events gives the lie to the idea that the war on Confederate monuments had any aim besides eradicating America's past.

It doesn't matter what side of the war you fought on. The California city of Arcata decided to pull down a statue of William McKinley, the twenty-fifth president of the United States, who had fought for the Union. The justification for this removal was that McKinley was racist toward American Indians because he annexed Hawaii. New York Mayor Bill de Blasio's commission to purge "symbols of hate," didn't stop at Christopher Columbus. It swept in Ulysses S. Grant, whose tomb resides in New York. Grant, who led the Army of the Potomac at the end of the Civil War, was the great architect of the Union victory. As president, he successfully worked to shatter the original Ku Klux Klan in the South. But at a New York City Council meeting when politically incorrect figures were brought up for review, Grant was added to the list of suspect characters. "In 1862, he signed general order 11, expelling Jews from Kentucky, Tennessee, and Mississippi. I wonder if you think that given the large number of Jewish, he should be buried in New York City," asked a reporter.[18] Grant actually regretted this anti-Semitic action, and when he became president, he went out of his way to apologize. But personal redemption is meaningless in this crusade. The joke, "Who's buried in Grant's tomb?" might not be so funny in the near future if this insanity is taken to its logical conclusion; protestors in Memphis, Tennessee, demanded that the body of Confederate general Nathan Bedford Forrest—at this point, nearly a century and half after his death, nothing more than dust—be dug out of his grave in a park and removed.[19]

Shockingly, even Abraham Lincoln, the Great Emancipator, has been targeted by campus radicals. Students at the University of Wisconsin—Madison (which wouldn't exist without Lincoln's Morrill Land Grant College Act) protested a monument to Abraham Lincoln at their school. During a Columbus Day protest in 2016, they hung a sign on his neck that read "#DecolonizeOurCampus." The activists said that Lincoln was complicit in the murder of American Indians because of his role in the Dakota War and that having his statue on campus was "belittling."

Beyond the Dakota war, one of the protest leaders actually said that Lincoln had owned slaves. "Everyone thinks of Lincoln as the great, you know, freer of slaves, but let's be real: He owned slaves, and as natives, we want people to know that he ordered the execution of native men," said one of the protestors.[20] This is nonsense. Lincoln never owned slaves. Ironically, slave ownership was quite common among Indian tribes, and many joined with the Confederacy.[21]

That wasn't the only Lincoln statue to be marked for destruction. In the wake of the Charlottesville protests, a Lincoln statue in Chicago was torched and vandalized with the words "Fuck Law," which is as good a representation of the ethos of the vandals as any.[22] Whether the work of militant activists, mindless vandals, or some combination of the two, the attacks on Lincoln only prove that virtually no figure in America's history is safe. Impressively, in less than six months, the movement to topple statues moved from Robert E. Lee to Abraham Lincoln. Its descent was so rapid it can hardly be called a slippery slope; it's an untethered elevator hurtling toward oblivion. The march to erase history—iconoclasm with no apparent rhyme or reason—continues.

One Great General Recognizes Another

Before America descends further into the hell of racial strife and an all-consuming culture war over its past, it's important to take a step back and learn from men who knew what it was like to go through a period where Americans were literally at each other's throats. The American Civil War was the great calamity of our nation, the product of a half-century cold war over what America was to be. Both sides were "conservative" in the sense that they both claimed to be preserving America, although one side, at its intellectual core, intended to replace the original foundation. Ultimately, and thankfully for Americans today, the Union triumphed. Abraham Lincoln emerged from the war as the man whose ideas were elevated by victory, but nearly as important, Robert E. Lee would go on to symbolize the best aspects of Confederate defeat. Both men were instrumental in recreating the United States from the ashes of cataclysmic war and making it the great, unconquerable force for good it became in the twentieth century. Instead of tearing down men who rose to prominence in our past, we should pay attention to why our society thought to raise them on a pedestal to begin with.

At the Republican National Convention in 1960, Dwight Eisenhower, America's most famous general and formerly the supreme allied commander in Europe, revealed on national television that in his office he had portraits of "four great Americans." Among them was Robert E. Lee, a seemingly odd inclusion.[23] Eisenhower had received a letter from a concerned New York dentist who was baffled by the choice of Lee and said he did "not understand how any American can include Robert E. Lee as a person to be emulated."

In his hometown of Abilene, Kansas, Eisenhower had grown up around Civil War veterans of both the Blue and the Gray and absorbed their stories. After World War II, he bought a house next in Gettysburg and became an expert on the battle. He relished taking world leaders on tours of the site.[24] Though he was busy on the campaign trail, Eisenhower took time to carefully respond to the dentist's questions and to defend Lee in the following letter:

August 9, 1960

Dear Dr. Scott:

Respecting your August 1 inquiry calling attention to my
often expressed admiration for General Robert E. Lee, I
would say, first, that we need to understand that at the
time of the War between the States the issue of secession
had remained unresolved for more than 70 years. Men of
probity, character, public standing and unquestioned loyalty, both North and South, had disagreed over this issue
as a matter of principle from the day our Constitution was
adopted.

General Robert E. Lee was, in my estimation, one of
the supremely gifted men produced by our Nation. He
believed unswervingly in the Constitutional validity of
his cause which until 1865 was still an arguable question
in America; he was a poised and inspiring leader, true to
the high trust reposed in him by millions of his fellow
citizens; he was thoughtful yet demanding of his officers
and men, forbearing with captured enemies but inge-
nious, unrelenting and personally courageous in battle,
and never disheartened by a reverse or obstacle. Through
all his many trials, he remained selfless almost to a fault
and unfailing in his faith in God. Taken altogether, he
was noble as a leader and as a man, and unsullied as I
read the pages of our history.

From deep conviction, I simply say this: a nation of
men of Lee's calibre would be unconquerable in spirit and
soul. Indeed, to the degree that present-day American
youth will strive to emulate his rare qualities, including

his devotion to this land as revealed in his painstaking efforts to help heal the Nation's wounds once the bitter struggle was over, we, in our own time of danger in a divided world, will be strengthened and our love of freedom sustained.

Such are the reasons that I proudly display the picture of this great American on my office wall.

Sincerely,

Dwight D. Eisenhower

Eisenhower believed that Lee, despite a war that split the country in two, was a great American, one whose life and character were worthy of study. Eisenhower was no Confederate apologist, nor was he blind to the horrors of slavery and segregation. And yet—at the very time when he gave the order for the 101st Airborne to forcefully desegregate schools in Arkansas—he intentionally and prominently displayed the portraits of his "four greatest Americans," including Lee, in the Oval Office.[25] Among the four was Abraham Lincoln, the Great Emancipator, a man upon whom he also lavished enormous praise.[26]

Eisenhower embraced Lee's bravery and devotion to duty—and also celebrated Lincoln's legacy of liberty and union. In a 1954 speech at Lincoln's birthplace, Eisenhower—who had become the Great Emancipator of the Old World—explained that legacy: "We remember his words because they still mean for us, and still explain to us, what this great country is: the greatest power on God's footstool that has been permitted to exist. A power for good, among ourselves, and in all the world. And he—this great Lincoln—was the one who did so much to give us the opportunity to live at a time when that would be so. When America's leadership in the world is necessary to the preservation of freedom and of liberty in that world, just as his presence in the [eighteen] sixties was necessary to the preservation of liberty and freedom and union of this Nation." Eisenhower represented the dominant opinion of Americans at the time, who could admire both Lincoln and Lee for their strengths and contributions to the development of the United States.

Today, the legacy of both men is under attack, though in different ways. The "myth of the kindly General Lee" as one author put it, is being replaced by the myth of the evil General Lee.[27] To even express the desire to preserve Lee's memory as anything other than a monster is heresy. Lee made many mistakes in life, but his critics have gone too far in making no distinction between him and the most ardent pro-slavery extremists. They also fail to understand the necessity of what they call the "myth" of Lee, which was essential to recreating a still imperfect but unified Republic in the wake of its near annihilation.

The Great Emancipator

Lincoln remains broadly popular, but his great accomplishments are often diminished, whether intentionally or not. Though he is given credit for defeating the Confederacy and saving the Union, his commitment to the anti-slavery cause is often questioned by modern audiences. And insofar as he is admired, Lincoln's presidency is portrayed as an early progressive triumph, bursting the bounds of the slavery-tainted Constitution. The truth is that Lincoln saw himself not as an innovator but as a guardian of the Founders' timeless principles. In that sense, he was deeply conservative.

Lincoln saw that slavery was incompatible with the principles of the Founding. Would the United States be a nation committed to the equal natural rights laid out by Thomas Jefferson in the Declaration, in which slavery would eventually go extinct, or would it be a slave-holders' republic where natural rights were irrelevant?

Slavery, Lincoln argued, existed in the United States due to positive, not natural law. That is, while protections for slavery remained on the books in the slave states, they were ultimately illegitimate. This didn't mean that those who opposed slavery needed to immediately march armies into the slave states, but that it was their duty to work within the Constitutional system to oppose further extension of the institution and put it on the road to extinction. This was the prudent and just path forward, as Lincoln asserted time and again. Lincoln knew that if this path were pursued, slavery would wither on the vine, and so did pro-slavery radicals—which is why they seceded from the Union after Lincoln was elected.

Lincoln had laid out his anti-slavery philosophy most notably in his debates with Stephen A. Douglas, but he had also done so in several other important orations. He had put the Founders firmly in the anti-slavery camp. He maintained the view that the simple statement from the Declaration of Independence that "all men are created equal" really did apply to everyone, not just white men, as both the defenders of slavery in the 1850s and many on the Left have maintained. As political philosopher and Lincoln historian Harry Jaffa has explained in his definitive account of the Lincoln-Douglas debates, "[Roger] Taney's decision in the case of *Dred Scott*—that the Founders believed the Negroes had no rights which white men were bound to respect—had now become the hallmark of official liberalism."[28] Strangely enough, that is, the Left has accepted Taney's decision in that infamous case as the correct way to view the Founders. But this wasn't Lincoln's view.

Notions that Lincoln "evolved" on the slavery issue are simply wrong. In fact, he remained remarkably consistent in explaining that slavery was an evil that eventually must die out in a free country. Before the war, Lincoln had argued against those who were morally indifferent to slavery, most famously Stephen A. Douglas, who thought the issue should be left to the states, right or wrong. Lincoln shredded this idea in his debates with Douglas. Ultimately, Douglas's so-called "popular sovereignty" would have led to slavery every-where.[29] Lincoln also attacked the other more militant school of thought associated with Southern statesman John C. Calhoun, who argued that slavery was a "positive good" rather than an evil.

Lincoln had to convince the public that failing to repudiate pro-slavery doctrines would lead to a loss of liberty everywhere. He explained that adhering to the Missouri Compromise of 1820, which kept slavery to the Southern states, was the best way to put it on the path to extinction. The country couldn't ultimately remain half slave and half free, he explained by means of a commonly understood Bible reference.

In his June 1858 "House Divided" speech, Lincoln avowed his commitment to the enduring Union while explaining that the time was coming when the issue of slavery would have to be resolved one way or another. "A house divided against itself, cannot stand," Lincoln said to Illinois Republicans upon receiving their nomination to run for senator. "I believe this government cannot endure, permanently, half slave and half free. I do not expect the Union to be dissolved—I do not expect the house to fall—but I do expect it will cease to be divided. It will become all one thing or all the other. Either the opponents of slavery will arrest the further spread of it, and place it where the public mind shall rest in the belief that it is in the course of ultimate extinction; or its advocates will push it forward, till it shall become lawful in all the States, old as well as new—North as well as South."

It was a bold speech, and one for which he was labeled a radical. But it established Lincoln as one of the foremost anti-slavery men in the country. After his unsuccessful senate run, this speech and his series of debates with Douglas made him a presidential contender on the Republican ticket. Uniting "Conscience" Whigs, anti-slavery and pro-union Jacksonian Democrats, and even some nativist Know Nothings, Lincoln was propelled to the presidency. (Lincoln only won about 37 percent of the vote, but the Democratic Party had split and fielded several candidates, so Lincoln won in the Electoral College—which is how American presidents are elected. Those today calling for abolishing the Electoral College as unfair and anti-democratic should remember that without it, Abraham Lincoln might not have become president.) When Lincoln was elected, the Southern states seceded and geared for war.

Lincoln had embraced Thomas Jefferson's Declaration of Independence and the natural rights philosophy based on equal, God-given natural rights as truth. He believed this philosophy was the soul of the Republic: the "apple of gold" to the Constitution's "frame of silver." Pro-slavery radicals understood this too, which is why they founded the Confederacy on explicitly different ideas. The Confederate constitution explicitly defines and protects slavery while the US Constitution scrupulously avoids the topic and never even mentions the word "slave."

Confederate Vice President Alexander H. Stephens, strangely enough, affirmed Lincoln's belief that the Founders were anti-slavery. The Confederacy, he said, would have to be founded upon a new philosophy of "science," explicitly opposed to natural rights as defined in the Declaration of Independence. The races were inherently unequal. This made the concept of God-given rights nothing but a farce.

Stephens had once been a member of the defunct Whig Party and a political ally of Lincoln. Conflict over slavery led them to split. The "Cornerstone Speech," which Stephens delivered shortly after the Confederate states began to secede, articulates what was at the heart of this new nation, not only in stark contrast but in acknowledged contradiction to the one created by the Founding Fathers. Stephens had never been an ardent secessionist, but he was forthright about his understanding of what was dividing the nation:

The prevailing ideas entertained by [Jefferson] and most of the leading statesmen at the time of the formation of the old constitution, were that the enslavement of the African was in violation of the laws of nature; that it was wrong in principle, socially, morally, and politically," Stephens said. "It was an evil they knew not well how to deal with, but the general opinion of the men of that day was that, somehow or other in the order of Providence, the institution would be evanescent and pass away.

Stephens admitted that the Founding Fathers—despite their allowances and even some protections for it in the original Constitution—were opposed to the continuance of slavery. They had understood it was a great evil that the nation had been born with. "Those ideas, however, were fundamentally wrong," Stephens said. "Our new government is founded upon exactly the opposite ideas; its foundations are laid, its cornerstone rests, upon the great truth that the negro is not equal to the white man; that slavery, subordination to the superior race, is his natural and normal condition. This, our new government, is the first, in the history of the world, based upon this great physical, philosophical, and moral truth. This truth has been slow in the process of its development, like all other truths in the various departments of science."

This was what the Civil War was about. This four-year conflict was ultimately over whether the central tenets of the Declaration of Independence were true, or false. Thus, the Gettysburg Address is the perfect summation of a generation of debate over slavery and the nature of the Union:

Four score and seven years ago our fathers brought forth on this continent a new nation, conceived in Liberty, and dedicated to the proposition that all men are created equal.

Now we are engaged in a great civil war, testing whether
that nation or any nation so conceived and so dedicated, can
long endure. We are met on a great battlefield of that war.

Ronald Reagan said it best in a 1987 speech to high school students in Indiana: "This is Lincoln's greatest lesson, this lesson in liberty. He understood that the idea of human liberty is bound up in
the very nature of our nation. He understood that America cannot
be America without standing for the cause of freedom. He had often
asked himself, Mr. Lincoln once said, what great principle or idea it
was that held the Union together for so long. 'It was not,' he said, 'the
mere matter of the separation ... from the motherland." It was something more. It was "... something in that Declaration of Independence
giving liberty, not alone to the people of this country, but hope to the
world ... it was that which gave promise that in due time the weights
should be lifted from the shoulders of all men."

While many modern historians see Lincoln's actions as president—particularly his Emancipation Proclamation only near the end
of the war—as evidence of his evolution on the issue, this is far from
the truth. Unlike the radicals of his day, Lincoln believed that slavery
could be driven to extinction in America only under the Constitution, and the careful path he trod to that end was the wise statesmanship of principled prudence, not evidence of evolution or flip-flopping on slavery. Absolute moral righteousness, regardless of the
actual consequences, is the standard by which the leftist iconoclasts
judge historical figures today—rather than wise statecraft, leadership,
or even practical results in achieving the goals they claim to care
about. Lincoln knew that liberty, for the slaves and everyone else, was
not possible without the Union and the Constitution. And Lincoln
freed the slaves—while these vandals have done nothing more
impressive than tear down statues of great Americans.

It's easy for modern Americans to be moral absolutists about the past—given our separation from the world in which slavery was the reality and the lack of consequences for taking any extreme position. Naturally, today's Left prefers the most radical abolitionists to Lincoln. But if emancipation had depended on those extremists, there would likely be no United States—and there might possibly still be slavery in the Americas today.

American Hero

Southern heroes are treated even more uncharitably than the Great Emancipator. Confederates like Lee are condemned as uniquely evil men whose motivations were confined entirely to saving the wicked institution of slavery.

For those looking back on history with 20/20 vision, it is easy to see the outcome of the Civil War, Emancipation, and the ultimate triumph of Civil Rights for Black Americans as foregone conclusions. The reality wasn't so neat and tidy. It is far more difficult to rebuild a civilization than destroy it. There was no guarantee that the United States would ever recover from its Civil War, but recover it did. Without men like Abraham Lincoln and, yes, Robert E. Lee, things might have turned out very differently.

It may seem odd to pair Abraham Lincoln and Robert E. Lee together as positive symbols of the Civil War. After all, they represented opposing sides in an incredibly bloody conflict. In fact, it's nearly incredible that both figures could be celebrated by future Americans in what one historian called the "cult of Lincoln and Lee,"[30] but they certainly were.

As the decades wore on after Union victory and the passions of both sides began to fade, Americans of the early twentieth centruy eventually came to a healing understanding of the conflict as a whole.

Northerners and Southerners came to share what has been called the "nationalist interpretation" of the Civil War—an understanding that while irrepressible differences between the sections over culture and particularly over the evil of slavery had led inevitably to violence, ultimately all Americans could celebrate the triumph of the Union, the end of slavery, the birth of modern America—and the honorable service of soldiers on both sides of the conflict.[31]

Americans could accept that slavery had been a terrible evil and cheer its demise and yet acknowledge that not everyone who fought on the other side was evil. That was a necessary condition for accepting them back as fellow countrymen. In this reconciliation that took place in the decades after the Civil War, Lincoln and Lee became powerful symbols of the best of both sides.

Lee had not led the slave states out of the Union. In fact, he had discouraged secession as a great error.[32] He had never belonged to the clique of militant defenders of slavery who celebrated it as a positive good.[33] Yet he still fought on the wrong side of this great struggle. Lee owned slaves, resigned his Army commission when his state of Virginia seceded, and then reluctantly fought for the Confederacy until he was defeated. Shall he be remembered in history as at best a Benedict Arnold? Americans after the Civil War came to a very different estimation of his place in history—and we are better as a nation for it.

Though he was a general and not the president of the seceded states, late in the war, Lee *was* the Confederacy, the man who had the most power to sway the minds of the Southern people. And Lee's example to a defeated South was almost unique in human history. When some Southerners wanted to keep fighting a guerilla war, he urged them to accept defeat, reconcile with their fellow countrymen, and to abandon animosities and "make your sons Americans."[34]

As one writer for the *Atlantic Monthly* wrote in 1911, "What finer sentence could be inscribed on Lee's statue than that?"

Lincoln, too, was a proponent of reconciliation. He waged the war in a spirit of "malice toward none" and "charity for all," in the moving words of his Second Inaugural Address.

In the early twentieth century, the Arlington Memorial Bridge over the Potomac River was built as a symbol of reconciliation between North and South, Yankees and Confederates, Lincoln and Lee. It joins the seat of the federal government in Washington, D.C., to Virginia, the home of the Confederate government, and links the Lincoln Memorial with Arlington House, Robert E. Lee's home.

Thus a spirit of honor and forgiveness prevailed, a willingness to overlook past grievances to reunify the nation. Sometimes, it is best to forget the ugliness of past differences, find the best in old opponents, and move on to a better future. From that impulse, Lee became almost as important a figure to Northerners as Southerners. Together, Lincoln and Lee gave America a joint future. In fact, without them, the US might have had no future at all.

That spirit of reconciliation is now under attack. Though we are now much farther removed from the bloody conflict of the Civil War than the Americans—both North and South—who unashamedly venerated Lincoln and Lee, we have embraced the idea that forgiveness is unacceptable. Americans must take up old grievances, argue with the past, and once again be at war with one another.[35] Mutual respect and acceptance are gone with the wind. Racial conflicts and resentments over the history of slavery and must be carefully guarded and fanned into new flames, never forgotten and forgiven.

Appomattox, and the Union Restored

It was early April 1865. The Army of Northern Virginia, which had fought and often won against great odds for four years, was dissolving. There would be no reinforcements this time. This withered,

starving army of 28,000 men was being countered by the well-sup-
plied and confident Army of the Potomac, at least 150,000 strong.

In their final gasp, the Army of Northern Virginia battled it out
near Appomattox Courthouse in Virginia. The now ragtag Confederate Army could put up little resistance against the swollen ranks of
Federal soldiers who were quickly bearing down to annihilate what
was left of the bedraggled holdouts. One Union officer noted that the
Rebel lines appeared to have more battle flags than soldiers, a sign of
their pathetically decimated state.[36]

On April 9, Palm Sunday, Lee saw that the game was up. He
would do what he had to do to ensure that his men would live to see
Easter. Lee called for a meeting with Union General Ulysses S. Grant,
the final and most successful commander of the Army of the
Potomac, to negotiate the terms of surrender. The two entered Appomattox Courthouse on that day as pictures in contrast.

Grant wrote of this remarkable meeting that, dressed in a "rough
traveling suit, the uniform of a private with the straps of a lieutenant-
general, I must have contrasted very strangely with a man so hand-
somely dressed, six feet high and of faultless form."[37] An outside
observer, not knowing the details of the war, might have concluded
from the two men's appearance that it Lee who was leading the victorious army and Grant who was leading the rag-tag ranks of the
defeated.

Grant noted that, in what was in many ways a rewarding moment
of victory and a sure sign that the war would be concluded soon, he
found it difficult to glory in the downfall of Lee, a man he had served
with over a decade earlier in the Mexican-American War. "I felt like
anything rather than rejoicing at the downfall of a foe who had fought
so long and valiantly, and had suffered so much for a cause, though
that cause was, I believe, one of the worst for which a people ever
fought, and one for which there was the least excuse. I do not

question, however, the sincerity of the great mass of those who were opposed to us," Grant said.

Lee was in some ways the picture of an American aristocrat, a stereotypical Southern gentleman in the best sense. His family was among the most prominent in the Commonwealth of Virginia. Lee's father, "Light Horse" Harry Lee, had served under George Washington, and Lee had even married into Washington's family. Lee admired Washington greatly, and he shared many traits of the great man's character.

Countless volumes have been dedicated to Lee's battlefield exploits. Even the abridged version of historian Douglas Southall Freeman's three-volume set of books on Lee's days leading the Army of Northern Virginia runs a staggering 912 pages.[38]

Numerous historians have praised Lee as one of the finest generals in the war. As a military leader, there is much to study and admire about Lee. But it is ultimately what he did after the fighting was over that has secured his important place in American history. Lee's greatest triumph, the achievement that deserves the respect and gratitude of modern Americans, has little to do with his exploits at Chancellorsville or any other battlefield. Instead, it was his actions at the end of the war and in the years that followed that cemented his place in our history. This is not to say that everything Lee did was right or correct or that he didn't make a mistake in abandoning the United States in favor of the Confederacy in the first place. Alas, Lee was no George Washington; the "country" he led was built upon a false edifice; his defeat, not his victory, would be a blessing to humanity.

Lee had called slavery a moral and political evil while believing that African slaves were better under this system than they were in Africa because they would be Christianized. While Lee's position on slavery fell short of recognizing its true horrors, he never adopted the more radical doctrine of his day that embraced it as a positive good.

Human bondage has never been a kindly institution, but slavery was so entrenched in American life that it was difficult for slaveowners, even those who saw that it was evil, to disentangle themselves. It was legally challenging to near impossible to release slaves. Some pulled it off, but often the freed slaves ended up in situations nearly as bad as bondage, as in the case of the slaves freed by John Randolph of Roanoke, for instance, who were ejected from the property he had purchased for them in the free state of Pennsylvania.[39] Such unfortunate occurrences were common in a nation dealing with the legal consequences of being half slave and half free.

Though Southern radicals undoubtedly saw slavery as *the* reason to break the Union and wage war, Lee had never been in their camp. Instead, he was a reluctant rebel, having long held out hope that America's politicians would resolve the sectional crisis before it turned to war. For Lee, the critical decision on which way to go was made when he was asked by Francis Preston Blair, a former adviser to President Andrew Jackson who had been authorized to contact Lee by President Lincoln, to lead the Union Army. Lee said, "Mr. Blair, I look upon secession as anarchy. If I owned the four millions of slaves at the South, I would sacrifice them all to the Union; but how can I draw my sword upon Virginia, my native State?"[40] Lee resigned his commission almost immediately thereafter, returned to private life, and prayed that he would never have to take up arms again. But he was quickly enlisted by his state, which had joined secession, and went on to serve in the doomed effort of the Confederacy. Through the war, he never quite came to the point of thinking Union soldiers his "enemies," and he clearly, carefully avoided the term. He referred to his battlefield opponents as "General Meade's people," "General Grant's people," or our "friends across the river."[41]

To twenty-first-century Americans, Lee's allegiance to his state over his country seems obviously wrong. The question of slavery, which had provided the kindling for a sectional conflict that had been a generation in the making, is what we focus on the most.

Those who say that the Civil War was over slavery are correct. This supercharged debate was tearing at the national soul and making compromise impossible. Issues such as "states' rights" and tariffs were simply policies that were interconnected with slavery, not the casus belli. On the other hand, it's a mistake to assign the motives of individuals who participated in the war to this reason alone. For most, interlocking and sometimes competing factors went into their difficult decisions. Loyalty to community and family were often of equal or greater concern. For some, the issue of slavery, whether right or wrong, was absolute, and they would go with whatever side aligned with their beliefs. Others saw the Union as the only consideration and stuck with their country no matter their opinion on slavery. More than a few, like Lee, saw their state as their "country" and would rally around that regardless of whether it was right or wrong. In one humorous story, a Maryland officer, upon reading that his state had seceded from the Union, resigned his commission and sought to join the Confederacy. When he learned that the reports of secession were false, he went back and tried to get his commission back. In some cases, men actually joined a side because they saw more opportunity for advancement in one army or the other.[42]

Sometimes even stranger occurrences took place. A group of black citizens in New Orleans, led by veterans of Andrew Jackson's victory over the British in the War of 1812, enthusiastically gathered up a regiment to volunteer to fight for the Confederacy. The unit, called the Native Guard Regiment, was well received in New Orleans but rejected by Confederate leadership. This same group of men joined with the Union Army when the Federals took the city. Again, the motivations of individuals are often more complex than the simple ideological convictions we would like to ascribe to them.[43]

From Lee's perspective, the grand mistake was in allowing secession to occur in the first place. He believed that once states began to break from the Union, the entire American experiment would be over. If he had gone with the Union instead of Virginia, he would have risked not only fighting against his home state in war but also being forever separated from it—a tall order for a man like Lee. He was not just a Virginian—he was a Lee. For generations, the Lees had been among the most prominent families in the Commonwealth. Should he have abandoned his Virginian heritage and sided with the Union? Yes, but one can at least see that the decision wasn't so clear-cut for him and why going with his "country," Virginia, seemed to him to be the honorable thing to do.

It's hard to imagine what might have happened if Lee had led the Union army from the beginning. Having an able commander from day one instead of a string of mediocrities certainly could have hastened the war's end and Union victory. On the other hand, an extension of the war allowed Lincoln to push the abolition of slavery to the forefront with the Emancipation Proclamation. The Union might have been saved with slavery left intact. History can be complicated.

It was in the final days of his command, while the war was slogging on toward its conclusion, that Lee made a decision that ultimately began the long process of rebuilding the country. Confederate President Jefferson Davis planned to continue the Civil War by disbanding regular armies and waging a guerilla war against the Union Army. In a letter to Davis, Lee recommended against such a strategy. Lee told Davis that such a war would only delay the inevitable defeat and perpetuate more suffering for everyone.

"A partisan war may be continued, and hostilities protracted, causing individual suffering and the devastation of the country, but I see no prospect by that means of achieving a separate independence," Lee wrote in an April 20 letter. "It is for Your Excellency to decide, should you agree with me in opinion, what is proper to be done. To save useless effusion of blood, I would recommend measures be taken for suspension of hostilities and the restoration of peace."[44]

Ultimately, Davis came around and turned against the idea of waging guerilla war. This was just the first step in the last and greatest chapter of Lee's life, which began quickly as the war came to a close.

He was horrified, in the last days of the war, to hear that President Lincoln had been shot. Lee called Lincoln's assassination a "crime previously unknown to the country, and one that must be deprecated by every American."[45]

Lincoln's assassination leaves us with unanswered questions about whether Reconstruction would have gone more smoothly with stronger presidential leadership. His successor, Andrew Johnson, though a patriot and a brave man who had stayed on and risked his life as a unionist governor of Tennessee when the state had descended to secession, left much to be desired as a leader after the war.

The nation was exhausted, and much of the former Confederate states, which now had to be reintegrated into the union, were in shambles. A generation of young men had lost their lives, including many who were leaders in their respective communities.

Lee played a quiet but vital role in restoring some semblance of leadership to the war-torn Southern states.

Lee worked hard to convince the ablest men in the South to stay in the United States instead of abandoning it for Mexico or Canada. After the war, many Southerners were bitter about the outcome and wanted nothing to do with the United States. Lee believed their duty was to their homes in America. Even more, he thought they should accept the terms of rejoining the Union. He hoped that the Constitution and free institutions would survive the cataclysm of war. He worked diligently to make the country whole again.

"Although the South would have preferred any honorable compromise to the fratricidal war which has taken place, she now accepts in good faith its constitutional results, and receives without reserve the amendment which has already been made to the constitution for the extinction of slavery," Lee wrote to the British Lord Acton. "That is an event that has been long sought, though in a different way, and by none has it been more earnestly desired than by citizens of Virginia. In other respects I trust that the constitution may undergo no change, but that it may be handed down to succeeding generations in the form we received it from our forefathers."

Lee was likely overstating the amount of anti-slavery opinion that had existed in Virginia in the days before the war. But his sentiment that the Union must be restored and the country be allowed to move on was quite sincere. A reporter who interviewed Lee after the war said that what was most remarkable about his conversation with Lee was that the former Confederate general "talked throughout as a citizen of the United States. He seemed to plant himself on the national platform, and take his observations from that standpoint."[46]

Though many former Confederates attempted to enlist Lee as the symbol of the "Lost Cause"—a revisionist narrative of a war of Southern resistance against Northern aggression—Lee's actions worked against them. "He was very careful not to attend public meetings that might seem to oppose the government, or to extol the cause of the Confederacy. When I had the privilege after his death of examining his private letter-book I found it literally crowded with letters advising his old soldiers and others to submit to . . . authority and become law-abiding citizens," wrote one editor of Lee's private papers.[47]

Lee actually worried about erecting monuments that might cause lingering animosity among Americans. He was asked by the Gettysburg Battlefield Association to come to Gettysburg in 1869 to push for permanent memorials on the site. The event included both

Unionists and Confederates and proved acrimonious, likely due to the fact that it was less than five years after the war had concluded. Lee declined the invitation, saying that there was little he could add to the occasion. Lee thought it "wiser, moreover, not to keep open the sores of war but to follow the examples of those nations who endeavored to obliterate the marks of civil strife, to commit to oblivion the feelings engendered."[48]

Does this mean Lee would have wanted to take down his statues today? Not necessarily. He was concerned about smoothing over animosities among Americans in his own time. He thought that stirring up acrimony while the country was so fragile would do more damage than good. Many Democrats and Confederates at the time undoubtedly wanted to avoid tributes to Gettysburg and the war because they had lost. Immediately after the war, tributes were likely to be celebrations of Union victory.

So, ironically, Lee's chief reason for trepidation about building Civil War monuments is partly why we should leave up his monuments today. While statues built in the immediate aftermath of the war occasionally served to "keep open the sores of the war," it is the act of pulling down the statues now that is becoming the source of acrimony.

Lee also had another reason for shooting down ideas to build Confederate monuments in the immediate years after the war. It wasn't that he didn't want appreciation of his former comrades but that he thought the war-torn South was in no position to use what few resources it had on statues. Lee thought it wrong to spend lavishly on the dead when the living were starving. This might be a good lesson for modern cities spending lavishly on monument removals or changing city and school names when their budgets are a mess and their streets filled with crime,[49] as is the case with modern New Orleans.[50]

Lee's hesitancy about building statues in the days just after the war helps explain why most of the Confederate statues we have today were built at later dates. The Southern Poverty Law Center and other groups claim this is because the statues had more to do with enforcing white supremacy in the Jim Crow Era or during civil rights agitation, but that explanation misses the mark.[51] In the 1860s and 1870s, the South, as Lee understood, was simply too poor to be constructing expensive memorials and would have been foolish to do so at a time when the region had so many other concerns. Statues went up for various reasons at later dates, mostly through the work of the Daughters of the Confederacy, a women's heritage group. Many monuments were built to celebrate the fifty- or one-hundred-year anniversary of the war or for other general commemorations, not for the purpose of championing white supremacy, as detractors claim. "Because the Charlottesville Lee went up in 1924, at the apex of Jim Crow, it is easy to suppose that it was designed to reinforce white supremacy," historian Allen Guelzo has written. "But the dedication ceremonies featured high-school bands, cadets from the Virginia Military Institute, university faculty, and the American Legion—not the Ku Klux Klan."[52] Guelzo, who is no fan of the Confederacy, nevertheless explains that the reasons behind the building of each statue were diverse.

A prime example is the heated battle over the "Silent Sam" statue at the University of North Carolina at Chapel Hill, which ended with a mob toppling the hundred-year-old monument. The statue, which was dedicated to the Carolina students who fought for the Confederacy in the Civil War, was erected by the United Daughters of the Confederacy and other groups and individuals in 1913. Journalists and historians have pointed out that at the statue's dedication ceremony, Julian Shakespeare Carr, a KKK member, former Confederate soldier, and one-time vice presidential candidate on the Democrat

Party ticket, made numerous racist comments, came out in support of white supremacy, and said at one point that he had "horse-whipped a negro wench until her skirts hung in shreds," after, he said, she "had insulted and maligned a Southern lady."[53]

As noxious as these comments were, Carr was just one of numerous individuals who spoke at the dedication of the monument, and most made no reference to white supremacy or anything like it. North Carolina governor Locke Craig, the principal speaker at the event, only discussed the bravery and devotion of the young men who had left the school to fight for the Confederacy—most of whom never returned—and made no reference to white supremacy or the Lost Cause.[54] Craig noted how, following the war, "the University mourned in silent desolation. Her children had been slain." For many, this was the meaning of Silent Sam. Carr's white supremacist speech went unremembered until it was rediscovered by a graduate student in 2011.[55] Why should it be the one thing that defines the statue today?

Yes, there were militant racists who wanted to memorialize prejudice, Jim Crow, and white supremacy. But there were plenty of others at the time who erected the monuments to pay tribute to fathers and grandfathers who had died in the war, to honor the soldiers' memory as men and human beings—and to celebrate the reconciliation of the two sides as equally American.

We sometimes forget it, but even into the twentieth century, America was in the process of healing from a savage war in which hundreds of thousands died, violence and death were a part of daily life, and the country had been shattered into pieces. The construction of monuments and statues was a crucial matter of paying tribute to the reality that a generation had fought, suffered, and often died in the most violent conflict in the history of our civilization.

In 1914, black civil rights activist Booker T. Washington personally donated to the construction of a Confederate monument in Alabama because, as Washington explained, Confederate general George Paul Harrison Jr. and "men like him" had been "true friends of our race," and "any monument that will keep the fine character of such heroes before the public will prove helpful to both races in the South."[56]

Certainly not everyone who contributed to the erection of Confederate memorials was a proponent of civil rights, as Carr's screed at the dedication of Silent Sam attests, but Washington's comments bear witness to the complexity of the meaning behind the statues lost on the zealots who wish them all to come down. Some were built to support white supremacy, others were built to honor the virtues of ancestors, and some were built by groups of people who had differing motivations—some noble, some ignoble, and some in between.

Historian Allen Guelzo has addressed the question of whether Lee's statue in Charlottesville serves the purpose of promoting white supremacy. "The answer would be yes only if we believed that 1865 and 1873 were yesterday, and that everything about the past is a statement of power (or a clever concealment of power) in the present," Guelzo wrote for the *Wall Street Journal*. "This is what links the monument-smashers to the campus deniers of free-speech: They understand monuments and speech solely as manifestations of power, which only can be confronted and silenced by power."

Honoring a Vanquished Foe

It is notable that one of the primary proponents of putting up statues to the Confederacy's most famed general wasn't a Confederate at all.

Charles Francis Adams Jr. was the great-grandson of Founding Father John Adams, the grandson of President John Quincy Adams, and the son of Charles Francis Adams Sr., a noted diplomat. The famous Massachusetts family name was nearly synonymous with the cause of ending slavery. John Adams had called slavery "hateful" and believed it would quickly die out.[57] After his one-term presidency, John Quincy Adams had gone back to Congress and become one of the most vociferous and certainly most articulate anti-slavery men in the country. And Charles Francis Adams Sr. had served as a diplomat to England under President Abraham Lincoln during the Civil War. The Adamses were about as far removed from the Confederacy and "the slave power" as a family could be.

Charles Francis Adams Jr. enlisted in the 1st Massachusetts Volunteer Cavalry during the Civil War and was present at the battles of Gettysburg and Antietam. He had volunteered out of a sense of duty, even against the wishes of his family. He led a black regiment during the war when he was assigned to guard Confederate POWs, which he did proudly.[58] Adams was anti-secessionist and anti-slavery by birth and by personal conviction. Having fought against Lee's Army of Northern Virginia, he had no personal reason to view its commander charitably. When the war ended, Adams Jr. went back to civilian life. He became a businessman and a historian. He eventually served on the Massachusetts Park Commission, where he had the task of designing public parks. Few men were as uniquely qualified to comment on Civil War memorials from the point of view of an opponent of slavery and a defender of the Union.

And in a 1902 speech delivered to the Phi Beta Kappa Society of the University of Chicago, Adams made the argument that Americans should build a statue to Lee and perhaps other prominent Confederates. Adams noted that Lee and his home state of Virginia had not been ardently in favor of secession. Slavery had been less commercial and in some ways more feudal, primitive, and familial in Virginia than in the Deep South states like Louisiana. In Virginia, it was a dying institution in a declining state rather than an integral part of the booming cotton economy. Virginians had less of a financial interest in militantly extending and preserving slavery. When Virginians did decide to secede, it was only when war seemed inevitable and partly out of the fear that if they stayed in the Union they would be isolated from their Southern brethren and might even be forced into war against them. Lee's decision to leave the Army was much like his state's decision to leave the Union.

Adams then turned to the question of why Lee chose secession when fellow Virginians Winfield Scott (famed general of the Mexican-American War and architect of the Union war strategy) and George H. Thomas (who would become an acclaimed general in his own right during the war) stood by the United States. Adams explained that Scott had actually been apart from his state for decades and had only shallow roots in the Commonwealth of Virginia. Of Thomas, Adams said that he was one of the most deeply respected and admired men of the Union and certainly had some roots in Virginia, but there were, he said, "Virginians and there were Virginians. Thomas was not a Lee." Breaking with his home state was far simpler for Thomas than it would have been for Lee, who was the "very quintessence of Virginia."

State loyalty had great meaning to Adams. As an Adams, he was tied to Massachusetts in the same special way that Lee was tied to Virginia. Adams noted how this very question of loyalty to state or nation had come up for Massachusetts nearly half a century earlier, when his state had threatened secession during the War of 1812. Ultimately, his grandfather John Quincy Adams chose nation before state, something that damaged his political career. And the speaker himself said that he would have ultimately sided with country over state, but that it was difficult to come down too hard on those who chose otherwise. And it was even harder to define Lee as a "traitor."

The legal question of citizenship was still complicated in Lee's day.[59] It was not unreasonable for an American of Lee's time to consider state citizenship a priority over national citizenship.

Adams noted how, when Lee was president of Washington College (now Washington and Lee University), he rebuked a student who had delivered a tribute to the "Lost Cause": "General, then President Lee sent for the student, and, after praising his composition and delivery, seriously warned him against holding or advancing such views, impressing strongly upon him the unity of the Nation, and urging him to devote himself loyally to maintain the integrity and honor of the United States" Adams said. This was "true patriotism: the pure American spirit." Though Lee had joined the Confederate cause, it was mistaken to lump him in with conniving traitors like Benedict Arnold. "His lights may have been wrong, according to our ideas then and now they are wrong—but they were his lights, and in acting in full accordance with them he was right." This was not "moral indifference" on the question of secession, which Adams called a "slaveholders' rebellion, conceived and put into action for no end but to perpetuate and extend a system of human servitude, a system the relic of barbarism, an insult of advancing humanity."

But good men sometimes fight for bad causes, just as sometimes bad men fight for good ones. Adams celebrated the fact that slavery had been conquered forever, and he believed the terrible price paid to eliminate it had been worth it. Yet he also wanted to celebrate the good qualities of his Confederate opponents, who had become his fellow countrymen once more. Americans should be as "brave, chivalrous, self-sacrificing, sincere, and patriotic," as many of the men he fought. "So I look forward with confidence to the time when they too will be represented in our national pantheon," Adams said. He anticipated the day when the "bronze effigy of Robert E. Lee, mounted on his charger and with the insignia of his Confederate rank, will from its pedestal in the nation's [capital] look across the Potomac at his old home at Arlington.''

Adams concluded, "When that time comes, Lee's monument will be educational,—it will typify the historical appreciation of all that goes to make up the loftiest type of character, military and civic, exemplified in an opponent, once dreaded but ever respected; and, above all, will symbolize and commemorate that loyal acceptance of the consequences of defeat, and the patient upbuilding of a people under new conditions by constitutional means, which hold to be the greatest educational lesson America has yet taught to a once skeptical but now silenced world."

There may have been Southerners who saw statues of Lee and other Confederates as memorials of defiance, but Adams saw things quite differently. He saw their existence as a tribute to Union victory. Right makes might, as Lincoln said in his Cooper Union address, and the Confederacy was defeated.[60] But that victory would be hollow if former enemies couldn't be reintegrated into a re-forged nation. Even those as honorable as Lee could choose wrongly, but we are a lot poorer as individuals and as a nation if we cannot recognize that the country needed both its Lees and its Lincolns after the bloody war was over.

A Nation that Needs Lincoln and Lee

This isn't to say that every aspect of national reconciliation was successful or beneficial. Despite attempts by Northern and a few Southern Republicans, including former Confederate General James Longstreet, to protect the civil rights of black Americans in the South after the war, many of the former slave states resisted. They successfully stripped black Americans of rights and initiated the so-called Jim Crow era, which lasted nearly a century. Perhaps in large part because of this, the South remained an economic backwater beset by racial violence. It's hard for your economy to prosper when you suppress a large part of your population from getting jobs or participating in civil society. But as bad as that was, things could have been much worse had the South turned to mass guerilla warfare and failed to be reintegrated into the Union, extending an already bloody war and wrecking any chance of rebuilding the nation. In the end, the national reconciliation after the Civil War laid the groundwork not just for regional reintegration but for racial reconciliation as well.

If today we can't include men like Robert E. Lee in the list of men we choose to honor, or at least respect, then perhaps we've forgotten the lessons of the four-year bloodbath of our Civil War. What will we have gotten after we destroy the statues to Lee and his fellow Confederates? Will we have ended racism and racial division? Will we have taught the dead a lesson? Will we have made America a better and more united place of "malice toward none and charity for all?" It's doubtful.

It's a mistake to think that giving into the demands of the statue topplers will ratchet down tension and rage in the body politic. The vandals' anger is directed at America in general. The statues are simply scapegoats standing in for our guilty nation.

The American, and one might say Christian, idea of forgiveness is a far better attitude than vengeance if we intend to continue living as countrymen. Otherwise, the only answer in the end is divorce and separation. At the time of the Civil War, this meant secession. During Jim Crow, it meant segregation. Is that truly the direction we want America to go in? This is the logical end game of identity politics, which teaches that the races are inherently different, that there will always be oppressors and oppressed, and that racial colorblindness is not only impossible but actually racist. Perhaps instead, like Robert E. Lee, we should aim to raise our children to be simply Americans.

Many in Lincoln's day, and a few in ours, thought it would have been best to simply let the South go, save nearly a million lives, and make the messy and only partially successful process of national reconciliation unnecessary. If, instead, we believe that restoration of the union, annihilation of slavery, and a future world in which the United States is both the most formidable power on earth and a bastion for the free world, were the better outcomes, then men like Lincoln and Lee deserve respect and admiration a century and a half later. Together, and only together, they represent American restoration in full. Without Lincoln, there would have been no new birth of freedom placed on a cornerstone of liberty, the principles of Thomas Jefferson and the Founders.[61] Without Lee, America could not be great because it may have been permanently rent by perpetual civil feud.

Lincoln and Lee were both great men in their own way, each of whom, were truly unlike modern iconoclasts, very much committed to healing and reconciliation after the Civil War. Instead of tearing down old statues of Lee and other Confederates, it would be better to recommit ourselves to Lincoln's timeless principles, which are daily under attack. The greatest threat to Lincoln's philosophy is not now coming from a handful of neo-Confederates or members of the alt-right, but from broadsides in academia and the media. America's elite institutions now treat the concept of natural, God-given rights as a joke and teach Americans that their rights come from government and not nature and nature's God.[62]

Yet it is Lincoln's restoration of the Founders' conception of natural rights that has been the deepest fount of liberty in our nation's history, the ultimate justification for the elimination of slavery as well as other forms of tyranny. Embracing Lincoln and the Founders means abandoning the identitarian, collectivist impulses of the left and the alt-right, which lead to nothing but nihilistic and unending racial strife. To ultimately defeat these doctrines, this country desperately needs a revival of Americanism, with the philosophy of Lincoln at its core.

CHAPTER 6

The War on Patriotism

Our allegiance must be purely to the United States. We must unsparingly condemn any man who holds any other allegiance. But if he is heartily and singly loyal to this Republic, then no matter where he was born, he is just as good an American as any one else.

—Theodore Roosevelt, October 12, 1915

Mount Rushmore is a kind of national pantheon of great presidents. The massive sculpture in the Black Hills of South Dakota is one of America's most iconic pieces of art. It depicts four presidents familiar to almost everyone: George Washington, Abraham Lincoln, Thomas Jefferson, and Theodore Roosevelt. The first three choices on this list may seem obvious: George Washington the Father of Our Country and universally admired; Jefferson, the author of the Declaration of Independence and American liberty; Abraham Lincoln, the savior of the Union who ushered in a new birth of freedom. But what about Roosevelt?

Mount Rushmore was the brainchild of Gutzon Borglum, a famed sculptor who aimed to create a modern marvel that would exemplify the fast-rising America of the early twentieth century. When he launched the construction of the incredible artwork in 1927, he wanted to depict timeless Americana and pay tribute to some of the young nation's heroes. His final choice of Roosevelt has in part been attributed to his personal relationship with the recently deceased president—Borglum was a lifelong friend of Roosevelt's who had worked on Teddy's quixotic Bull Moose presidential campaign in 1912.[1] Roosevelt, though a New Yorker by birth, also had deep ties to the Dakotas, having spent time there as a young man after his first wife died. But Borglum insisted that Roosevelt's inclusion was not just due to a personal relationship; instead, it was because he was an "all American President" who had established America as a world power, in part by creating the Panama Canal.[2] Roosevelt was the symbol of a bold, confident America that had finally "made it" on the world stage.

Roosevelt had detractors in his own time. His outsized personality led him to sharp fights with other leading men of the day. He seemed reckless and outrageous, too much of a tempest to be trusted with power. He was a morally upright man—some would say obnoxiously so—who committed himself to causes he believed unquestionably right. He was a masterful political reformer, but many of his reforms would leave things worse than they were before. A political "Progressive," he pursued some policies that have been associated with the American Left over the last century. At the same time, his core instincts could be deeply conservative. Teddy Roosevelt was a militant defender of American civilization, unquestionably patriotic, and even nationalistic. His social conservatism would have put him deeply at odds with the modern Left—and perhaps with modernity in general. But at the end of the day, he was a brilliant and consequential leader.

Roosevelt had his flaws, undoubtedly, but he is worthy of respect as an "all American" president who exemplified the time he lived in. But that's not good enough for the modern Left, who couldn't care less about his contributions to his country. As with Columbus, Confederates, Andrew Jackson, and the problematic Founders, his time for erasure has come.

Beloved Progressive No More

In New York City, where Christopher Columbus statues are being reviewed for removal, Roosevelt is also threatened. In particular, a statue of Roosevelt standing in front of the American Museum of Natural History, created by James Earle Fraser and erected in 1939, has come under withering fire from activists and vandals. In life, Roosevelt braved real gunfire with panache, but unless we are willing to defend him from attack now, his monuments won't survive. The Roosevelt statue in front of the Natural History museum was vandalized in the immediate aftermath of the Charlottesville protest.

The ten-foot-tall bronze statue portraying Roosevelt on a massive steed, flanked by an Indian on one side and a black man on the other, had already drawn the ire of activists. And after Charlottesville, as attacks on statues and calls for their removal became more rampant, Roosevelt became a major target, despite the fact that he had nothing to do with the Confederacy. Protestors consider the statue racist because it portrays Roosevelt in the saddle and people of color on foot on either side. This has become a pattern: out-of-context criticism of a statute gathers a mob and when nothing can or will be done to take it down legally, lawless individuals simply take the statue's destruction into their own hands. A protest broke out at the museum on Columbus Day in 2017. The protestors didn't just want to get rid of the statue; they wanted to remove any connection between the museum and Roosevelt, who they said had been essentially genocidal toward Indians. "Teddy Roosevelt's nature was not empty wilderness. It was and is indigenous land," said one of the activists. "Taken through violence. Just like Columbus who came to enslave. To take their gold and their bodies and their souls."[3] If their fellow citizens didn't want to take part in the crusade, the protesters indicated that they wouldn't take no for an answer. One of the protesters said, of bringing down the Roosevelt statue and others, "It's way overdue. We're going to pull them down if you don't take them down."[4] Not long after this event, the statue was vandalized with red paint.

The protesters and the vandals have been egged on by reasonable-sounding professors who insist that while they don't want to destroy the statue, it should be moved to a museum to "contextualize" it. In a letter to New York Mayor Bill de Blasio, a hundred professors called for the removal of the statue and demanded that it be placed in a museum where Roosevelt, along with other great figures of the American past, can presumably be shamed for their sins. "The Roosevelt monument by James Earle Fraser could be profitably displayed alongside Fraser's *The End of the Trail* in the Metropolitan Museum, for example, so that viewers could explore how race and eugenics were visualized in the period," the professors wrote.[5]

There are certainly cases in which it's reasonable to provide context for statues. It's also a good idea to build new statues for the purpose of portraying views that counter those of the old. But the impulse to force monuments of yesteryear into a setting where far-left professors can simply tell a captive audience what to believe about the past is hardly better than bulldozing them. In some ways, it's worse. While studying the mistakes of previous generations is critical, putting America's past on trial is an entirely unproductive way to treat our statues and monuments. One way or another, though, the Roosevelt statue won't be left alone unless we come to its defense.

There would be something particularly sad about removing Roosevelt's connection to the Natural History Museum, which was originally conceived by his father, Theodore Roosevelt Sr. Like Jefferson, young Teddy was fascinated by the natural world and had a small collection of taxidermied animals. TR's father envisioned a larger museum that could entertain and educate the people of New York, so in 1869, he helped draft a charter for the American Museum of Natural History.[6] The younger Roosevelt would continue to be involved with the museum his entire life, contributing many of the specimens used in its exhibits. That connection seems to matter very little to the brigade of angry activists.

Roosevelt maintains a fair amount of popularity across the political spectrum, but as we've seen with other once universally venerated heroes like Thomas Jefferson, support without informed understanding can erode quickly.[7] Though the American hard Left is leading the charge to boot Roosevelt from his place of honor in our history, many on the American Right have been hesitant to defend him. His progressive political swing, especially late in life, runs afoul of the limited government beliefs of modern conservatives. The Left has even more reasons to let Teddy go. Roosevelt was a firm believer in a powerful military and peace through strength, and he had an overabundance of what now would be called "toxic masculinity."[8] His views on marriage, the family, and especially birth control—he thought it was evil, and even sparred with Planned Parenthood founder Margaret Sanger on the issue—put him somewhere to the right of most modern social conservatives.[9] Certainly, some of his views on race, which drew from the Social Darwinist movement popular among the American elite at the time, are shocking. In the early twentieth century, progressivism and "scientific" racism were often linked, an uncomfortable fact for their progressive ideological descendants. Nevertheless, Roosevelt should not be cavalierly dismissed. Though some of his views make modern Americans on both the left and right blanche, the best of his philosophy is highly applicable today. It's not necessary to accept everything about people of the past to celebrate and learn from them.

The United States has had few leaders as charismatic and iconic as Theodore Roosevelt. He was not just a consequential president—though he was that—he was a dazzling personality who, in his relatively short life, managed to be not just a politician but a soldier, rancher, big game hunter, and talented historian. His book on the War of 1812 has rightly been called a "masterpiece."[10] It's not a stretch to say that Roosevelt was one of the best-read men who ever presided in the White House—not forgetting bookish types like Thomas Jefferson and James Madison. Of course, Roosevelt was not just a bookworm. He was one of the county's most famed outdoorsmen, an advocate of "the strenuous life"—a phrase that became the title of his short book about living a life of hard work, both mental and physical. Though he was born into an extremely wealthy family dynasty, he resisted using that privilege to coast through life. As he wrote, "A mere life of ease is not in the end a very satisfactory life, and, above all, it is a life which ultimately unfits those who follow it for serious work in the world."[11] This did not suit Roosevelt, who was ever the man "in the arena."[12]

TR was a character; his boyish antics, unmistakable grin, and memorable phrases have sparked the imaginations of generations of schoolchildren. But it would be incorrect to think that this is his main contribution to American history. Roosevelt arrived on the American political scene as the country was in a period of transition. After generations of development and explosive growth, America was coming into its own as an international power. No longer a country that was merely proud of holding its own against European leviathans, the US was taking its place as an equal in the global arena, and Roosevelt was ready to lead Americans in that arena.

Many of America's great leaders, including George Washington and Andrew Jackson, had believed wholeheartedly that the United States was destined to be the world's preeminent power—not just a beacon of liberty but an unmatched tower of strength. Roosevelt and Americans of his time found themselves in an America that was not only a promised land for the people of the world but also reaching the pinnacle of power in relation to nations across the globe. From this new vantage point, a once-scrappy underdog set course in a world far less intimidating than it had been for previous generations. The issue facing the nation was what to do with its newfound clout. For good—and sometimes ill—it was Roosevelt and his contemporaries who ushered in the American century.

But his greatest contribution to America may have been at home. Roosevelt offered an inclusive vision of American nationalism. This, even more than the statues and monuments built to honor Roosevelt, is what the Left is attempting to tear down—they see the "cultural imperialism" that demands immigrants assimilate to the country and flag that they live under offensive. Until recently, there was a common consensus about immigration. Immigrants were allowed in based on what was good for the country as a whole. In addition, there was the strong expectation that new arrivals would attempt to conform to American culture, learn English, and assimilate to their new county.

Today, the very term "melting pot" is considered a "microaggression" on some college campuses; the idea of assimilation borders on hate speech.[13] Roosevelt would have found this sort of progressivism bewildering, to say the least. His idea of progress was unity, not division. Like many in his generation, he had lasting memories of a time when the nation, hopelessly divided, went to war with itself and left scars that had never fully healed. He offered a vision for America to become both a nation of immigrants and a nation of citizens with undivided loyalty—Americanism pure and simple.

Few championed the American melting pot more aggressively than Roosevelt. For him, *e pluribus unum* was America's strength, and bold Americanism would provide the glue to keep the country together through any trial. Though there were flaws in the way Roosevelt looked at the world, and though some of his policies did great harm, we have good reason to uphold and carry on this aspect of his legacy today.

America Rising

When Theodore Roosevelt was born, the United States was on the brink of a Civil War that would divide regions and families and leave over half a million Americans dead. Its continued existence as one country was very much in doubt; the experiment in liberty seemed just about over. By the time Roosevelt died, the country was a united superpower emerging victorious in what was, at that point, the largest-scale war in human history. The United States was among the handful of most powerful countries in the world, and to keen observers of the day, it was clearly *the* most powerful.

As we have seen, rebuilding the American nation from the shards that survived the Civil War was a monumental task. That the free institutions created by the Founders survived and were in some ways improved upon was nearly a miracle. In the process of restoring the Union, the United States took another step in its development.

The country was growing explosively in the late nineteenth century. It was at this time that the United States quietly surpassed the United Kingdom in raw economic output. The territorial advances it had made in a century, expanding beyond the Eastern Seaboard all the way to the West Coast, showed the world that the United States was capable of becoming a continental empire that could use its central location between Asia and Europe to be a force in both the East and the West. Prodigious economic growth was propelling America past the most prosperous economies of the world, and the nation was settling into a new position. Combine these factors with an unparalleled system of government and the still-young country had the potential to become something rare in human civilization: a global hegemon.

But the fulfillment of that potential depended on national unity and the patriotism of all Americans—sons and daughters of the North and the South as well newcomers to US soil.

Theodore Roosevelt was born in 1858, the most tumultuous time in American history. He was a toddler when the great armies of the North and South battled across the country. His father, a wealthy New Yorker, paid for a substitute to fight in his place, so he never served in the war. This practice, although common at the time, embarrassed Roosevelt, who overcompensated throughout his life with his own military service.

Young Roosevelt idolized Abraham Lincoln, and the depth of his admiration only grew. As president, he wrote that he believed George Washington and Abraham Lincoln to be among the highest class of statesmen who ever lived and far more worth emulating for a free people than ancients like Caesar, Alexander the Great, and Napoleon. "The more I study the Civil War and the time following it, the more I feel (as of course everyone feels) the towering greatness of Lincoln, which puts him before all other men of our time," Roosevelt wrote.[14]

True to his core value of national unity, Roosevelt was no fan of secession; in fact, he considered it one of the most terrible political crimes ever committed. His public attacks on former Confederate President Jefferson Davis were so caustic that he received what he called an "undignified" letter from Davis demanding an apology for comparing him to infamous American traitor Benedict Arnold. But Davis received no apology, only a curt return letter asking for no further communication.[15] Later in life, Roosevelt would have a change of heart about Davis, but he never relented in his belief that secession was a catastrophe for the United States. While Roosevelt generally castigated Confederate political leadership, he was quite generous in sentiment toward former Confederate soldiers, especially those he believed had simply done their duty to their state. Among these men, Roosevelt held Robert E. Lee in high esteem.[16]

Roosevelt's generation had to pick up the pieces of a shattered nation. He dealt with this matter delicately, refusing to move an inch on what he believed was the justice of the Union cause while acknowledging the humanity and qualities of those who fought for the Confederacy. It is easy to condemn those of the past who did not follow what we see as the right path. Americans of Roosevelt's time were dealing not with abstract ideas but with their flesh-and-blood countrymen. The Civil War didn't end with one side in triumph and the other eliminated from the Earth. Instead, it ended with mortal foes once again living under the same government, the same Constitution, and the same flag. Roosevelt understood this, and he helped complete Abraham Lincoln's task of truly putting the Union back together.

But he did not turn his back on the Americans for whom the bloodiest war in American history had, for the most part, been fought.

Roosevelt routinely reminded his countrymen that the cause of racial equality was essential to the nation's future success and existence. To deny the rights of some Americans based on their skin color, race, or country of origin was cancerous to the republic and dishonored the great task with which Lincoln had charged us in the Gettysburg Address. As Roosevelt explained in one of his best but often overlooked speeches, at a 1905 Lincoln Dinner for the Republican Party of New York, one of "the gravest problems before our people" was "the problem of so dealing with the man of one color as to secure him the rights that no one would grudge him if he were of another color."[17]

Roosevelt believed that the nation couldn't right itself until it became fully committed to equal rights for all citizens. Though Roosevelt used paternalistic terminology about the duty of white Americans to black Americans, he had an unwavering commitment to make equal treatment of the races a reality. He explained why in that stirring New York speech, which deserves quoting at length:

> Neither I nor any other man can say that any given way of approaching that problem will present in our time even an approximately perfect solution, but we can safely say that there can never be such solution at all unless we approach it with the effort to do fair and equal justice among all men; and to demand from them in return just and fair treatment for others. Our effort should be to secure to each man, whatever his color, equality of opportunity, equality of treatment before the law. As a people striving to shape our actions in accordance with the great law of righteousness we cannot afford to take part in or be indifferent to the oppression or maltreatment of any man who, against crushing disadvantages, has by his own industry, energy, self-respect, and perseverance struggled upward to a position which would entitle him to the respect of his fellows, if only his skin were of a different hue.

Every generous impulse in us revolts at the thought of thrusting down instead of helping up such a man. To deny any man the fair treatment granted to others no better than he is to commit a wrong upon him—a wrong sure to react in the long run upon those guilty of such denial. The only safe principle upon which Americans can act is that of "all men up," not that of "some men down."[18]

This gets to the heart of Roosevelt's beliefs—not only about racial equality between white and black Americans, but his overall belief in Americanism, the melting pot, and individualism. To live up to its Founding principles, America must treat people equally and on their merits as individuals. Roosevelt tried to do this in his own life. He caused a stir when he invited black civil rights activist and educator Booker T. Washington to eat with him at the White House in 1901. TR was stunned by the negative reaction to this action, which he "did not devote very much thought to" initially.[19] The president expressed befuddlement at the negative reaction to such a simple gesture and frustration with the entire race problem. The "only wise and honorable and Christian thing to do," he said, was to "treat each black man and each white man strictly on his merits as a man, giving him no more and no less than he shows himself worthy to have." Roosevelt noted that if he was wrong about this, then his whole outlook on life was wrong. In response to the complaints about Washington, the president said he had meant no offence to anyone, but he also didn't "intend to allow their prejudices to make me false to my principles."[20]

Unfortunately, Roosevelt bought into some of the "science" of his day that claimed that black people as a whole were "as a mass" inferior to whites (a salutary warning about the dangers of basing public policy on the contemporary scientific consensus). But to Roosevelt, it ultimately didn't matter what the differences between the races were. They provided no justification for denying individuals the equal rights afforded to all Americans.[21]

A Champion of the Old West, a Symbol of America

Though a through-and-through New Yorker, Roosevelt was also a great booster of the West. After his wife and mother both died on Valentine's Day 1884, the distraught Roosevelt sought escape out West. He retreated to a piece of land he had acquired in the Dakota territory and lived the life of a rancher. To his neighbors, he must have seemed at first like an eccentric Easterner who treated life in the wilder parts of the country as a hobby, but he worked and lived like they did and earned the respect of many.[22]

Roosevelt's interest in Western life did not end with ranching. He fell in love with the beauty and romance of America's wild lands, becoming one of the country's most famed naturalists. He was a fierce proponent of national parks who spearheaded the federal protection of land across the Western states. However, as historian Daniel Ruddy has noted, Roosevelt's intent when creating these parks was not simply to create vast spaces of uninhabited land in the US. "While the recreational angle is part of the story," Ruddy wrote, "TR's overriding objective was to protect the natural wealth of the nation. He wanted to maintain a few special forests.... But the rest of his goal was to 'allow marketable timber to be cut everywhere without damage to the forests.'"[23] For Roosevelt, conservation of the nation's great natural heritage meant preserving not only its beauty but also its wealth and strength.

Roosevelt admired the harsh lives of Westerners and saw the American frontier experience as a defining feature of the country. He mostly accepted the famed "Frontier Thesis" of historian Frederick Jackson Turner, who theorized that America's unique cultural and democratic heritage stemmed from its frontier experience.[24] Though many over the years have questioned Turner's thesis, there is no doubt that the push West left an indelible mark on the

American psyche. One only has to watch a John Ford Western from the mid-twentieth century to understand that the Western is an allegory for America.

It is telling that when TR finally got his chance to see battle in the Spanish-American War, he called the unit he formed the Rough Riders, a name that drew upon his love of the West. The regiment, drawn from all over the country, was composed of the element that Roosevelt saw as the strength of America: hardy men from all walks of life who could find common cause fighting for their country. Roosevelt wrote of his beloved unit, "All—Easterners and Western-ers, Northerners and Southerners, officers and men, cowboys and college graduates, wherever they came from, and whatever their social goal—possessed in common the traits of hardihood and a thirst for adventure."[25]

The Roosevelt's regiment had colorful nicknames that would have fit into a Hollywood Western—Happy Jack of Arizona, Smoky Moore, Rattlesnake Pete. They were a diverse lot, but they were thoroughly American.[26] One man who served in the Rough Riders wrote that it was composed of "millionaires, paupers, shyster lawyers, cowboys, quack doctors, farmers, college professors, miners, adventurers, preachers, prospectors, socialists, journalists, insurance agents, Jews, politicians, Gentiles, Mexicans, professed Christians, Indians, West Point graduates, Arkansas wild men, baseball players, sheriffs, and horse thieves."[27] In other words, it was pure Americana.

E Pluribus Unum

It was during Roosevelt's heyday that the United States emerged as an international power. America had always been expansionist to a certain extent. A purely isolationist country would not have emerged from the thin strip of territory on the East Coast to extend from sea to shining sea in the course of a century. But most Americans envisioned the expansion as limited to the North American continent. As the country reached its natural continental confines, though, many began to see them as a limitation rather than a blessing for a nation in a sea of aggressive imperialist powers. It is noteworthy that whenever the United States let up on enforcing the Monroe Doctrine—formulated by Secretary of State John Quincy Adams to ward off aggressive European expansion in the Americas—or appeared to be faltering—as during the Civil War—European nations swooped in to gobble up as much of the New World as they could.[28]

Roosevelt has often been labeled a reckless meddler, an imperialist, and a militarist for his foreign policy. But his views weren't so far outside the norm of American history. Even the famed and sometimes maligned "Roosevelt corollary" to the Monroe Doctrine was for the most part used as a deterrent to European powers not to cross American interests, rather than as a dictum for remaking the Americas in our image.

Roosevelt believed that, for the United States to remain strong and independent, it had to be able to project that strength from time to time. It also had to be strong within. At a time when America was taking in large numbers of immigrants from nations that sometimes clashed with American interests, Roosevelt championed a philosophy that may be his greatest legacy to us today—if we don't lose sight of it.

No speech better sums up Theodore Roosevelt's philosophy than one he delivered on October 12, 1915, to the Knights of Columbus. As we have seen, the Knights of Columbus was no ordinary fraternal organization. Because it was Catholic, groups such as the Ku Klux Klan frequently attacked it as un-American. Hostilities between Protestants and Catholics in that day were far more intense than our own. So it was noteworthy that former president Roosevelt, a fervent Protestant, would make an appearance before the group.[29]

Roosevelt began by crediting Columbus for the discovery of America that had led to the creation of the United States. He found it appropriate that he should pay tribute in English to a great Italian who had sailed to the New World under a Spanish flag. It all fit in with his view of America as a country crafted from a mosaic of many peoples into one.

Roosevelt explained, "Our nation was founded to perpetuate democratic principles. These principles are that each man is to be treated on his worth as a man without regard to the land from which his forefathers came and without regard to the creed he possesses. If the United States proves false to these principles of civil and religious liberty, it will have inflicted the greatest blow on the system of free government that has ever been inflicted.... Our duty is to secure each man against injustice by his fellows."

This was a powerful statement of support for the Catholic group and a stinging rebuke to the Klan and other organizations that would have excluded them from American life. Roosevelt added, "Any political movement directed against any body of our fellow citizens because of their religious creed is a grave offence against American principles and American institutions." Then he addressed the question of what a true American is, condemning both nativists and those who refused to identify as simply Americans. TR had no tolerance for what he called "hyphenated Americans":

> What is true of creed is no less true of nationality. There is no room in this country for hyphenated Americanism. When I refer to hyphenated Americans, I do not refer to naturalized Americans. Some of the very best Americans I have ever known were naturalized Americans, Americans born abroad. But a hyphenated American is not an American at all. This is just as true of the man who puts "native"

before the hyphen as of the man who puts German or Irish or English or French before the hyphen. Americanism is a matter of the soul. Our allegiance must be purely to the United States. We must unsparingly condemn any man who holds any other allegiance. But if he is heartily and singly loyal to this Republic, then no matter where he was born, he is just as good an American as anyone else.[30]

To Roosevelt, being an American was about more than asserting your rights. It was about your duty to the country—the burden of citizenship. Those patriots who demonstrated devotion to their country were due respect and equal treatment from their fellow citizens. This did not just apply to European immigrants, who were more common at that time. Roosevelt became livid when a concerted movement—he attributed it to labor and trades unions—began targeting Japanese on the West Coast. Boycotts were organized against the businesses of Japanese immigrants, and Japanese children were forced out of local public schools. Worse, mobs went on the attack, triggering Roosevelt's ferocious defense of law and order.[31]

This is not to say that Roosevelt believed that all people everywhere should be let into the United States or were willing and able to act as free people living in a democratic republic. But he did believe that once immigrants became American citizens, they should be treated equally with all other citizens. That meant full rights and responsibilities as Americans—and nothing but Americans: neither a reduction of rights nor additional privileges that were not afforded to others.

If there is one concept that Americans today must salvage from Roosevelt, it is this concept of assimilation and nationhood. Of course, from the country's earliest days, there was a strong widespread belief that a diverse America needed to embrace *e pluribus unum.* Some Founders emphasized America's English heritage. John Jay wrote in Federalist 2 that Americans are "a people descended from the same ancestors, speaking the same language, professing the same religion."[32] But the truth is that we've been a fairly polyglot assortment from day one. White Anglo-Saxon Protestants dominated, but among the Founding generation, there was already a heterogeneous mix of ethnicities—English, Scotch, Irish, German, and Dutch, among others—religions, and creeds among the general population. As the country grew enormously in size and population in the nineteenth century, this ethnic and religious diversity also greatly increased. How was such a country to maintain anything like a unity of purpose?

Roosevelt had an answer to this question. He had an expansive view of who could become an American, though he never assumed that all people everywhere would be willing and able to adapt to our ways. American citizens had developed norms for living under our unique system. Native-born Americans had a duty to teach and transmit the best of who we are, and newcomers had a reciprocal duty to learn from their predecessors and carry on this now-shared tradition.

In a letter to his friend Richard Melancton Hurd just after World War I, Roosevelt noted that just because the war was over, it did not mean that the country should slide back into recognizing dual loyalties. On the other hand, it was unacceptable bigotry to reject an American because of where he was born. "We should insist that if the immigrant who comes here does in good faith become an American and assimilates himself to us, he shall be treated on an exact equality with everyone else, for it is an outrage to discriminate against any such man because of creed, or birthplace, or origin."[33] But acceptance would come with some stipulations: " ... this is predicated upon the man's becoming in fact an American and nothing but an American. If he tries to keep segregated with men of his own origin and separated from the rest of America, then he isn't doing his part as an American." He stressed that there "could be no divided allegiance here."

"Any man who says he is an American but something else also, isn't an American at all," Roosevelt said. In an additional jab at communists, he added, "We have room for but one flag, the American flag, and this excludes the red flag which symbolized all wars against liberty and civilization just as much as it excludes any foreign flag of a nation to which we are hostile." Roosevelt said that the only language for Americans would be English. And finally he warned Americans not to abandon these principles: "We intend to see that the crucible turns our people out as Americans, of American nationality, and not as dwellers in a polyglot boarding house; and we have room for but one soul loyalty, and that loyalty is to the American people."[34]

Roosevelt's outlook is considered hopelessly offensive by many today. The idea that newcomers should abandon their national and ethnic loyalties and identify as Americans like anyone else is seen as retrograde, bigoted, and oppressive. Americans are constantly reminded about what makes us different from each other, not of the qualities that bind us together. But Roosevelt's vision of a united America might just save us from the kind of vicious ethnic hatred that bedevils countries all over the world, wherever different nationalities share a single government. The ethos of Americanism could provide a healthy alternative to the multiculturalism that is breeding noxious forms of tribal identity politics.

TR loathed the concept of being a "citizen of the world." In one editorial, he called the "cult of internationalism" a "doctrine of fatal sterility."[35] Roosevelt lamented the fact that the "educated classes" made themselves odious to the general population due to their "queer lack of Americanism"[36]—even in his day! Roosevelt was not worried that the world lacked humanitarian feeling. On the contrary, he was concerned that America suffered from too much "ill-regulated milk and water philanthropy which makes us degrade or neglect our own people by paying too much attention to the absolutely futile task of trying to raise humanity at large."[37]

"Our business is with our own people," Roosevelt wrote. "If we can bring up the United States we are doing well; yet we can't bring it up unless we teach its citizens to regard the country, and the flag which symbolizes that country, with the most genuine fervor of enthusiastic love." This was not to say that Roosevelt believed citizens should not be critical of their country—far from it. It was the duty of every citizen to help correct the country's shortcomings, but we have "absolutely no ground to work on if we don't have a firm and ardent Americanism at the bottom of everything." Roosevelt compared the concept of being a citizen of the world to a person who denounces monogamous marriage as a selfish and archaic practice: "I regard the man who holds up to admiration adultery and robbery, for instance as being but an indifferent moral teacher. In the same way, I feel that the lack of patriotism shows an absolute defect in any national character."[38]

In his famed "Citizenship in a Republic" speech in Paris in 1910 (more commonly known as the "Man in the Arena" speech), Roosevelt explained the correct relationship between Americans and the so-called international community. He was no fan of "foolish cosmopolitanism": "I believe that a man must be a good patriot before he can be, and as the only possible way of being, a good citizen of the world. Experience teaches us that the average man who protests that his international feeling swamps his national feeling, that he does not care for his country because he cares so much for mankind, in actual practice proves himself the foe of mankind; that the man who says that he does not care to be a citizen of any one country, because he is the citizen of the world, is in fact usually an exceedingly undesirable citizen of whatever corner of the world he happens at the moment to be in."[39]

Contrast these remarks with President Barack Obama's 2013 speech in Berlin, in which he said, "We are not only citizens of America or Germany—we are also citizens of the world. And our fates and fortunes are linked like never before."[40]

Roosevelt was very clear about the fact that devotion to the flag and the country are the signs of a good citizen, and that these loyalties should be cultivated among both new arrivals to the country and the young. Global citizenship was a farce, a dangerous, empty creed of the untrustworthy.

America has found a way to blend the most diverse assortment of people in a single nation. It accomplished this by building a unique system of government that divides political power through federalism, protects individual liberties (of, for instance, citizens of differing religious beliefs), and fosters a welcoming culture that is certainly among the most strongly assimilatory in human history. These factors make America both an unrivaled superpower and a highly desirable place to live. One cannot simply become Chinese or Japanese, German or French, in the same way that anyone with the right mindset can, in time, become an American. This is a great strength of the Republic. But that is not to say that every person who steps on American soil can immediately become fully American in every aspect the moment he arrives—an increasingly common assumption with no basis in reality.

All men are created equal, with equal natural rights, but not all cultures are equal. As we have seen, it was the unique American culture, which predated even the creation of the United States, that produced the men who signed onto the natural rights in the Declaration of Independence and a transformational political document like the Constitution. America may have been the *only* place in the late eighteenth century where these things could have succeeded—as the great failure of Revolutionary France would demonstrate.

This does not mean that individuals from other places aren't equally hardworking and decent as Americans. It simply means that ideas don't exist in a vacuum; culture and civilizational traditions matter. And only the American people have the right to decide for ourselves which newcomers will fit in under a shared free government; we alone determine who will strengthen America and who will weaken it. Teddy Roosevelt understood this truth far better than many today.

Roosevelt didn't see all immigrants as an unqualified blessing. He worried that Chinese and Japanese immigrants on the West Coast were not assimilating—even going so far as to sign and praise an exclusionary immigration bill in 1907 while he was president. He was quite concerned to learn that three-quarters of New York's population was foreign born or the child of immigrants. Yet Roosevelt remained optimistic that the awesome assimilatory power of American culture and institutions would win out and lambasted the militant nativists of his time who wanted to put a halt to accepting newcomers.[41]

In his important 1894 speech "True Americanism," Roosevelt explained that it was often necessary to regulate and restrict immigration for a variety of reasons, but that Americans must "freely extend the hand of welcome and of good-fellowship to every man, no matter what his creed or birthplace, who comes here honestly intent on becoming a good United States citizen like the rest of us."[42] The immigrant, in turn, must give up the prejudices and quarrels of his former home and fully embrace his new country, including the all-important rule of law.

Roosevelt then quoted the German-born representative Richard Guenther, who had explained to his fellow immigrants,

We know as well as any other class of American citizens where our duties belong. We will work for our country in time of peace and fight for it in time of war, if a time of war should ever come. When I say our country, I mean, of course, our adopted country. I mean the United States of America. After passing through the crucible of naturalization, we are no longer Germans; we are Americans. Our attachment to America cannot be measured by the length of our residence here. We are Americans from the moment we touch the American shore until we are laid in American graves. We will fight for America whenever necessary. America, first, last, and all the time. America against Germany, America against the world; America, right or wrong; always America. We are Americans.[43]

Roosevelt's patriotic vision for America is the element of his ideas most worth preserving for our own and future generations. As radicals and activists in modern American try to tear down the foundations of the American creed and American history piece by piece, the patriotic notions of Teddy Roosevelt are a revitalizing alternative.

Citizenship and identity are serious business, as TR knew full well. That's why he used his advantages as a member of the American elite to promote the gospel of Americanism, so that generations long after him could inherit the same great country he loved. This is the duty of responsible citizens. Unfortunately, America's elites are more contemptible than admirable today. They consider patriotism beneath them. And they would never ask new immigrants to give up their loyalties to their former homes and embrace the American way of life. Until this dynamic changes, populist convulsions will continue unabated.

Roosevelt, a patrician New Yorker whose family had been in America since before the founding of the Republic, cared little if those who came to America were rich or poor, as long as they wanted to be Americans and nothing else. He promoted a belief system that allowed every newly arrived immigrant to see George Washington as the father of *his* country too. This can still happen if there are those like Roosevelt, ready to impart the values of "true Americanism," and immigrants who are willing to listen and embrace that legacy.

Roosevelt offered this vision at the dawn of the twentieth century, at a time when the United States was on the cusp of playing a much larger role in world affairs. The upstart nation destined to be in the middle of the most important events in world history would benefit from this strong uniting ethos as it went through a dramatic period of economic transformation, global involvement, regional factionalism, racial conflict, and rapidly changing demographics.

Times have changed. Today, the patriotic spirit of Theodore Roosevelt is being purged from American life. Our elites, our educational institutions, and the engines of popular culture prefer demonstrating their left-wing *bona fides*. Even US government officials rush to placate international audiences.[44] But freedom for Americans won't be upheld by the "international" community if American citizens give up on transmitting Roosevelt's values.[45]

Social commentators denounce America as intolerant and xenophobic—a nation devoted to "white supremacy" at its core. But they couldn't be farther from the truth. Yes, there were many moments of ugly nativism and racial prejudice in our history. At times, there was even targeted violence against ethnic and religious minorities. But these were the exceptions, not the rule in the United States. Prejudice, oppression, and violence have been more or less universal across all civilizations and peoples on this earth from the dawn of human civilization. Liberty and justice are rare gifts.

At one time, most Americans understood this. Despite the difficulties and prejudice that many immigrants faced in America, they were willing—more than willing—to face those challenges for the privilege of becoming Americans. And they did so mostly by leaving countries where they had been surrounded by people of their own race and their own faith. They knew that it was better to live under the American flag and the Constitution rather than under the rule of their own ethnic kin. It is telling that twenty-first-century activists condemn America and its immigration laws as racist yet at the same time demand that more people from allegedly oppressed groups be brought into the country through an open border. If they really believed that America was so truly awful, they would be desperately trying to get racial minorities out of this country instead of in.

Jews did not demand to be let into Nazi Germany. From the time this country was founded, people have risked their lives to get into America. And no wonder. It is almost infinitely better to be a person of Mexican heritage living in the United States than a Mexican living in many parts of Mexico beset by anarchy, gang violence, and little hope for economic betterment. The reason for that is the unique cultural, legal, economic, and constitutional traditions of the United States, the ones that Roosevelt extolled and attempted to pass on.

It is desperately important that we continue to uphold the uniting traditions of American pride and patriotism. We can cultivate a genuine love of country though civic rituals, like standing for the national anthem before a ball game or saying the Pledge of Allegiance.[46] And yet these uniting practices are increasingly seen as examples of ugly, chauvinistic nationalism.[47]

The freedom we enjoy does not come from an international community of nations. It comes from our sovereign nation, which, through the Constitution, is designed to protect our individual rights based on the equality of citizenship. Perhaps, at a time when we face the challenge of mass immigration in an increasingly globalized world, we would be better served by re-embracing Roosevelt's legacy of patriotic assimilation rather than by tearing down his statues. If we return to Teddy's conviction that the American way of life should be proudly cultivated in every citizen, new or old, we will assuredly have yet another American century—and humanity will be better for it.

CHAPTER 7

The War on the American Century

The American war production job was probably the great-est collective achievement of all time. It makes the "seven wonders" of the ancient world look like the doodling of a small boy.

— *Donald Nelson, head of the War Production Board[1]*

W hy is America the most powerful nation on earth? Other countries have more people, and many are nearly as rich in natural resources. America's unique cultural, constitutional, and legal system allowed it to create the most dynamic and productive economy in world history. And when that system was challenged in the twentieth century, it pre-vailed over all rivals. The United States military and the free economy that supports it are the symbols of American prosperity and might.

World War II is almost universally considered the "good war." Even today, most across the political spectrum agree that American defeat of the Axis powers in the 1940s was a positive thing. By the time the war ended, the United States had risen to a level of international preeminence virtually unmatched in human history. Americans who have lived in the post-war world can hardly even imagine what it was like not to think of our country as the economically and militarily dominant nation. Many who resent America's status as the only superpower would rather see the US as merely one among equals—a state of affairs they assume would make the world a more peaceful place.

It's rare for the US role in World War II to be questioned outright. The trend is to diminish what made it possible for America to defeat fascism. Community organizers, social justice warriors, and street thugs did not bring down the Third Reich. Instead, it was our uniquely American heritage: The independent New World, born from the seeds of discovery in 1492. It was the sons of the Puritans, who fled the gripping vise of Old World autocrats and built a promised land across the sea as a shining city upon a hill. It was the Constitutional Republic, created by the Founders, saved by Lincoln, and committed to Jefferson's timeless principles of individual liberty. It was the Jacksonian spirit of the American people who refused to be tread on by tyrants. And it was the Rooseveltian patriotism that allowed a diverse country to act in concert against its enemies.

Remembering the Bad, Forgetting the Good, Losing Sight of How We Got Here

In an age of historical ignorance, in which fewer Americans are taught about America's wars and the generation that fought World War II is fading from national consciousness, we are losing touch with what exactly the world faced at that time and why we defeated our enemies. Polls on American knowledge of the Second World War are downright embarrassing. According to one study, two-thirds of millennials didn't know what Auschwitz was.[2] Young Americans learn little about Normandy and Midway in classrooms. In their place are tales of Japanese internment and the immorality of using atomic weapons without the larger context of the threat America faced or the evils only the United States could counter.

America's accomplishments are diminished, and even when they are acknowledged, credit for success is almost entirely misplaced.

A militant left-wing activist group calling itself "Antifa," short for "anti-fascist," has been at the forefront of instigating the destruction of historical statues. This organization, which became particularly active after the election of President Donald Trump, has at various times claimed that it's fighting fascism, white supremacy, and capitalism.

Though many on the American Left keep their distance from this extremist group, others praise what it stands for. Representative Keith Ellison, a Minnesota Democrat who is the deputy chair of the Democratic National Committee, posted a picture of himself holding the "Antifa: The Anti-Fascist Handbook" and said that it would "strike fear" into the heart of Trump.[3]

Many in the media have taken Antifa at face value, portraying them as a genuine opposition to Nazis in defense of the American way of life. Some have even compared Antifa to the American soldiers who defeated Nazi Germany in World War II. *Atlantic* editor Jeffrey Goldberg tweeted a picture of American troops storming the beaches of Normandy on June 6, 1944, with this description: "Watching 'Saving Private Ryan,' a movie about a group of very aggressive alt-left protesters invading a beach without a permit."[4]

Comparing the Invasion of Normandy to Antifa or "Alt-Left" demonstrators became a viral meme. The obvious absurdity of claiming that attacking statues or duking it out with a handful of alt-right extremists can be compared to the bravery of soldiers who stormed the beaches of Normandy was bad enough. Insinuating that those soldiers—representatives of the wide swath of American society as it existed in the 1940s—were anything like a collection of left-wing political activists was laughably incorrect.

Antifa activists are more similar to the socialist street thugs who battled it out with fascists in the streets of Germany in the 1930s—many of whom found themselves comfortably within Nazi ranks before World War II was through. Mark Bray, the author of *Antifa: The Anti-Fascist Handbook*, notes how, back in the 1980s and 1990s, the precursors to the Antifa movement in Europe had to work to keep potential recruits from becoming neo-Nazis.[5] In America, to appeal to a different population, these groups painted themselves as "anti-racists," but their goals were mostly the same. The bottom line is that they bear little resemblance to the Allied soldiers who liberated Western Europe from tyranny. They are more like the communist thugs who worked with the Soviet Union to bring another repugnant tyranny to Eastern Europe when the war ended.

Antifa and other radical left-wing groups are dedicated to undermining the great pillars of American strength that made the defeat of the Third Reich possible. It was free enterprise and the United States military, two bugaboos of the far-Left, that brought down fascism. We should be thankful for both and thankful for the men who best represented them: Henry Ford and Dwight Eisenhower.

Henry Ford is regarded as one of America's great entrepreneurial geniuses, and for good reason. From humble beginnings on the farm, this man with an innate knack for things mechanical not only built the famed Model T but created the business model that brought it to Americans of almost any means. He was instrumental in ushering in the middle class economic prosperity that Americans—and now people across the globe—have come to expect: a house, a car in the garage, a steady job, and the means to enjoy leisure time outside that job. He opened up to the average person a world of material plenty that had once been unavailable to even the wealthiest upper crust. He employed men of all backgrounds and religions in his factories—something notable at a time when black Americans were excluded from many places of employment, particularly in the South.

But Ford had a dark side. He published anti-Semitic articles in his *Dearborn Independent* newspaper—tellingly reprinted under the title *The International Jew*. Though Ford likely didn't personally write any of the articles, he kept publishing them for years, stopping only after the pleading of two former presidents, Woodrow Wilson and William Howard Taft, the souring of relationships with Jewish friends, and eventually a libel lawsuit by a Jewish man saying he had been slandered.[6] Ford apologized and disbanded the paper, but it left a black mark on his legacy, especially given the rise of Nazi Germany and accusations that he was a German sympathizer.

So what should we make of this great but flawed man?

Eisenhower's reputation is less mixed. Few openly criticize the man who represents American military triumph in World War II and the high tide of our global dominance in the 1950s. The accomplishments of Eisenhower and his generation, instead of being attacked outright like those of Columbus or the Founders, are being gutted of their significance.

The most obvious example of this is the absurdist, postmodern Eisenhower Memorial proposed for the National Mall in Washington, D.C. The monstrous boondoggle, which is set to portray Eisenhower as a teenager, captures nothing of the greatness of the man or the men he fought with, and it has generally been opposed by his family.[7] It's the overpriced vanity project of a celebrity, Canadian artist Frank Gehry, who has compared President Donald Trump's speeches to those of Adolf Hitler in the 1930s.[8] It would appear that Eisenhower is unlikely to get the tribute he deserves.

The Great Republic

"The creation of the United States of America is the central event of the past four hundred years," wrote historian Walter A. McDougal. If a person were transported in time from the year 1600, McDougal theorized, besides the marvelous growth in the world's technology and population, most of the international landscape would look about the same. "The only continent that would astound the Renaissance time-travelers would be North America, which was primitive and nearly vacant as late as 1607, but which today hosts the mightiest, richest, most dynamic civilization in history—a civilization, moreover, that perturbs the trajectories of all other civilizations just by existing."[9]

That remarkable and mighty civilization came into its own in the twentieth century.

America's cultural traits, unique political system, and excellent geographic location—which had allowed the country to expand enormously in size since the time of the Founding—produced an energetic young nation of remarkable growth in the nineteenth century. The Civil War ended the existential crisis over slavery and freedom, the crisis of the house divided. While fissures in American life remained deep as the United States entered the twentieth century, it nevertheless emerged as a powerful and unified country, a magnet for immigrants, and, especially after the Spanish-American War, a nation that Old World imperialists were unlikely to trifle with.

The nineteenth century represented America in its youth—a plucky underdog of seemingly limitless potential for both growth and implosion. In the century that followed, the United States became something else. The twentieth century was the American century, the time when the world's youngest civilization rose to become its greatest—certainly its most influential. The heart of American strength, the reason it leapfrogged over Great Britain and ultimately defeated the twin evils of fascism and communism, is in part the astounding and transformative nature of the American economic system. No people were better able harness the awesome power of the market economy than Americans.

Alexis de Tocqueville, who was so perceptive about American life, believed that the middle class could become the nation's Achilles's heel. He feared that its steady growth, which he observed in the Jacksonian era, would lead to general mediocrity at the expense of greatness. Tocqueville may have been right in some respects. Aristotle, however, wrote that a polity with an expansive middle class was likely to be the greatest and most stable of any political system.[10] Perhaps a nation of these middling men would better protect liberty than a society of lords and serfs. For most of history, hardly any city or nation—especially one of considerable size—could sustain a large, prosperous middle class. That changed with the rise of the United States.

The famed economist Adam Smith once called Great Britain a "nation of shopkeepers," a phrase that may have been used derisively by Napoleon Bonaparte to suggest that the British were commercial rather than martial. But it was British finance capitalism that allowed it to challenge and surpass the greatest empires of continental Europe, nations that had more resources and larger populations. The United States became a vast continent of shopkeepers, far exceeding what even the mighty British Empire was in its heyday. America was blessed with plentiful resources, gifted statesmen like Andrew Jackson who fought for and secured American interests in a sea of foreign competitors, a legal system dedicated to protecting private property, and cultural values that encouraged enterprise.

Smith may have been the first to describe how a market economy works in his masterpiece book *The Wealth of Nations*, fittingly published in 1776, and Americans took to his doctrines whether they read his treatise or not. They fit in perfectly with the ethos of the new nation and by the nineteenth century had become a central element of the American creed. The "self-made man," a celebrated trope of the Jacksonian era, became an archetype that Americans aspired to. And though Americans have always fought over the role of government in economics—some preferring higher tariffs and government sponsorship of projects that couldn't be financed by private citizens—overall, the United States maintained an incredibly free, "laissez-faire" economy, which made the country remarkably prosperous.

As much as American-style capitalism comes under fire today, as it has for a long time, there is no question that it has created more wealth for more people than any other system in human history. The United States has always been an economically dynamic country. The nation punches well above its weight in production per capita. This was already true throughout the eighteenth and nineteenth centuries, even when the country's chief economic enterprise was agriculture. The United States was prosperous, provided amply for its citizens, and became a magnet for immigrants who could find opportunities in the New World that were impossible to find elsewhere. As a result, the country grew phenomenally. The next stage of its economic development, at the dawn of the twentieth century, was even more transformative. No man represented this economic revolution better than Henry Ford.

Fordism: Capitalism for the Everyman

It is a curious thing that Henry Ford became the architect of modern life. Ford was born in Michigan in 1863, less than a month after the Union triumph at the Battle of Gettysburg. He grew up on a farm and was inculcated with the "cultural values pervasive among mainstream, middle-class Americans during most of the nineteenth century. Victorian culture 'as historians have termed it' forged a creed combining Protestant moralism, market individualism, the work ethic, and genteel restraint."[11]

In some ways, Ford was a man with a foot in both the past and the future. He hated farm work, preferring to have machines do labor in man's place, yet it is clear that he came to admire the old-fashioned rural lifestyle he rebelled against in his youth. Late in life, when he had more money than he knew what to do with, Ford turned to projects to preserve Americana.[12] Still, his understanding of history was often wanting. When, in a notable 1919 libel court case, he was grilled on basic facts of American history, he said he believed the American Revolution was in 1812 and that Benedict Arnold was "a writer, I think."[13] Whether Ford was being straightforward with these answers or not, the truth is that Ford was no scholar. Yet throughout his life, he maintained a firm belief that America was a great and good country. He tried to pass his love of his country on to other Americans by building a giant open-air museum called Greenfield Village, which features an impressive assortment of items of deep historical significance. He brought in the courthouse where Abraham Lincoln practiced law as a young man, the workshop of great inventor Thomas Edison, the schoolhouse from the short story "Mary Had a Little Lamb" by Sarah Josepha Hale, among a wide array of other historic buildings and antiques.

Ford was obsessed with the *McGuffey Reader*, ubiquitous in nineteenth-century American schools. He could recite from it at length throughout his life. But Ford wasn't simply a man looking backward. When Ford lectured a schoolboy about the virtues of the *McGuffey Reader* and the old-fashioned school rooms he had learned in, the boy blurted out, "But, sir, these are different times, this is the modern age and—" Ford interrupted the schoolboy mid-sentence.

"Young man, I invented the modern age," he said.[14]

This boast was not mere hyperbole. As Ford, sometimes ham-handedly, tried to preserve what he saw as the good elements of his country's past, he was unquestionably defining the distinctive features that would be the hallmarks of its future. As the world entered the peak of the industrial age, America hit its economic high point, thanks to "Fordism."

In the beginning, the automobile industry mostly catered to a few wealthy hobbyists who appreciated the novelty of the "horseless carriage." The vast infrastructure required to support a massive industry and make the car ubiquitous—roads and places to refuel—simply didn't exist at that point. Plus, car innovation was held back by a persistent patent troll, George B. Selden, who claimed to own rights to the patent on the internal combustion engine and worked with a cartel to extort the infant industry. Ford won a highly publicized legal victory against Selden, the cartel dissolved, and the car industry exploded. Ford became an immediate folk hero.[15]

But Ford's contributions to humanity were not limited to unshackling the auto industry. Though the originator of the "assembly line" concept is somewhat unclear—Ford often took credit for it publicly, despite the fact that others were using similar methods before him—there is no doubt that he was the one who initially made the most effective use of it. Ford's adaptation of this marvel of economic organization transformed the world forever. Steven Watts, author of *The People's Tycoon: Henry Ford and the American Century*, has called it "perhaps the most revolutionary development in industrial history. Rather than having teams of laborers doing many different jobs as they built a car from the ground up, this new process placed workers, each performing a minuscule task, at

stationary positions along a conveyor belt that moved the developing vehicle along. The relentless, steady accumulation of these tiny
jobs, performed incrementally, produced a finished automobile in
record time."[16]

Suddenly Ford cars, starting with the world-famous Model T,
could be produced so quickly and cheaply that they became a standard household item—helped along by Ford's ethos of getting his
creation into the hands of every American family, no matter where
they stood on the income ladder. The sales of his cars typically produced very thin profit margins because he insisted on keeping the
price at a bare minimum.

Ford also famously created the $5 workday in 1914—an astound-
ing amount of money for a factory worker at that time. The pay
increase even caused a riot when workers, many of whom had traveled from around the country just for a chance to get a job at the Ford
Motor Company, had to be turned away.

The $5 policy didn't just make employees happy; it was also a
shrewd business move. By paying workers more money, Ford was
able to hire and retain the best and most reliable workers, of all creeds
and races, thus stemming the turnover that harmed productivity. A
better paying job made it far less likely a worker would look elsewhere for employment. Because Ford paid his men more, they were
better able to afford more consumer goods and leisure time. This was
helping create the bulging middle class while producing items for
them to enjoy that had once been limited to only a wealthy elite. In
addition, he was fueling the growth of America's car culture, which
would allow workers who suddenly had more money in their pock-
ets to take vacations and travel—an activity once relegated to the
wealthy, but not anymore.

"Mr. Ford was saying that one ought to be one's own best cus-
tomer; that unless an industry keeps wages high and prices low, it

limits the number of its customers and destroys itself," said Charlie Sorensen, a top manager at Ford Motor Company in its heyday. "Thus the wage earner is as important as a consumer as he is as a producer; and that enlarged buying power by paying higher wages and selling at low prices is behind the prosperity of this country."[17]

In America, the working man would be middle class.[18]

America was ushering in the age of the producer-consumer and the dominant middle class. This wasn't all Ford's doing, of course. The other two of the "Big Three" automakers, General Motors and Chrysler, were also propelling the enormous boom in the consumer economy, and other industries ramped up production as well. But Ford—the man and the company—were the originals, and they symbolized this market transformation. It was American capitalism at its finest—creating wealth and distributing its blessings to people of every background.

Dark Clouds Gather

As American-style capitalism was driving economic growth, other creeds that would challenge it in the twentieth century were gaining traction. First came the threat of communism, which took root in Russia under the sclerotic czarist regime at the end of World War I. The other was fascism, a state-based style of socialism that took root in Europe during the Great Depression.[19] These ideologies, both of which challenged the notions of the Founding Fathers—that individual rights were God-given and that government derived its power from the consent of the governed—would pose the ultimate threat to the American system. But bizarrely, Adolf Hitler and Stalin, dictators of fascist Germany and the communist Soviet Union respectively, quoted Ford favorably and claimed to be building their regimes on his principles.[20] It isn't hard to see why others wanted to copy American success even while gutting other ideas that have made the country distinct. A massively productive economy made one powerful, and authoritarian regimes have been happy to copy our success as long as they can find ways to circumscribe our ideas about liberty and self-government. Are things so different with Communist China today?

Before America's fundamental institutions and economic system were challenged abroad, they were first challenged at home. The Wall Street crash of 1929 famously sent the United States and most of the world into economic chaos. Many questioned whether the American system of free enterprise was really superior, and some began to wonder whether collectivism and strong men might be the way of the future, as nations around the globe fell under various forms of authoritarian government.

Limited government, private property rights, and a free economy—along with strong civil society outside of government involvement—which had been our secret sauce to prosperity, came under attack as the financial crash spiraled into an appalling decade-long Depression. Around the globe, relatively free governments were replaced with dictatorial ones, and some in America thought the writing was on the wall. Many believed America must adapt and embrace an empowered government with fewer restrictions, accepting the government's "scientific" management of the economy, which could more fairly and efficiently foster the nation's wealth than the unfettered economy and the profit motive. An ascendant executive branch and armies of bureaucrats, who would require little more than a rubberstamp from Congress, would impose their will on the American people.

"Congressional government is incompetent to deal with the many, urgent, and specialized problems of administering a large and varied country..." wrote far-left New Deal proponent Jay Franklin in 1940. "This means that the president should exercise, through the

Federal bureaucracy, the real powers of American government.... Modern political administration is a continuous process, and the needs of the people do not always wait for the election returns or the passage of a bill."[21]

The fact that millions of Americans couldn't find work and many were left destitute in the 1930s made them open to the idea that the government needed to step in to provide. Many of President Franklin Roosevelt's New Deal programs, such as unemployment benefits and Social Security, were justified as a kind of insurance—rather than mere handouts—to people the industrial economy had failed. These were among the least intrusive and most widely accepted New Deal programs; others went much further. But as many accepted this growth of government as necessary in a time of desperation, others became fervent in opposition to programs that appeared to be a violation of the Constitution and American principles. One of those was Henry Ford.

Ford blasted Roosevelt's programs, in particular the National Industrial Recovery Administration, or NIRA. The NIRA was the most expansive New Deal program, with power over almost every element of the American economy. The Ford Motor Company released a statement saying the head of the NIRA was "assuming the airs of a dictator" and that the program was fundamentally shifting the American way of life.[22]

Ford himself was even more caustic about the program, telling the *New York Times* that the NIRA would destroy the American competitive spirit so that "the world will not progress."[23] He thought the most aggressive New Deal programs were meant to fundamentally change America for the worse and make us dependent on government from cradle to grave. Roosevelt's Second Bill of Rights used the rhetoric of the Founders but directly countered their principles. Instead of protecting liberty and equality under law, the government would take away American liberty to promote a forced social equality. This was the philosophy behind FDR's most aggressive reforms, and it triggered a more-than-half-century battle over the nature of government and the Constitution, with similar battle lines standing today.[24]

The NIRA was eventually struck down by the Supreme Court in the famed *Schechter Poultry Corp. v. United States* case, which prompted Roosevelt to unsuccessfully attempt to pack the Court with additional justices. His scheme failed, and the inertia behind the New Deal slowed.

Despite years of experimentation, the New Deal failed to jump-start the economy. In fact, there was yet another recession in 1937—nearly a decade after the initial Wall Street crash—that was perhaps the lowest point of the Great Depression. Tellingly, in 1939, Roosevelt's treasury secretary, Henry Morgenthau Jr., who was a fervent New Dealer, admitted in a private meeting with the House Ways and Means Committee that the programs weren't working.

"Now, gentlemen, we have tried spending money. We are spending more than we have ever spent before and it does not work..." Morgenthau said to the committee. "I say after eight years of this administration we have just as much unemployment as when we started."[25]

"And an enormous debt to boot!" replied Robert L. Doughton, a Democratic congressman from North Carolina—to which Morgenthau concurred. Of course, Morgenthau suggested doubling efforts to tax the rich to take care of the debt issue, but the moment was revealing. Despite the popularity of Social Security and some other programs, the economy was flat on its back and not looking up. Industrial output wasn't increasing, and unemployment was still at stunningly high rates, despite a little movement downward.[26]

But the American people have always been the bane of socialists, Marxists, and economic levelers. Despite the constant pressure to adopt increasingly aggressive left-wing policies, the United States didn't go as far as other countries in handing power to the government. In the 1920s, American Communists bemoaned the lack of desire for revolution in the US, to which Soviet dictator Joseph Stalin replied that they needed to dispel the "heresy of American exceptionalism." The American Communists knew better. Capitalism worked for the working man. He had no taste for revolution or the dogmas of radical theorists. Even in the depths of the Depression of the 1930s, there was a limit to how far he would go.

So what finally turned things around? The answer is somewhat complicated and still debated by historians. But a number of factors seem important. The onset of World War II certainly played a part. Many have attributed the wartime boom to the demand created by the war, arguing that the New Deal failed because the government hadn't spent enough. Others disagree and say that government meddling had actually prolonged the Great Depression and made recovery difficult, and the economy roared to life during the war because at that point, desperate to produce needed war materiel, the FDR administration dialed back its aggressive regulation of and rhetorical attacks on American business.[27]

Regardless, it's a good thing that turnaround came. The country was about to face the gravest external threat since the British burned down Washington, D.C. Fortunately, the nation was filled with men like Andrew Jackson, who, thrown to the ground, would rise again and fight with savage ferocity.

A Sleeping Giant Stirs and Slays the World's Monsters

John Quincy Adams, one of the greatest foreign policy minds in American history, said in an 1821 speech to the House of Representatives that the United State shouldn't go out into the world "in search of monsters to destroy."[28]

Through most of our history, that has been the case. Blessed with incredible affluence—a product of the industrious American spirit—and imbued with the notion that it was best to steer clear of Old World foreign policy machinations, as George Washington made clear in his farewell speech—Americans and our leaders generally avoided foreign entanglements when possible.

The same was true on the eve of World War II and well into its early days. Though some have maligned this reluctance to enter the war as isolationism, that is an unfair caricature.[29] The United States has historically been willing to use its military and economic power to protect its interests and rights around the globe. Recall when Andrew Jackson nearly called on the United States to go to war with France over unpaid spoliation claims, for instance.

Following the bloodbath of World War I, in which over one hundred thousand Americans died, the American people had an understandable reluctance to jump into a conflict that initially seemed to be a replay of a costly war from just a few decades earlier. Americans did not wish to solve the world's unending problems. But a number of dramatic incidents around the globe eventually made it clear that freedom for all people everywhere, even in the United States, was under grave threat. First was Nazi Germany's non-aggression pact with the Soviet Union, which allowed these two brutal regimes to carve up and plunder their neighbors unimpeded, starting with Poland. This coincided with Imperial Japan swallowing up parts of China and Asia in an attempt to subsume the continent under their brutal East Asia Co-Prosperity Sphere. Then came the fall of France—which had fought valiantly while being bled white in World War I—after just three weeks of combat with the Germans. It was at this point, when Great Britain stood virtually alone, that Winston Churchill spoke of England's defiance of evil but also carefully alluded to the free world's only hope of salvation. It certainly wasn't the Soviet

Union, led by merciless dictator Joseph Stalin, who had gladly worked with Hitler and Nazi Germany when it allowed him to subsume more people and resources into his evil empire.

No, it was the United States, with all its power and might, that provided the last and really only hope for mankind. The moment of salvation was ensured when, in their hubris, the Axis foolishly chose war with America, first through a tactically brilliant and strategically catastrophic attack on Pearl Harbor by Japan and then by an even more foolish declaration of war on the United States by Germany and Italy. This came after Nazi Germany recklessly decided to invade the Soviet Union.

The Axis powers, by choice, had drawn the greatest economic superpower in history into a total war. This was perhaps in part because they didn't quite grasp the capacity of the United States, exemplified by one great American city in particular, and they deeply underestimated the will of its people.

Detroit at its height, was one of the great cities of the world and an engine of the US economy. The city reached its zenith during World War II. In 1941, Detroit had a bigger economy than all but four *nations*—Britain, France, Germany, and the Soviet Union.[30] The Ford Motor Company alone would produce more war material than all of fascist Italy.[31] And Ford's production, as incredible as it was, was still less than that of General Motors.[32]

The American economy as a whole was even more amazing. It emerged from the depths of the Depression as the most decisive factor in favor of the Allies in the war. It was not the New Deal but American businessmen and the legions of factory workers of all backgrounds who aided them that drove America's wartime economy. Unlike our day, when most of our country's successful corporations—like Google and Apple—are global rather than American—patriotic American businessmen put their feelings about the New Deal aside to come to the aid of their country in time of need: men like William Knudsen, the former president of General Motors, who worked with the administration to get American business to ramp up war production; Henry Kaiser, an industrialist who contracted to build the Hoover Dam and created the shipbuilding facility in Richmond, California, that produced staggering number of Liberty ships (one every four days at its peak); and Edsel Ford, who took over for his father as head of Ford Motor Company and whose Willow Run plant incredibly produced a bomber an hour at the height of production.

Though Roosevelt and New Dealers took credit for creating the "Arsenal of Democracy," as FDR called it in a famous fireside chat, it was truly American free enterprise that made it possible. It was likely Knudsen, one of the great unsung heroes of World War II, not Roosevelt, who initially coined the term "Arsenal of Democracy."[33] Knudsen convinced Roosevelt that to create the kind of production that would be needed to win the war, the government would have to stop meddling in the American economy as it had done the previous decade. "Mr. President, do you want statistics, or do you want guns?" Knudsen asked.[34] The president wisely chose guns, and an economic miracle followed.[35]

Incredibly, while the American economy was supplying the Arsenal of Democracy for the world, production of domestic consumer goods continued to climb during the war. Nothing like this was possible in the authoritarian economies of Nazi Germany or the Soviet Union, which had been turned entirely toward war production at the expense of everything else. Unlike those economies, which relied on force, regulation, and subsidies, the American economy was generally given a free hand during the war, with businesses providing the tools and government providing the organization to bring the fruits of manufacture to the battlefield. "The dream of an economy vibrant enough to produce both guns and butter had been realized thanks to American business…" as Arthur Herman, the author of *Freedom's Forge: How American Business Produced Victory in World War II*, has concluded. "No one had foreseen this except Bill Knudsen. He had sensed from the beginning that Washington didn't have to command or ride herd over the American economy to achieve new heights of production, even after a decade of depression. All you had to do was put in the orders, finance the plant expansion, then stand back and let things happen. And they did, in prodigious amounts."

Stalin himself told Roosevelt, Winston Churchill, and other leaders at the Tehran Conference late in the war that it was the American economic might that ultimately guaranteed victory. "I want to tell you," Stalin said to the audience in a toast. "From the Russian point of view, what the President and the United States have done to win the war. The most important thing in this war are machines. The United States has proven that it can turn out 8,000 to 10,000 airplanes per month. Russia can only turn out, at most, 3,000 a month. England turns out 3,000 to 3,500…the United States, therefore, is the country of machines. Without the use of these machines, through Lend-Lease, we would lose the war."[36]

What was critical about American wartime production, what separated it from the Axis powers and Soviet Russia, was that, like Great Britain, it was powered by free men and women working for a free country. This set the US apart from, for instance, Nazi Germany, which forced millions of European slave laborers to produce for the German war effort. An economy of free people can unleash productivity in ways that a society built on slavery can't.

German leaders seemed to be particularly clueless about the depth of American industrial strength, which perhaps was one reason why they so quickly declared war on the United States after Japan bombed Pearl Harbor. Hermann Göring, commander of the Luftwaffe—the German air force—mockingly said in 1942, "Americans only know how to make razor blades."[37]

"What can the USA do faced with our arms capacity?" wrote Nazi propagandist Joseph Goebbels in his diary. "They can do us no harm. [Roosevelt] will never be able to produce as much as we, who have the entire economic capacity of Europe at our disposal."[38]

It seems that German high command badly underestimated the sheer depth and capability of American economic might, and so did Japan. Even in the depths of the Depression, when many American industries, including the automotive sector, had been halved since the crash of 1929, the United States was by far the most productive economy on earth.

In World War II, American underwent what political scientist Walter Russell Mead described as a kind of "Jacksonian" awakening.[39] America had not sought conflict with the monsters of the world, but now our homeland was under attack; our way of life was threatened with annihilation. American industrial might, one of the wonders of the world, would be thrust into action. But machines alone could not produce victory. Dispirited nations, regardless of wealth, don't win wars on the magnitude of what the US faced following the Pearl Harbor attack on December 7, 1941.

"The Eyes of the World Are Upon You"

An initially reluctant generation of Americans, galvanized to action by the imminent threat to their way of life, was enlisted in a crusade to save human civilization from Japanese imperial aggression and Hitler's so-called Thousand Year Reich—which would have surely plunged the world into a thousand years of darkness. But the darkness would be quickly dispelled. The shining city on a hill would shine brighter. For the desperate people living under the shroud of evil, morning would come.[40]

While Great Britain kept Germany occupied in the skies above London and the Soviet Union was engaged in the great bloodbath of the Eastern Front, the United States, new to the conflict, had to coordinate and execute a plan to wage war across two oceans. It was a monumental undertaking, especially given the challenge of mobilizing what had been a tiny pre-war military. American leaders settled on a Germany-first approach, focusing on the greater threat of Nazi Germany than the more immediate threat of Japan.

It was eventually decided that a knockout blow could be delivered to Germany by landing in France and driving to Berlin. The plan was initially opposed by the British. Prime Minister Winston Churchill thought the Allies were not prepared for such an undertaking in 1942 and that an invasion of Italy would be a better place to plow through the "soft underbelly" of Europe. The Allies settled the disagreement by planning an operation to first drive the Axis out of North Africa, land in Italy, then commit to the landing in France.

North Africa proved a difficult but important lesson in warfare for the American military; Italy turned into a quagmire and mostly a sideshow to the greater struggle with Germany. Meanwhile, Soviets died by the millions battling Germany through Eastern Europe. The next phase would be the all-important landing in France. Army Chief of Staff, George Marshall, one of America's greatest war planners, was initially favored to lead the operation, but he was considered too valuable in Washington, D.C. In his place was put General Dwight Eisenhower, the man who would come to symbolize American and Allied victory.

Dwight Eisenhower was born in Texas but grew up in Abilene, Kansas. His parents were Mennonites of German descent, and his ancestors had arrived in America in 1741. He was a tall, athletic man and a graduate of West Point—which is likely where he grew fond of Robert E. Lee and Abraham Lincoln.[41] His West Point class of 1915 was full of distinguished military men, including Omar Bradley. It was called "the class the stars fell on" because it produced so many generals.

Though he never saw combat, Ike, a childhood nickname that became a popular moniker, rose quickly in the ranks and showed a marvelous aptitude for organization and diplomatic leadership—important skills for the coming conflict. When called on to lead the D-Day operation in France, he tackled the challenge with aplomb. Years of planning and buildup was required for an assault of this magnitude.

Eisenhower performed brilliantly in what was perhaps the most complex and important military operation in human history. Some believe that there were better battlefield commanders than Ike and that he had flaws as a leader and tactician. But it's unlikely that anyone could have cobbled together the polyglot group of Allies—Americans, British, Canadians, Free French, and countless others—and carried out Operation Overload, as the landing was called, better than Eisenhower.[42]

As thousands of ships and over one hundred thousand men waited in ships and planes off the coast of France, Eisenhower delivered a message to the troops to explain to them the great importance of their undertaking. Three centuries earlier, a tiny flotilla of ships had crossed the Atlantic and delivered a handful of Puritan pilgrims to the shores of the New World. John Winthrop told them that they ought to be as a shining city upon a hill; the eyes of the world would be upon them. In 1944, the ships went the other way. With this vast collection of free men under arms led by an American commander, the New World, which had been through its history a refuge for those escaping oppression, came to liberate the Old.

Channeling Winthrop, Eisenhower said to the men,

You are about to embark upon the Great Crusade, toward which we have striven these many months. The eyes of the world are upon you. The hopes and prayers of liberty-loving people everywhere march with you. In company with our brave Allies and brothers-in-arms on other Fronts, you will bring about the destruction of the German war machine, the elimination of Nazi tyranny over the oppressed peoples of Europe, and security for ourselves in a free world....

Good luck! And let us beseech the blessing of Almighty God upon this great and noble undertaking.[43]

Though Eisenhower had great confidence in the men he led, he understood that even the greatest of plans and military operations could fail. In the days leading up to the operation on June 6, 1944, bad weather had plagued the English Channel, and the invasion had been delayed. He alone was tasked with making the consequential decision to go ahead with the landing or risk further delays. In a tribute to Eisenhower after the German surrender, Churchill described the gravity of the situation facing the Supreme Allied Commander. "It was one of the most terrible decisions, and the decision was taken by this man—this very great man..." Churchill said. "Not only did he take the risk and arrive at the fence, he cleared it in magnificent style."[44]

Eisenhower knew full well the consequences of defeat. Recall that Ike admired the leadership of Robert E. Lee. He wrote a note that would be delivered to the public, accepting blame if D-Day failed, just as Lee had accepted total responsibility for defeat at Gettysburg. "Our landings in the Cherbourg-Havre area have failed to gain a satisfactory foothold and I have withdrawn the troops," Eisenhower's letter read. "My decision to attack at this time and place was based upon the best information available. The troops, the air and the Navy did all that Bravery and devotion to duty could do. If any blame or fault attaches to the attempt it is mine alone."[45] Fortunately, he never had to deliver this message.

Ike would take blame for defeat if Operation Overlord failed, but he knew where the credit belonged if it succeeded. It belonged with the countless men of unimaginable bravery who faced the vicious teeth of the Atlantic Wall, ran into the machine gun fire that sprang from it, dropped into darkness through the flak-filled skies, and scaled the cliffs at Pointe du Hoc. It would be their victory. It was not without suffering, death, and destruction. The German Army fought ferociously, and there was much chaos, confusion, and failure for the Allied armies. But eventually they prevailed.

The brave and the free who fought and died on the beaches of Normandy and throughout Europe were a testament to the strength and spirit of the people of the United States. Behind them was the awesome force of the American economy, which furnished the tools of war that no nation—or perhaps even collection of nations—could ever match.

"There was no sight in the war that so impressed me with the industrial might of America as the wreckage on the landing beaches," Eisenhower wrote of the Normandy beaches in his memoirs. "To any other nation the disaster would have been almost decisive. But so great was America's productive capacity that the great storm occasioned little more than a ripple in the development of our build-up."[46]

Liberators, Not Conquerors

From the beaches of Normandy, the Allies made the long slog to push Nazi forces out of France and back to Berlin. Much has been made of the Soviet destruction of the German war machine on the Eastern Front. It is true that the Soviets killed far more German soldiers than the Western Allies did—and with many times greater

sacrifice in their own blood. But it should also be remembered that
the Soviet Union began the war in a pact with the Nazi regime, only
flipping sides when Hitler invaded in June of 1941. The Soviets,
who had signed non-aggression pacts with Germany and Japan,
were largely responsible for the war becoming a global, all-consuming struggle.[47]

The USSR devoured Eastern Europe along with the Nazis, then
continued after the Germans turned on them. Stalin killed nearly as
many of his own people in the conflict as Hitler's forces. The Soviets
proceeded to plunder occupied nations for half a century before their
empire collapsed from economic and spiritual exhaustion. The Soviets liberated some, including the Jews at Auschwitz, then put everyone under the thumb of a new communist master.

The United States and Great Britain not only freed the people of
Europe, they went about giving them protection from the Soviet
menace after the war. This included their Axis foes, Germany and
Japan, which were occupied after the war but put on a path to inde-
pendence. The American victors were true liberators, not conquerors.
The distinction between them and the Soviets couldn't be starker.

Defeating Nazi Germany wasn't the only problem to solve. America had to finish business with the country that dragged it into war
to begin with. The dropping of atomic bombs on Hiroshima and
Nagasaki in August of 1945 after years of bitter war that was inten-
sifying as American armed forces neared the Japanese homeland was
not seen then as a great moral dilemma, as it is today. Dropping the
bombs ended the war within a month. President Harry Truman's
decision to use nuclear weapons has come under increasing scrutiny
in recent years. In some quarters, it is used to draw moral equivalence
between the United States and the Axis powers. That is absurd.

Given what a good international citizen Japan has been over the
past seventy-five years, it's easy to forget just how malignant the

country had become in the 1930s and 1940s. While we remember the genocidal policies of Nazi Germany—the extermination of millions of Jews and other "undesirables"—we tend to forget even the most notorious of Japan's atrocities: the "Rape of Nanking" following Japan's invasion of Manchuria in 1931, which horrified even Nazi observers.[48] This is not to mention the barbarous acts committed on American, British, and other prisoners of war.[49]

Dropping the A-bombs was merely the final act in the bloodiest war in human history, in which an estimated 50 to 80 million people died. The casualties from those two blasts were actually far fewer than those in the fire bombings of Japan in the months before—and also less than would have been produced by a full-scale invasion. Despite contentions that the United States was targeting civilians, both of the cities hit with the nuclear bombs were significant military targets. Some have used comments by General Curtis LeMay, one of the most aggressive military commanders of the war, to "prove" that the use of nuclear weapons was unnecessary. About a month after they were dropped, LeMay said that "the atomic bomb had nothing to do with the end of the war at all."[50] LeMay had actually wanted to step up the firebombing, which, given the effect of previous campaigns, would likely have caused far more devastation and casualties than the dramatic nuclear displays. Eisenhower, too, also after the war, privately doubted the need for using the bombs.[51] But given the enormous daily loss of life toward the end of the war and the increasing ferocity of Japanese resistance, President Harry Truman would have found it hard not to use the most awesome weapon at his disposal. The gruesome casualties at Okinawa and Iwo Jima and the horror of kamikaze suicide attacks were a preview of what was in store if the US couldn't end the war more through definitive means.[52]

The debate over America's use of atomic weapons has been distorted by the hindsight of seventy-five years' separation between

World War II and our comfortable world. The bottom line is that the use of atomic weapons against Japan was the result of Pearl Harbor and the total war that followed. As naval historian Samuel Elliot Morrison said of the attack on Pearl Harbor, "Never in modern history was a war begun with so smashing a victory by one side, and never in recorded history did the initial victor pay so dearly for his calculated treachery."[53] Millions of Japanese and American people are likely alive today because of Truman's decision to drop the bombs and put a decisive end to the conflict.

Without America, the product of Columbus's great discovery, the civilized world wouldn't have triumphed over brutal Japanese imperialism and Nazi genocide. America's Puritan faith, founding principles, Jacksonian spirit, Union, and Americanism brought about the victory of free people over fascism and then communist tyranny. It was only because Abraham Lincoln preserved the Union, Robert E. Lee showed Southerners how to raise their sons to be Americans, and TR embraced immigrants as real Americans that the descendants of Union soldiers, Confederate rebels, and second-generation Americans would march up the beaches of Normandy side by side. This should be a lesson to modern statue-topplers—or, if not to them, at least to people open-minded enough to consider that heroes don't have to be correct about everything to be great.

Despite Henry Ford's anti-Semitism, the Ford Motor Company became a key cog in the destruction of Nazi Germany. The machines built by a company owned by an anti-Semite bombed the most anti-Semitic regime in history to smithereens. History can be complicated like that.

Like Ford, the nation that annihilated the fascist powers and rid the world of their barbarity was not perfect. Nor was it a country that modern social justice warriors would approve of. The American military was largely segregated, traditional gender norms were rarely questioned, popular culture was full of racially insensitive material, and civil liberties were sometimes suppressed—such as, infamously, in President Franklin Roosevelt's internment of Japanese citizens.

Does this lessen America's achievements in World War II? Does it make America's moral authority illegitimate and our victory hollow? This is the issue at the heart of our current war on history. We now ruthlessly attack the sins of the past with no context and little understanding of the world previous generations inhabited. Instead of feeling smug self-righteousness about our superiority and selectively combing through history to find fault, perhaps it is better to take a step back and recognize that the good and the great can exist in a flawed world.

What unimaginable evils would have come to pass if Nazi Germany had ultimately dominated Europe? It is not a stretch to imagine our own time as, in the warning of Winston Churchill in his "Finest Hour" speech, "a new Dark Age made more sinister, and perhaps more protracted, by the lights of perverted science." Churchill knew that this bleak future could only assuredly be prevented by bringing into the war the unconquerable power of America.

The United States emerged from World War II as the sole nuclear nation and, unquestionably, the most powerful country on earth. By the end of war, in some raw capacities—such as in numbers of ships and planes—the US had a military larger than the rest of the world combined.[54] This set the stage for the half-century-long struggle between the United States and the other power that emerged from the war: the Soviet Union.

The collapse of the Berlin Wall in 1989 was the last chapter of the "terrible twentieth Century," as Churchill called it.[55] Once again, the two great factors that had made victory in World War II possible— free enterprise and the United States military—proved decisive. In the great military buildup of the 1980s, the Soviet Union simply couldn't compete because all that it produced for war came from a shrinking pie while its people lived in deprivation.

It was a victory for capitalism over communism in the rawest sense: capitalism could produce far more than any top-down economy, and the Soviet Union's economy sputtered. But under the surface was something more than a simple contest of raw production. The American system was more moral than the communist one. America was one nation, under God, the Soviet Union was a nation in which the state was god. It wasn't just raw commercial success that triumphed. Communism had sapped the spirit from the Russian people. This was the message President Ronald Reagan communicated to the world with his reference to "the Evil Empire" and his challenge: "Mr. Gorbachev, tear down this wall!" A system that threw millions of political dissenters into prison for questioning the state and had to construct a wall to keep its own people from escaping would inevitably collapse.

In stark contrast, America, the shining city upon a hill, was—and today still is—attractive because it allows for a good and moral life in which men are free, religion can thrive, a man can keep the products of his labor and build for his family, and his government is held tightly in check. His God-given rights are protected from violation, and his fellow citizens—committed to the great nation that encompasses all of those things—willingly fight to defend them at home and abroad.

Our great nation—like everything else in this world—is fundamentally imperfect. But, to quote Abraham Lincoln, who corrected America's deepest flaw and saved it from the gravest existential threat it has faced up to our own day, "the last, best hope of earth" deserves to be defended. We Americans who love our country, know its history, and understand its unique place in the world must defeat the ignorant, ungrateful, and shortsighted vandals who are making war on our history.

Was America Ever Great?

"We're not going to make America great again. It was never that great," said New York Governor Andrew Cuomo on the campaign trail in late 2018 to an audience of mixed cheers and groans. "We have not reached greatness. We will reach greatness when every American is fully engaged."

It was a revealing moment. Cuomo backtracked after making the comment, acknowledging that perhaps America was great but had failed to meet his laundry list of ideological demands. Despite his later flip-flopping, it's clear that Cuomo originally thought his line questioning American greatness would resonate with voters. And with some, it probably did.

A reporter for the conservative media website Campus Reform went out into Washington Square Park in New York City to ask people if they thought America was great. The answers—from people in one of the wealthiest and most privileged cities in the United States—were disheartening to say the least.

"The idea that there was this once great America is pointing towards this false sense of nationalism.... What, it's talking about white America? Yeah, it's not great," said one person.

When they were asked whether they had learned about the concept of "American Exceptionalism" in school, their answers were equally disappointing. "I've never heard of it before.... I personally wasn't taught American Exceptionalism because I went to a very forward thinking liberal school."[56]

These interviews could perhaps be written off as anecdotal evidence. But a Gallup poll on the question "Are you proud to be an American?" has shown a rising trend of people saying, "No." In 2018, the number of Americans saying they were "extremely proud to be an American" hit an all-time low—with the numbers lowest among the youngest generations.[57]

If many Baby Boomers didn't quite hate America, they certainly didn't teach their children to love it. And therein lies the problem. Informed but unambivalent patriotism is being replaced with moral equivalence, ignorance, and outright hostility toward our country and its history.

Unfortunately, returning to Ronald Reagan's farewell address, this means we have done a poor job of transmitting an "informed patriotism" to future generations.

"[A]re we doing a good enough job teaching our children what America is and what she represents in the long history of the world?" Reagan asked. He noted that his generation, the one that won World War II, had received a love of country and an understanding of their past through family, schools, and even popular culture. But that was changing as the century was winding down.

"Younger parents aren't sure that an unambivalent appreciation of America is the right thing to teach modern children," he said. "And as for those who create the popular culture, well-grounded patriotism is no longer the style. Our spirit is back, but we haven't reinstitutional-ized it. We've got to do a better job of getting across that America is freedom—freedom of speech, freedom of religion, freedom of enter-prise. And freedom is special and rare. It's fragile; it needs protection."[58]

Reagan was right, but his warning went mostly unheeded. The fruit of that failure is that, thirty years later, there is an aggressive movement committed not only to attacking America's history, obscur-ing or distorting its foundational ideas, and maligning its culture, but to literally knocking the physical symbols of our past off their pedes-tals. These radical demands are met with ambivalence and often encouragement on the part of school administrations and administra-tors and with silence from those who have been cowed by fear.

America now looks at an uneasy future in which its best men and ideas are being forgotten or maligned. The United States is bringing in more immigrants than at any time since the turn of the twentieth century, and many of the newcomers are from non-Western environments with little connection to a culture of liberty, civic participation, and free government.[59] Are there any Theodore Roosevelts around to infuse them with the spirit of Americanism?

It's a sobering thought, but not all hope is lost. The first stage in American restoration lies in rekindling informed patriotism. Making America great again isn't about returning to a fanciful past; rather, it's about restoring a better way of looking to the future.

American history is not an unending trail of rosiness, success, and progress. But focus too much on what is unexceptional about America—the flaws in human nature that are universal to mankind—and we can easily miss what is exceptional.[60] Human history is filled with atrocity. Real genocides occur all over the world, including today. These ugly realities are a part of the human condition. Civilization, freedom, peace, prosperity, and security are the outliers.

Today, we look at history backwards. Instead of trying to understand why America has produced so much good, we reject the past wholesale because it doesn't meet an impossibly high, ever-evolving standard. Tearing down great Americans isn't just harmful to our understanding of the past; it is poisoning our bonds of citizenship in the present and threatening to destroy our future.

It wasn't a handful of Constitution-shredding fanatics who liberated the slaves and saved our nation. It was the Union Army and the careful statesmanship of Abraham Lincoln.

It wasn't "alt-left" street punks who brought down Nazi Germany. It was hundreds of thousands of men in uniform—most of whom were racist by any modern definition—and the overwhelming force of American-style free enterprise. Compare the bravery of the Boys of Pointe du Hoc, who scaled cliffs at Normandy under heavy fire, to modern social justice warriors kicking an inanimate statue. Who has done more to make the world a better place? Deep down, perhaps, what the statue topplers are rebelling against is their own failure to accomplish anything of note. The only way for some of them to make themselves feel better about not overcoming any great challenges is to diminish great Americans who actually accomplished significant things and made enormous sacrifices to improve their country.

Raising statues to the heroes of our past is about more than just teaching history. It's about reminding new generations of Americans that we stand on the shoulders of giants—that to make our country better, we must have valor and courage, we must distinguish what's right from what's wrong, and we must do our best to carry on the best ideas and traditions of the people who came before us. This outlook enrages those who want to eliminate our history. In their minds, heroism implies inequality and perpetuates the notion that great individuals, not just historical forces, can move the world of men.

No one believes that the actions and views of even the greatest men of the past should be exempt from scrutiny. But that doesn't necessitate subscribing to the insane notion that they should be wiped from memory like Party hacks who lost Stalin's favor and were disappeared from photos in the Soviet Union.

The destructive urge of those who war on our history ultimately arises out of malice. It is driven by caustic feelings not just toward Americans of earlier times but toward their neighbors and countrymen. They have little in common with now celebrated critics of America such as Frederick Douglass—the escaped slaved turned abolitionist turned prophet of the American idea—and Martin Luther King Jr., a man who dared to dream of an America that would finally, fully commit to the idea that all men are created equal and deserve to be treated as individuals.

These men, while criticizing the unequal application of our principles, nevertheless committed to celebrating and expanding those ideals. Theirs was a philosophy of building up what was special and redemptive about this country, not tearing down old heroes or calling our foundations fraudulent. One doesn't have to be uncritical of America—past or present—to have a deep love and appreciation for its merits. That healthy attitude is being drowned out by the illiberal actions of mobs and grievance merchants. While we should publicly debate the actions, good and bad, of America's heroes, it is foolish to give in to the demands of such unreasonable people.

Instead of committing to the raw power politics of destruction and annihilation, it would be wiser for us to impart an appreciation and understanding of the great figures of our past. Regardless of the complexities, mistakes, and failings of the heroes in our history, it is undeniable that the United States was great from the moment of its conception and that it has been a remarkable force for good ever since. Just as undeniable is that fact that America is the greatest country for *anyone* to live in today, as immigration numbers prove; people from Asia, Africa, Central and South America, and all over the globe are desperately fighting to get into the United States because they know there is no better land of opportunity. It's telling that those who say that America and its past only stand for white supremacy and oppression would demand that these people be let in instead pleading for themselves to be let out.

If our country cherishes its past as it looks to its future, it will produce more Americans who deserve to be celebrated as greats: men and women who can inspire future generations as did Christopher Columbus, William Bradford, Thomas Jefferson, Andrew Jackson, Abraham Lincoln, Robert E. Lee, Theodore Roosevelt, Henry Ford, and Dwight Eisenhower. But if our country foolishly commits to erasing its history, it will have no future worthy of its past.

It is the duty of those of us who still believe that America was and is great to do a better job of defending what it means to be an

American, preserving the heroes of our history, and boldly going on offense as apostles of Americanism. We must demand that our institutions—our education system, media, and popular culture—quit attacking our heritage, restore what has been lost, and ensure that our future will not be a slow slide into the well-trodden and bloody paths of most of human history. Only by taking up this challenge can we reject civilizational suicide and win the war for our history.

Notes

Introduction

1. "Transcript of Reagan's Farewell Address to American People," *New York Times*, January 12, 1989, www.nytimes.com/1989/01/12/news/transcript-of-reagan-s-farewell-address-to-american-people.html.

2. "Abraham Lincoln's Lyceum Address," Abraham Lincoln Pre-Presidential Political Timeline, Abraham Lincoln Online, http://www.abrahamlincolnonline.org/lincoln/speeches/lyceum.htm.

3. Victor Davis Hanson, "Obama: Transforming America," *National Review*, October 01, 2013,. https://www.nationalreview.com/2013/10/obama-transforming-america-victor-davis-hanson/.

4. Potus8blog, "Barack Obama's Small Town Guns and Religion Comments," YouTube, April 11, 2008, https://www.youtube.com/watch?v=DTxXUufI3jA.

5. Katie Reilly, "Hillary Clinton Transcript: 'Basket of Deplorables' Comment," *Time*, September 10, 2016, http://time.com/4486502/hillary-clinton-basket-of-deplorables-transcript/.

6. Elliott Robinson, "Mayor Calls for Removal of Lewis and Clark Statue," *Charlottesville Tomorrow*, November 06, 2018, https://www.cvilletomorrow.org/articles/mayor-calls-for-removal-of-lewis-and-clark-statue/

7. Joy Pullman, "Mayor Proposes Grinding Thomas Jefferson's Birthday Into the Dust," *The Federalist*, June 19 2019, thefederalist.com/2019/06/14/mayor-hometown-proposes-grinding-thomas-jeffersons-birthday-dust/.

Chapter 1: The War on America

1. Ronald Reagan, "Proclamation 4873—Columbus Day, 1981," Ronald Reagan Presidential Library and Museum, October 9, 1981, https://www.reaganlibrary.gov/research/speeches/100981d.

2. Michael Pollak, "Columbus in Hiding," *New York Times*, October 09, 2005, http://www.nytimes.com/2005/10/09/nyregion/thecity/columbus-in-hiding.html.

3. "Columbus Triangle Statue—Astoria NY," Living New Deal, March 3, 2014, https://livingnewdeal.org/projects/columbus-triangle-statue-astoria-ny/.

4. Adam Brinklow, "San Jose Votes to Boot Christopher Columbus from City Hall," Curbed SF, January 31, 2018, https://sf.curbed.com/2018/1/31/16956286/san-jose-columbus-city-hall.

5. Jarrett Stepman, "What We Lose When We Take Down Statues of Men Like Columbus," The Daily Signal, February 01, 2018, http://dailysignal.com/2018/02/01/san-jose-caves-to-iconoclasm-will-remove-columbus-statue-from-city-hall/.

6. Cameron Cawthorne, "San Jose City Council Votes to Remove Christopher Columbus Statue" Washington Free Beacon, February 01, 2018, http://freebeacon.com/issues/san-jose-city-council-votes-remove-christopher-columbus-statue/.

7. "De Blasio Names Members Of Commission That Will Review Statues, Plaques Across NYC," CBS New York, September 08, 2017, http://newyork.cbslocal.com/2017/09/08/mayor-public-art-commission-christopher-columbus/.

8. Tina Moore, "Another Christopher Columbus Statue Gets Vandalized in NYC," *New York Post*, September 25, 2017, https://nypost.com/2017/09/25/another-christopher-columbus-statue-gets-vandalized-in-nyc/.

9. Joe Tacopino, "Vandals Behead Christopher Columbus Statue in Westchester," *New York Post*, August 30, 2017, https://nypost.com/2017/08/30/vandals-behead-christopher-columbus-statue-in-westchester/.

10. Associated Press, "Vandals Target Christopher Columbus Statues," *New York Post*, October 09, 2017, https://nypost.com/2017/10/09/vandals-target-christopher-columbus-statues/.

11. Jarrett Stepman, "I Went to a Vandalized Columbus Monument. Here's What I Saw," The Daily Signal, August 23, 2017, http://dailysignal.com/2017/08/23/went-vandalized-columbus-monument-heres-saw/.

12. Claire Voon, "225-Year-Old Columbus Monument in Baltimore Attacked with Sledgehammer," Hyperallergic, August 21, 2017, https://hyperallergic.com/396743/christopher-columbus-baltimore-attack/.

13. Carol Lawson, "History Proving Harder to Celebrate," *New York Times*, August 14, 1988, 2018. http://www.nytimes.com/1988/08/14/us/history-proving-harder-to-celebrate.html.

14. "Political Correctness: There Go the Coat Sales," *Time*, January 27, 1992, http://content.time.com/time/subscriber/article/0,33009,974727,00.html.

15. Nolan Feeney, "Indigenous Peoples Day: How the Columbus Day Alternative Came to Be," *Time*, October 13, 2014, http://time.com/3495071/indigenous-peoples-day/.

16. G. Scott Thomas, "54 U.S. Communities Carry Columbus' Legacy in Their Names," The Business Journals, October 10, 2011, https://www.bizjournals.com/bizjournals/on-numbers/scott-thomas/2011/10/54-us-communities-carry-columbuss.html.

17. David Zahniser, "L.A. City Council Replaces Columbus Day with Indigenous Peoples Day on City Calendar," *Los Angeles Times*, August 30, 2017, http://www.latimes.com/local/lanow/la-me-ln-indigenous-peoples-day-20170829-story.html.

18. See, for example, Deborah Netburn, "More than 140 Children May Have Had Their Hearts Removed in Ancient Sacrifice in Peru," *Los Angeles Times*, March 6, 2019, www.latimes.com/science/sciencenow/la-sci-sn-child-sacrifice-hearts-peru-20190306-story.html.

19. Phillis Wheatley, "To S. M., A Young African Painter, on Seeing His Works," Poets.org, January 04, 2016, https://www.poets.org/poetsorg/poem/his-excellency-general-washington.

20. Edward Burmila, "The Invention of Christopher Columbus, American Hero," The Nation, October 13, 2017, https://www.thenation.com/article/the-invention-of-christopher-columbus-american-hero/.

21. Brian J. Jones, *Washington Irving: The Definitive Biography of America's First Bestselling Author* (New York: Arcade Publishing, 2011), 233.

22. Jones, Washington Irving, 249.

23. Washington Irving, *The Life and Voyages of Christopher Columbus* (Forgotten Books, 2017), 4.

24. Howard Zinn, *A People's History of the United States* (New York: Harper, 2017), 1–9; Stepman Jarrett, "How a Radical Left-Wing Historian Birthed the Anti-Columbus Crusade," The Daily Signal, September 27, 2017, http://dailysignal.com/2017/09/25/radical-left-wing-historian-birthed-anti-columbus-crusade/.

25. Ross Wolfe, "Soviet Avant-Garde Submissions for the 1929 Memorial to Christopher Columbus in Santo Domingo," The Charnel-House, October 10, 2016, https://thecharnelhouse.org/2012/09/19/soviet-avant-garde-submissions-for-the-1929-international-competition-to-design-a-memorial-to-christopher-columbus-in-santo-domingo/.

26. Jarrett Stepman, "The Truth About Columbus," The Daily Signal, October 07, 2017, 2018, http://dailysignal.com/2017/10/06/the-truth-about-columbus/.

27. "K. of C. History Revisionists Taken to Task," Fellowship: The Forum, July 22, 1922.

28. "Benjamin Harrison: Proclamation 335-400th Anniversary of the Discovery of America by Columbus—July 21, 1892," The American Presidency Project, http://www.presidency.ucsb.edu/ws/?pid=71118.

29. Carold Lowery Delaney, *Columbus and the Quest for Jerusalem* (London: Duckworth, 2013), 1.

30. Carold Lowery Delaney, *Columbus and the Quest for Jerusalem*, 18.

31. Samuel Eliot Morison, *The Great Explorers: The European Discovery of America* (New York: Oxford University Press, 1986), xii.

32. Samuel Eliot Morison, *Admiral of the Ocean Sea: A Life of Christopher Columbus* (Little, Brown and Company), 24.

33. Zinn, *A People's History*, 3–4.

34. John Michael Cohen and Christopher Colombo, *The Four Voyages of Christopher Columbus: Being His Own Log-book, Letters and Dispatches with Connecting Narrative Drawn from the Life of the Admiral by His Son Hernando Colon and Other Contemporary Historians* (London: Penguin Books, 2008), 38.

35. Carol Lowery Delaney, *Columbus and the Quest for Jerusalem* (London: Duckworth, 2013), 29.

36. *The Travels of Sir John Mandeville* (Robbins Library Digital Project), http://d.lib.rochester.edu/crusades/text/the-travels-of-sir-john-mandeville.

37. James Reston, *Dogs of God: Columbus, the Inquisition, and the Defeat of the Moors* (London: Faber, 2007), 135.

38. Reston, *Dogs of God*, 166.

39. Irving, *The Life and Voyages of Christopher* Columbus, 42–43.

40. Morison, *Admiral of the Ocean Sea*, Boston: Little, Brown, 89.

41. Reston, *Dogs of God*, xvii.

42. John Fiske, *The Discovery of America: With Some Account of Ancient America and the Spanish Conquest* (Boston and New York: Houghton, Mifflin, and Company 1897), Gutenberg, https://www.gutenberg.org/files/27253/27253-h/27253-h.htm.

43. Morison, *Admiral of the Ocean Sea*, 26.

44. Reston, Dogs of God, 13.

45. "Santa María," Encyclopædia Britannica, April 08, 2016, https://www.britannica.com/topic/Santa-Maria-ship.

46. *The Columbus Encyclopedia* (New York, NY: Simon & Schuster, 1992), 515.

47. Morison, *Admiral of the Ocean Sea*, 183–95.

48. Ibid., 195.

49. Ibid., 215.

50. Delaney, *Columbus and the Quest for Jerusalem*, 91.

51. Cohen and Colombo, *The Four Voyages of Christopher Columbus*, 39.

52. Delaney, *Columbus and the Quest for Jerusalem*, 181.

53. Morison, *Admiral of the Ocean Sea*, 669.

54. Ibid., 671.

55. Bartolomé De Las Casas, *The Devastation of the Indies: A Brief Account* (Baltimore: Johns Hopkins University Press, 1996), 3.

56. Cohen and Colombo, *The Four Voyages of Christopher Columbus*, 56.

57. Delaney, *Columbus and the Quest for Jerusalem*, 238.

58. "Why Columbus Sailed," Knights of Columbus Home, http://www.kofc. org/en/columbia/detail/2012_06_columbus_interview.html.

59. Irving, *The Life and Voyages of Christopher* Columbus, 320.

60. Ibid., 75.

61. Delaney, 99.

62. Ibid., 142.

63. Ibid.

64. Lawrence H. Keeley, *War before Civilization: The Myth of the Peaceful Savage* (Oxford University Press, 1996), 105.

65. David Carrasco, *City of Sacrifice: The Aztec Empire and the Role of Violence in Civilization* (Boston: Beacon Press, 2000), 67–68.

66. Morison, *The Great Explorers*, xvii.

Chapter 2: The War on Thanksgiving

1. Belen Fernandez, "Giving Thanks and Whitewashing Genocide," Al Jazeera, November 23, 2017, https://www.aljazeera.com/indepth/opinion/ thanksgiving-annual-genocide-whitewash-171120073022544.html.

2. Glen Ford, "American Thanksgiving: A Pure Glorification of Racist Barbarity," Global Research, November 26, 2014, https://www. globalresearch.ca/american-thanksgiving-a-pure-glorification-of-racist-barbarity/5359622.

3. Rob Shimshock, "Yale Covers Up Gun in Stone Carving of Puritan, Indian," The Daily Signal, August 11, 2017, https://www.dailysignal. com/2017/08/11/yale-covers-up-gun-in-stone-carving-of-puritan-indian/.

4. Kyle Smith, "Yale's Disgraceful Whitewashing of History Continues," *National Review*, August 14, 2017, https://www.nationalreview. com/2017/08/yale-erases-history-campus-statue-covered-appeasing- activist-mob/.

5. Mark A. Branch, "Disarmament (Updated)," Yale Alumni Magazine, August 9, 2017, https://yalealumnimagazine.com/blog_posts/2695- disarmament.

6. Amity Shlaes, *The Forgotten Man* (HarperCollins, 2013), 20.

7. "Calvin Coolidge: Address to the American Society of Newspaper Editors, Washington, D.C.—January 17, 1925" The American Presidency Project, http://www.presidency.ucsb.edu/ws/?pid=24180.

8. Joseph Lynn Dubbert, *The Puritan in Babylon: William Allen White* (Toronto: Macmillan Company, 1967), 173.

9. Edmund Sears Morgan, *The Puritan Dilemma: The Story of John Winthrop* (New York: Pearson Longman, 2007), xi.

10. Walter A. McDougall, *Freedom Just around the Corner: A New American History*, 1585–1828 (New York: Perennial, 2005), 106–9.

11. Walter A. McDougall, *Freedom Just around the Corner*, 22–23.

12. Rod Gragg, *The Pilgrim Chronicles: An Eyewitness History of the Pilgrims and the Founding of Plymouth Colony* (Perseus Distribution Services, 2014. 49–50.

13. Gragg, *The Pilgrim Chronicles*, 87–98.

14. Nathaniel Philbrick, *Mayflower: A Story of Courage, Community, and War* (New York: Penguin Books, 2007), 7.

15. William Bradford, *Of Plymouth Plantation* (Great Neck Publishing, 2009), xi.

16. Gragg, *The Pilgrim Chronicles*, 101.

17. Philbrick, *Mayflower*, 46.

18. Bradford, *Of Plymouth Plantation*, 43.

19. "Mayflower Compact : 1620," Avalon Project: Documents in Law, History and Diplomacy, accessed August 31, 2018. http://avalon.law. yale.edu/17th_century/mayflower.asp.

20. Philbrick, *Mayflower*, 41.

21. Jarrett Stepman. "The Latest Political Correctness Crusade Targets Sessions for Using Term Obama Also Used," The Daily Signal, February 13, 2018, https://www.dailysignal.com/2018/02/13/latest-political-correctness-crusade-targets-sessions-using-term-obama-also-used/.

22. Bradford, *Of Plymouth Plantation*, 50.

23. Ibid., 52.

24. Philbrick, *Mayflower*, 117.

25. Michael Franc, "Pilgrims Beat 'Communism' With Free Market," The Heritage Foundation, https://www.heritage.org/markets-and-finance/commentary/pilgrims-beat-communism-free-market.

26. Bradford, *Of Plymouth Plantation*, 75.

27. "How Private Property Saved the Pilgrims," Hoover Institution, https://www.hoover.org/research/how-private-property-saved-pilgrims.

28. Bradford, *Of Plymouth Plantation*, 76.

29. Alexis de Tocqueville, *Democracy in America*, Gutenberg, August 31, 2018, https://www.gutenberg.org/files/815/815-h/815-h.htm.

30. Francis J. Bremer, *John Winthrop America's Forgotten Founding Father* (New York: Oxford University Press, 2005), 157.

31. Ibid., 159.

32. Ibid., 173–84.

33. "Copy of 1961-01-09 Massachusetts General Court," John F. Kennedy Presidential Library and Museum, https://www.jfklibrary.org/Asset-Viewer/ohJztSnpVo6qFJUT9etUZQ.aspx.

34. Tocqueville, *Democracy in America*.

35. Howard Zinn, *A People's History of the United States* (New York: Harper, 2017), 14–16.

36. Bremer, *John Winthrop*, 262–63.

37. H. R. Boughton, "The Pequot War," Howard Zinn Refuted, January 01, 1970, http://howardzinnrefuted.blogspot.com/2017/02/the-pequot-war.html.

38. Lawrence H. Keeley, *War before Civilization: The Myth of the Peaceful Savage* (Oxford University Press, 1996), 88–89.

39. Keeley, *War before Civilization*, 108–12

40. Ibid., 169–71

41. Howard Zinn, *A People's History of the United States* (New York, NY: Harper, 2017), 16.

42. Winston Churchill, *The Great Republic* (New York: Random House, 2000), 35.

43. "Thanksgiving Proclamation, 3 October 1789," Founders Online, National Archives and Records Administration, https://founders. archives.gov/documents/Washington/05-04-02-0091.

44. Sanford Kessler, "Tocqueville's Puritans: Christianity and the American Founding," Journal of Politics 54, no. 3 (1992): 776–92, doi:10.2307/2132311.

45. Robert V. Remini, *Daniel Webster: The Man and His Time* (New York: W. W. Norton, 2015), 178-79.

46. "The Plymouth Oration (December 22, 1820)," Column Chromatography, https://www.dartmouth.edu/~dwebster/speeches/ plymouth-oration.html.

47. "Sarah Josepha Hale," Godey's Lady's Books, http://www.uvm.edu/~hag/ godey/hale.html.

48. Peggy M. Baker, " The Godmother of Thanksgiving: The Story of Sarah Josepha Hale," Pilgrim Hall Museum, 2007, http://www. pilgrimhallmuseum.org/pdf/Godmother_of_Thanksgiving.pdf.

49. Abraham Lincoln, "Thanksgiving Proclamation," Abraham Lincoln Pre-Presidential Political Timeline, http://www.abrahamlincolnonline.org/ lincoln/speeches/thanks.htm.

50. Catey Hill, "Americans Are the Most Generous People in the World," MarketWatch, June 16, 2015, https://www.marketwatch.com/story/ americans-are-the-most-generous-people-in-the-world-2015-06-16.

51. Daniel J. Mitchell, "Americans Are More Charitable than 'Socially Conscious' Europeans," Foundation for Economic Education, February 03, 2017, https://fee.org/articles/americans-are-more-charitable-than-socially-conscious-europeans/.

52. Paul Bedard, "Americans Are World's Most Charitable, Top 1% Provide 1/3rd of All Donations," *Washington Examiner*, January 19, 2016,

https://www.washingtonexaminer.com/americans-are-worlds-most-charitable-top-1-provide-1-3rd-of-all-donations.

53. Brian Doherty, "The Corporate Christian Conspiracy?" Reason, November 22, 2015, https://reason.com/archives/2015/11/22/the-corporate-christian-conspi/1.

54. Alexis Charles Henri Tocqueville, *L'ancien Regime: The Old Regime and the French Revolution* (New York: Doubleday, 1955), 208–11.

55. Kessler, "Tocqueville's Puritans," 776–92.

Chapter 3: The War on The Founding

1. Bernard Mayo, *Jefferson Himself* (University Press of Virginia, 1942).

2. Kristine Phillips, "Historians: No, Mr. President, Washington and Jefferson Are Not the Same as Confederate Generals," *Washington Post*, August 16, 2017, https://www.washingtonpost.com/news/retropolis/wp/2017/08/16/historians-no-mr-president-washington-and-jefferson-are-not-the-same-as-confederate-generals/?utm_term=.aac53e9332fb.

3. Ronald J. Pestritto and William J. Atto, *American Progressivism: A Reader* (Lanham, Maryland: Lexington Books, 2008), 91–95.

4. Alter A. McDougall, *Freedom Just around the Corner: A New American History*, 1585–1828 (New York: Perennial, 2005), 209.

5. Matthew Spalding, "A Republic, If You Want It," The Heritage Foundation, https://www.heritage.org/conservatism/commentary/republic-if-you-want-it.

6. James Thomas Flexner, *George Washington: The Indispensable Man* (Collins, 1996).

7. Stephen Dinan, "George Washington's Church to Tear down Memorial Honoring First President," *Washington Times*, October 27, 2017, https://www.washingtontimes.com/news/2017/oct/27/george-washingtons-church-tear-down-memorial-honor/.

8. Jill Tucker, "San Francisco School Board Votes to Destroy Controversial Washington High Mural," *San Francisco Chronicle*, June 26, 2019,

https://www.sfchronicle.com/bayarea/article/San-Francisco-school-board-votes-to-destroy-14050025.php?psid=bKEYP.

9. Jarrett Stepman, "The War on History Comes for George Washington," *The Daily Signal*, May 20, 2019, https://www.dailysignal. com/2019/05/20/the-war-on-history-comes-for-george-washington/.

10. Henry Wiencek, "The Dark Side of Thomas Jefferson," Smithsonian, October 01, 2012, https://www.smithsonianmag.com/history/the-dark-side-of-thomas-jefferson-35976004/.

11. James Truslow Adams, Thomas Jefferson, and Alexander Hamilton, *Jeffersonian Principles and Hamiltonian Principles: Extracts from the Writings of Thomas Jefferson and Alexander Hamilton* (Boston: Little Brown & Comapny, 1932), xvii.

12. Francis D. Cogliano, *Thomas Jefferson: Reputation and Legacy* (Charlottesville, Virginia: University of Virginia Press, 2008), 137.

13. Angelina E. Theodorou, "Americans Are in the Middle of the Pack Globally When It Comes to Importance of Religion," Pew Research Center, December 23, 2015, http://www.pewresearch.org/fact-tank/2015/12/23/americans-are-in-the-middle-of-the-pack-globally-when-it-comes-to-importance-of-religion/.

14. Rex Bowman and Carlos Santos, *Rot, Riot, and Rebellion: Mr. Jefferson's Struggle to Save the University That Changed America* (London: University of Virginia Press, 2015), 135.

15. Ibid., 34.

16. Sanjay Suchak and Hayley Martin, "Mr. Jefferson Makes His Triumphant Return," UVA Today, July 27, 2016, https://news.virginia.edu/content/mr-jefferson-makes-his-triumphant-return.

17. Spencer Culbertson, "Board of Visitors Approves Design for Memorial to Enslaved Laborer," *Cavalier Daily*, June 12, 2017, http://www.cavalierdaily.com/article/2017/06/board-of-visitors-approves-design-for-memorial-to-enslaved-laborers.

18. Debbie Truong, "Thomas Jefferson Statue at U-Va. Shrouded in Black," *Washington Post*, September 13, 2017, https://www.washingtonpost.

com/news/grade-point/wp/2017/09/13/thomas-jefferson-statue-at-u-va-shrouded-in-black/?utm_term=.8383182f14e4.

19. Jarrett Stepman, "Thomas Jefferson Is Politically Incorrect at School He Founded," The Daily Signal, November 15, 2016, http://dailysignal. com/2016/11/15/thomas-jefferson-now-politically-incorrect-at-university-he-founded/.

20. Fox News. "Thomas Jefferson Must Be Rolling Over in His Grave," *New York Post*, November 15, 2016, https://nypost.com/2016/11/15/ president-of-school-founded-by-jefferson-told-to-stop-quoting-jefferson/.

21. Kyle Smith, "Al Sharpton Puts Jefferson Memorial on Notice," *National Review*, October 10, 2017, http://www.nationalreview.com/ corner/450537/al-sharpton-opposes-jefferson-memorial.

22. Forrest McDonald, *Novus Ordo Seclorum: The Intellectual Origins of the Constitution* (Lawrence, Kansas: University Press of Kansas, 1987), 287.

23. Thomas Jefferson, "From Thomas Jefferson to George Rogers Clark, 25 December 1780," Founders Online, https://founders.archives.gov/ documents/Jefferson/01-04-02-0295.

24. "John F. Kennedy: Remarks at a Dinner Honoring Nobel Prize Winners of the Western Hemisphere—April 29, 1962," The American Presidency Project, http://www.presidency.ucsb.edu/ws/index.php?pid=8623.

25. "Ice Cream," Thomas Jefferson Foundation, https://www.monticello.org/ site/research-and-collections/ice-cream.

26. Thomas Jefferson, *Writings*, ed. Merrill D. Peterson (New York: Library of America, 2011), 165–99.

27. Thomas Jefferson, "Letter to Henry Lee, May 8, 1825," Teaching American History, http://teachingamericanhistory.org/library/ document/letter-to-henry-lee/.

28. Charles Kesler, "The Nature of Rights in American Politics: A Comparison of Three Revolutions," The Heritage Foundation, September 30, 2008, https://www.heritage.org/political-process/report/ the-nature-rights-american-politics-comparison-three-revolutions.

29. Martin Luther King Jr., "I Have a Dream, August 28, 1963," The Avalon Project, http://avalon.law.yale.edu/20th_century/mlk01.asp.

30. "Trans-Atlantic Slave Trade—Estimates," Slave Voyages, http://www.slavevoyages.org/assessment/estimates.

31. Kate Hardiman,"Most College Students Think America Invented Slavery, Professor Finds," The College Fix, https://www.thecollegefix.com/college-students-think-america-invented-slavery-professor-finds/.

32. Abraham Lincoln, "Fragment on the Constitution and the Union," *The U.S. Constitution: A Reader* (Hillsdale College, 2012), https://online.hillsdale.edu/document.doc?id=216, 67–68

33. Dumas Malone, *Jefferson and His Time: Jefferson the Virginian* (Charlottesville, Virginia: University of Virginia Press, 2006), 228.

34. Thomas G. West, *Vindicating the Founders: Race, Sex, Class, and Justice in the Origins of America* (Lanham, Maryland: Rowman & Littlefield Publishers, 2001), 2.

35. Bernard Bailyn, "The Central Themes of the American Revolution: An Interpretation" in *Essays on the American Revolution* (University of North Carolina Press, 1973).

36. John B. Boles, *Jefferson: Architect of American Liberty* (New York: Basic Books, 2017), 59.

37. Boles, *Jefferson*, 471.

38. Ibid., 310.

39. Alex Storozynski, *The Peasant Prince: Thaddeus Kosciuszko and the Age of Revolution* (New York: Griffin, 2010), 279.

40. Boles, *Jefferson*, 287.

41. Boles, *Jefferson*, 470.

42. Annette Gordon Reed, "Thomas Jefferson and Sally Hemings: An American Controversy," The University of Virginia Press, http://www.upress.virginia.edu/title/2650.

43. Robert F. Turner, *Report on the Jefferson-Hemings Matter to the Thomas Jefferson Heritage Society, Thomas Jefferson Foundation and the Monticello Association,* April 12, 2001, (Charlottesville, VA: Thomas Jefferson Heritage Society, 2001).

44. Turner, *Report on the Jefferson-Hemings Matter*

45. Boles, *Jefferson*, 152–53.

46. Ibid., 153–54.

47. Bernard Mayo. *Jefferson Himself: The Personal Narrative of a Many-sided American* (Charlottesville, Virginia: University Press of Virginia, 1998), 109.

48. Ibid., 338.

49. Allen C. Guelzo, "What Did Lincoln Really Think of Jefferson?," *New York Times*, December 21, 2017, https://www.nytimes.com/2015/07/04/opinion/what-did-lincoln-really-think-of-jefferson.html.

50. Abraham Lincoln, "Letter to Henry L. Pierce and Others [April 6, 1859]," Abraham Lincoln Pre-Presidential Political Timeline, http://www.abrahamlincolnonline.org/lincoln/speeches/pierce.htm.

51. Malone, *Jefferson and His Time*, 226–27.

52. Eric Scheiner, "Jackson Lee: Abortion a 'Needed Action'; Refers to Babies' Heartbeats as 'Sounds,'" CNS News, October 17, 2011, https://www.cnsnews.com/news/article/jackson-lee-abortion-needed-action-refers-babies-heartbeats-sounds.

53. Ed Stoddard, "Obama Says Pointed Abortion Query 'above His Pay Grade,'" Reuters, August 16, 2008, http://blogs.reuters.com/talesfromthetrail/2008/08/16/obama-says-pointed-abortion-query-above-his-pay-grade/.

54. Thomas Jefferson, "From Thomas Jefferson to Pierre Samuel Du Pont De Nemours, 1 November 1803," Founders Online, https://founders.archives.gov/documents/Jefferson/01-41-02-0482.

55. Jarrett Stepman, "Louisiana Democrats Purge Thomas Jefferson, the Man Who Acquired Louisiana," The Daily Signal, July 19, 2017, https://www.dailysignal.com/2017/07/19/louisiana-democrats-purge-thomas-jefferson-man-acquired-louisiana/.

56. Jonathan Zimmerman, "Where Does MLK Fit in Today's #MeToo World?" *Baltimore Sun*, April 6, 2018, www.baltimoresun.com/news/opinion/oped/bs-ed-op-0408-mlk-metoo-20180404-story.html; Bill Bostock, "Sealed FBI Audio Tapes Allege Martin Luther King Jr. Had

Affairs with 40 Women and Watched While a Friend Raped a Woman, a
Report Claims," *Business Insider*, May 28, 2019, https://www.
businessinsider.com/fbi-tapes-allege-mlk-watched-rape-2019-5?_
ga=2.169311336.855689297.1559041605-2034880592.1556701637.

57. Peter C. Myers, "Martin Luther King, Jr., and the American Dream," The
Heritage Foundation, March 28, 2014, www.heritage.org/political-
process/report/martin-luther-king-jr-and-the-american-dream.

Chapter 4: The War on the Common Man

1. William Garrot Brown, *Andrew Jackson: An Interpretation* (New York and
Chicago: Houghton, Mifflin and Company, 1900), 154–56.

2. Dylan Matthews, "Andrew Jackson Was a Slaver, Ethnic Cleanser, and
Tyrant. He Deserves No Place on Our Money," Vox, Apr. 20, 2016, www.
vox.com/2016/4/20/11469514/andrew-jackson-indian-removal.

3. Jarrett Stepman, "Why Are Democrats Purging the Memory of Jefferson
and Jackson?," *Newsweek*, July 29, 2017, www.newsweek.com/why-are-
democrats-purging-memory-jefferson-and-jackson-639736.

4. Kevin Litten, "Live Updates: Take Em Down NOLA Wants More
Monuments Removed," NOLA.com, August 17, 2017, www.nola.com/
politics/index.ssf/2017/08/confederate_monuments_city_cou.html.

5. Natalie Allison, "Andrew Jackson's Hermitage Tomb Vandalized with
Profanities, Police Report Filed," *The Tennessean*, April 27, 2018, www.
tennessean.com/story/news/crime/2018/04/27/andrew-jackson-tomb-
vandalized-nashville/560046002/.

6. James Parton, *Life of Andrew Jackson* (Mason Brothers, 1860), 698–99.

7. Dan McLaughlin, "Do Not Weep for Andrew Jackson," *National Review*,
October 10, 2017, www.nationalreview.com/corner/andrew-jackson-
20-not-bad-thing.

8. Dinesh D'Souza, "The Secret History of the Democratic Party," Fox
News Network, July 26, 2016, www.foxnews.com/opinion/2016/07/22/
dinesh-dsouza-secret-history-democratic-party.html.

9. Jarret Stepman, "The Republicans Should Be the Party of Lincoln-and Jackson," *National Interest*, May 14, 2017, nationalinterest.org/feature/the-republicans-should-be-the-party-lincoln%E2%80%94-jackson-20640.

10. Hendrik Booraem, *Young Hickory: The Making of Andrew Jackson* (Taylor Trade Publishing, 2001), 99–100.

11. Parton, *Life of Andrew Jackson*, 113.

12. Russell Kirk, *John Randolph of Roanoke: A Study in Politics* (Liberty Fund, 1997), 138–39.

13. Carl Schurz, *Life of Henry Clay: in Two Volumes* (Houghton Mifflin, 1915), 120.

14. "Andrew Jackson: A Resource Guide," Library of Congress, www.loc.gov/rr/program/bib/presidents/jackson/memory.html.

15. Joesph f. Stoltz, *A Bloodless Victory: The Battle of New Orleans in History and Memory* (Johns Hopkins University Press, 2017), 52–53.

16. Andrew Jackson, *The Papers of Andrew Jackson* (University of Tennessee Press, 1994), 176–77.

17. R. V. Remini, *Andrew Jackson and His Indian Wars* (Penguin Books, 2002), 55.

18. Rebecca Onion, "Andrew Jackson Adopted an Indian Son. Does That Really Mean He Felt Compassion for Indians?" Slate, 29 Apr. 2016, www.slate.com/articles/news_and_politics/history/2016/04/andrew_jackson_s_adopted_son_lyncoya_why_did_jackson_bring_home_a_creek.html.

19. R. V. Remini, *Andrew Jackson and the Course of American Empire* (Harper & Row Publishers, 1981), 193–94.

20. Remini, *Andrew Jackson and the Course of American Empire*, 144.

21. F. P. Prucha, "Andrew Jackson's Indian Policy: A Reassessment," *Journal of American History* 56, no. 3 (1969): 527–39, at 527, doi:10.2307/1904204.

22. Prucha, "Andrew Jackson's Indian Policy," 533.

23. Ibid.

24. R. V. Remini, *Andrew Jackson and the Course of American Freedom* (Harper & Row Publishers, 1981), 210.

25. Francis Paul Prucha, *The Great Father* (Lincoln, Nebraska: The University of Nebraska Press, 1984), 64.

26. Prucha, *The Great Father*, 65.

27. Jarrett Stepman, "Keep Andrew Jackson on the $20 Bill," Breitbart, March 14, 2015, http://www.breitbart.com/big-government/2015/03/14/keep-andrew-jackson-on-the-20-bill/.

28. "Inaugural Addresses of the Presidents of the United States: From George Washington 1789 to George Bush 1989," Avalon Project— Documents in Law, History and Diplomacy, http://avalon.law.yale.edu/19th_century/jackson1.asp.

29. Richard E. Ellis, *The Union at Risk: Jacksonian Democracy, States' Rights, and the Nullification Crisis* (New York: Oxford University Press, 1989), 31.

30. Gerard N. Magliocca, *Andrew Jackson and the Constitution: The Rise and Fall of Generational Regimes* (Lawrence, Kansas: University Press of Kansas, 2011), 49.

31. Magliocca, *Andrew Jackson and the Constitution*, 45.

32. John Sedgwick, *Blood Moon: An American Epic of War and Splendor in the Cherokee Nation* (New York: Simon & Schuster, 2018), 193.

33. Prucha, "Andrew Jackson's Indian Policy," at 534.

34. Sedgwick, *Blood Moon*, 194.

35. Ibid., 245.

36. Ibid., 313.

37. Prucha, "Andrew Jackson's Indian Policy," 537.

38. Ibid.

39. Ibid., 537–39.

40. William Perry Pendley, "The New Trail of Tears," *Washington Examiner*, February 28, 2017, https://www.washingtonexaminer.com/the-new-trail-of-tears.

41. Jarrett Stepman, "Andrew Jackson's Inauguration Set a Precedent." The Daily Signal, January 19, 2017, https://www.dailysignal.com/2017/01/19/heres-how-americas-first-outsider-president-set-a-precedent-for-inaugurations.

42. Carl Schurz, *Henry Clay*, vol. 1 (Cambridge: The Riverside Press, 1889), 322.

43. Remini, *Andrew Jackson and the Course of American Empire*, 9.

44. Remini, *Andrew Jackson and the Course of American Freedom*, 14–17.

45. Ibid., 27–28.

46. Jackson (pseudonym), "Jackson vs. Hamilton: From Centralization to Jacksonianism—a Response to Hamilton," Breitbart, July 11, 2013, https://www.breitbart.com/big-government/2013/07/10/jackson-v-hamilton-from-centralization-to-jacksonianism/.

47. Andrew Jackson, "Andrew Jackson: First Annual Message—December 8, 1829," The American Presidency Project, http://www.presidency.ucsb.edu/ws/?pid=29471.

48. Jarrett Stepman, "Here's How Andrew Jackson Drained the Swamp," The Daily Signal, January 25, 2017 https://www.dailysignal.com/2017/01/25/trump-to-put-andrew-jackson-portrait-in-oval-office-heres-what-jackson-said-about-draining-the-swamp/.

49. Inez Feltscher Stepman. "Civil Service Reform for the 21st Century: Restoring Democratic Accountability to the Administrative State," American Legislative Exchange Council, March 15, 2017, https://www.alec.org/publication/civil-service-reform-for-the-20th-century-restoring-democratic-accountability-to-the-administrative-state/.

50. Andrew Jackson, "President Jackson's Veto Message Regarding the Bank of the United States; July 10, 1832," The Avalon Project—Documents in Law, History and Diplomacy, http://avalon.law.yale.edu/19th_century/ajveto01.asp.

51. Jarrett Stepman, "The Media Have It Wrong: Andrew Jackson's Legacy Was Fighting Crony Capitalism," The Daily Signal, April 22, 2016, https://www.dailysignal.com/2016/04/20/the-media-has-it-wrong-andrew-jacksons-legacy-was-fighting-crony-capitalism/.

52. Andrew Jackson, "Andrew Jackson: Farewell Address—March 4, 1837." The American Presidency Project," http://www.presidency.ucsb.edu/ws/?pid=67087.

53. John M. Belohlavek, *Let the Eagle Soar! The Foreign Policy of Andrew Jackson* (Lincoln, Nebraska: University of Nebraska Press, 1985), 126.

54. Remini, *Andrew Jackson and the Course of American Freedom*, 27–30.

55. Carl Lane, *A Nation Wholly Free: The Elimination of the National Debt in the Age of Jackson* (Yardley, Pennsylvania: Westholme, 2014), 201

56. Maquis James, *The Life of Andrew Jackson: Complete in One Volume* (Garden City, New York: Garden City Publishing, 1940), 621.

57. Lily Rothman, "Donald Trump: Andrew Jackson Civil War Question Answered," *Time*, May 01, 2017, http://time.com/4761335/trump-jackson-lincoln-civil-war/.

58. James, *The Life of Andrew Jackson*, 622.

Chapter 5: The War on The Union

1. Gamaliel Bradford, *Lee the American* (The Riverside Press Cambridge, 1912), 98.

2. Jeff Greenfield, Jeremy B. White, Aaron David Miller, Richard Sokolsky, and David Andrew Stoler, "House Restores Citizenship to Robert E. Lee," July 22, 1975, About Us, July 22, 2010, https://www.politico.com/story/2010/07/house-restores-citizenship-to-robert-e-lee-july-22-1975-040085.

3. Russell Berman, "The Nation's Official Memorial to Robert E. Lee Gets a Rewrite," *The Atlantic*, August 18, 2017, https://www.theatlantic.com/politics/archive/2017/08/a-national-memorial-to-robert-e-lee-gets-a-rewrite/537237/.

4. "Letter: Arlington County Should Change Its Logo," ARLnow.com, June 27, 2018, https://www.arlnow.com/2018/06/27/letter-arlington-county-should-change-its-logo/.

5. Rich Lowry, "Mothball the Confederate Monuments," *National Review*, August 15, 2017, https://www.nationalreview.com/2017/08/charlottesville-virignia-robert-e-lee-statue-remove-right-decision-confederate-monuments-museums/.

6. Christopher Ingraham, "On Confederate Monuments, the Public Stands with Trump," *Washington Post*, August 17, 2017, https://www.washingtonpost.com/news/wonk/wp/2017/08/17/on-confederate-monuments-the-public-stands-with-trump/?utm_term=.cb9ccb59bb2a.

7. "POLL: Most Black Americans Don't Want Confederate Statues Removed," The Daily Caller, August 17, 2018, http://dailycaller.com/2017/08/17/poll-most-black-americans-dont-want-confederate-statues-removed/.

8. "Whose Heritage? A Report on Public Symbols of the Confederacy," Southern Poverty Law Center, https://www.splcenter.org/20160421/whose-heritage-public-symbols-confederacy.

9. Will Racke, "Woman Who Destroyed Durham Confederate Statue Is a Pro-North Korea Marxist," The Daily Caller, August 16, 2017, http://dailycaller.com/2017/08/16/woman-who-destroyed-durham-confederate-statue-is-a-pro-north-korea-marxist.

10. Matthew Haag, "ESPN Pulls Announcer Robert Lee from Virginia Game Because of His Name," *New York Times*, August 23, 2017, https://www.nytimes.com/2017/08/23/business/media/robert-lee-university-virginia-charlottesville.html.

11. Jarrett Stepman, "Here Are 8 Monuments That Have Been Attacked Since Charlottesville," The Daily Signal, August 22, 2017, https://www.dailysignal.com/2017/08/22/8-monuments-attacked-since-charlottesville.

12. "Abraham Lincoln's Lyceum Address," Abraham Lincoln Pre-Presidential Political Timeline, http://www.abrahamlincolnonline.org/lincoln/speeches/lyceum.htm.

13. Jarrett Stepman, "We Went to the Church That Will Remove the Washington and Lee Plaques. Here's What We Saw," The Daily Signal, November 01, 2017, https://www.dailysignal.com/2017/11/01/we-went-to-the-church-that-will-remove-the-washington-and-lee-plaques-heres-what-we-saw/.

14. Eli Rosenberg and Cleve R. Wootson Jr., "John Kelly Calls Robert E. Lee an 'Honorable Man' and Says 'Lack of Compromise' Caused the Civil War," *Washington Post*, October 31, 2017, https://www.washingtonpost.com/news/morning-mix/wp/2017/10/31/john-kelly-calls-robert-e-lee-an-honorable-man-and-says-lack-of-compromise-caused-the-civil-war/?utm_term=.4ef488aa09c3.

15. John Daniel Davidson, "Shelby Foot's Civil War History Defends U.S. Against Insatiable Haters," The Federalist, November 07, 2017, http://thefederalist.com/2017/11/02/shelby-footes-civil-war-history-defends-america-insatiable-haters-like-ta-nehisi-coates/).

16. Jeet Heer, "Let's Relitigate the Civil War," *The New Republic*, November 01, 2017, https://newrepublic.com/article/145587/lets-relitigate-civil-war.

17. Joe Concha, "April Ryan to Huckabee Sanders: Does Administration 'Think Slavery Is Wrong?'" The Hill, November 01, 2017, http://thehill.com/homenews/media/358086-april-ryan-to-huckabee-sanders-does-administration-think-slavery-is-wrong.

18. "New York City 'Symbols of Hate' Purge Could Target Columbus Statue, Grant's Tomb," CBS New York, August 22, 2017, http://newyork.cbslocal.com/2017/08/22/new-york-city-statue-removal/.

19. Jessida Chasmar, "Memphis Protesters Take Shovel to Nathan Bedford Forrest's Grave," *Washington Times*, July 24, 2015, https://www.washingtontimes.com/news/2015/jul/24/memphis-protesters-take-shovel-to-nathan-bedford-f/.

20. Jarrett Stepman, "University of Wisconsin-Madison Students Protest Abraham Lincoln Statue Because 'He Owned Slaves,'" The Daily Signal, October 25, 2017, https://www.dailysignal.com/2017/10/24/university-of-wisconsin-students-protest-abraham-lincoln-statue-because-he-owned-slaves/.

21. "Lincoln Memorial in Washington Defaced with Expletive," Reuters, August 16, 2017, https://www.reuters.com/article/us-washingtondc-memorial-idUSKCN1AV2E6.

22. "Lincoln Memorial in Washington Defaced."

23. Britishpathe, "Eisenhower Explains about General Lee (1957)," YouTube, April 13, 2014,2018, https://www.youtube.com/watch?time_continue=103&v=mOrtOlU8f9Y.

24. "Ike and the Civil War," National Parks Service, July 5, 2017, https://www.nps.gov/eise/learn/historyculture/ike-and-the-civil-war.htm.

25. Jim Newton, *Eisenhower: The White House Years* (New York: Anchor Books, 2012), 251.

26. "Dwight D. Eisenhower: Remarks at the Birthplace of Abraham Lincoln, Hodgenville, Kentucky—April 23, 1954," The American Presidency Project, http://www.presidency.ucsb.edu/ws/index.php?pid=10218.

27. Adam Serwer, "The Myth of the Kindly General Lee," *The Atlantic*, August 14, 2017, https://www.theatlantic.com/politics/archive/2017/06/the-myth-of-the-kindly-general-lee/529038/.

28. Harry V. Jaffa, *Crisis of the House Divided: An Interpretation of the Issues in the Lincoln-Douglas Debates: With a New Preface* (Chicago: University of Chicago Press, 1982), 12–13.

29. Harry V. Jaffa, *A New Birth of Freedom: Abraham Lincoln and the Coming of the Civil War* (Lanham, Maryland: Rowman & Littlefield, 2004), 68–69.

30. Thomas J. Pressly, *Americans Interpret Their Civil War*, (New York: Free Press, 1969), 222.

31. Pressly, *Americans Interpret Their Civil War*, 226.

32. J. William Jones, *Life and Letters of Robert Edward Lee: Soldier and Man*, (The Neale Publishing Company, 1906), 123–47.

33. Jarrett Stepman, "'The Very Best Form of Socialism': The Pro-Slavery Roots of the Modern Left," Breitbart, August 06, 2013, https://www.breitbart.com/big-government/2013/08/06/the-pro-slavery-roots-of-the-modern-left/.

34. Gamaliel Bradford, *Lee the American* (The Riverside Press Cambridge, 1912), 98.

35. Fraser McAlpine, "50 Sir Winston Churchill Quotes to Live By," BBC America, 2014, http://www.bbcamerica.com/anglophenia/2015/04/50-churchill-quotes.

36. Bruce Catton, *A Stillness at Appomattox,* (New York: Doubleday &, 1953), 377–78.

37. "Chapter LXVII: Negotiations at Appomattox—Interview with Lee at McLean's House—The Terms of Surrender—Lee's Surrender—Interview with Lee after the Surrender" in Ulysses S. Grant: Personal Memoirs, http://www.bartleby.com/1011/67.html.

38. Douglas S. Freeman, *Lee's Lieutenants: A Study in Command* (Simon & Schuster, 2001).

39. Russell Kirk, *John Randolph of Roanoke: A Study in American Politics, with Selected Speeches and Letters* (Indianapolis, Indiana: Liberty Fund, 1997), 189.

40. Elbert Benjamin Smith, *Francis Preston Blair* (New York: Free Press, 1980), 283.

41. Jones, J. William, *Life and Letters of Robert Edward Lee,* 398.

42. Gordon Chappell, *The Civil War in the American West: Civil War Sesquicentennial* (Oakland, California, 2012), 36–37.

43. Joseph F. Stoltz, *Joseph F. A Bloodless Victory: The Battle of New Orleans in History and Memory,* (Baltimore: Johns Hopkins University Press, 2017), 52–53.

44. "Robert E. Lee to Jefferson Davis, April 20th, 1865," American Battlefield Trust, April 01, 2017, https://www.battlefields.org/learn/primary-sources/robert-e-lee-jefferson-davis-april-20th-1865.

45. Julain A. Selby, "General Lee's Views," *Columbia Daily Phoenix,* May 26, 1865.

46. Charles Bracelen Flood, *Lee: The Last Years* (Boston: Houghton Mifflin, 1998), 51.

47. J. William Jones. *Life and Letters of Robert Edward Lee: Soldier and Man,* (Kessinger Publishing), 386.

48. SOL Guide, http://www2.vcdh.virginia.edu/saxon/servlet/SaxonServlet?source=%2Fxml_docs%2Fvalley_news%2Fnewspaper_catalog.xml&style=%2Fxml_docs%2Fvalley_news%2Fnews_cat.xsl&level=edition&paper=rv&year=1869&month=09&day=03&edition=rv1869%2Fva.au.rv.1869.09.03.xml.

49. "The Left's War on History Continues in Austin, Texas," CNS News, August 2, 2018, https://www.cnsnews.com/commentary/jarrett-stepman/lefts-war-history-continues-austin-texas.

50. Ellen Carmichael, "In New Orleans, Political Fashion (and Ambition) Clashes with Historic Preservation," *National Review*, August 14, 2015, https://www.nationalreview.com/2015/08/new-orleans-louisiana-robert-e-lee-monument-mayor-mitch-landrieu/.

51. "Whose Heritage," Southern Poverty Law Center, August 5, 2019, https://www.splcenter.org/data-projects/whose-heritage.

52. Allen C. Guelzo, "A Yankee Visits Charlottesville, Where Gen. Lee Is Under Cover," *Wall Street Journal*, September 29, 2017, https://www.wsj.com/articles/a-yankee-visits-charlottesville-where-gen-lee-is-under-cover-1506724000.

53. Eugene Scott, "Most People Mad at the Removal of UNC's Silent Sam Don't Know What It's Like to Walk past the Statue. I Do.," *Washington Post*, August 21, 2018, https://www.washingtonpost.com/politics/2018/08/21/most-people-mad-removal-uncs-silent-sam-dont-know-what-its-like-walk-past-statue-i-do/?utm_term=.fa2bcecd6c09%29.

54. "The Soldier's Monument Unveiled," The Alumni Review, https://archive.org/stream/alumnireviewseriv1i6chap#page/184.

55. Jane Stancill and Andrew Carter, "The Unfinished Story of Silent Sam, from 'Soldier Boy' to Fallen Symbol of a Painful Past," *News & Observer*, August 25, 2018, https://www.newsobserver.com/latest-news/article217247295.html.

56. Booker T. Washington, *The Booker T. Washington Papers*, ed. by Louis R. Harlan and Raymond Smock, vol. 13 (Urbana IL: University of Illinois Press, 1972), 64.

57. John L. Adams to George Churchman and Jacob Lindley, January 24, 1801, Washington, D. C.

58. "January 1865: "War Is Cruel in All Its Parts … " Massachusetts Historical Society: 54th Regiment, https://www.masshist.org/online/civilwar/index.php?entry_id=1167.

59. Allen C. Guelzo, "The Trial That Didn't Happen," *Weekly Standard*, April 16, 2018, https://www.weeklystandard.com/allen-c-guelzo/the-trial-that-didnt-happen.

60. Abraham Lincoln, "Cooper Union Address," Abraham Lincoln Pre-Presidential Political Timeline, February 27, 1860, http://www.abrahamlincolnonline.org/lincoln/speeches/cooper.htm.

61. Jaffa, *A New Birth of Freedom.*

62. Jarrett Stepman, "NBC's Chuck Todd Suggests the Constitution Excludes God-Given Rights," The Daily Signal, October 01, 2017, https://www.dailysignal.com/2017/09/30/nbcs-chuck-todd-suggests-constitution-excludes-god-given-rights/.

Chapter 6: *The War on Patriotism*

1. Daniel Ruddy, *Theodore the Great: Conservative Crusader* (Washington, D.C.: Regnery History, 2016), 9.

2. E. M. Halliday, "Carving the American Colossus," American Heritage, https://www.americanheritage.com/content/carving-american-colossus.

3. Mazin Sidahmed, "Take Down 'Racist' Theodore Roosevelt Statue, Activists Tell New York Museum," *Guardian*, October 11, 2016, https://www.theguardian.com/world/2016/oct/11/museum-natural-history-theodore-roosevelt-statue-protest.

4. Emma Whitford, "On Columbus Day, NYC Activists Target Teddy Roosevelt's Legacy," Gothamist, http://gothamist.com/2017/10/10/roosevelt_natural_history_museum.php#photo-1.

5. John Patrick and Mary Altaffer, "More than 100 Professors Call for the Removal of NYC Statues in Open Letter to Bill De Blasio," *Washington Examiner*, December 14, 2017, https://www.washingtonexaminer.com/more-than-100-professors-call-for-the-removal-of-nyc-statues-in-open-letter-to-bill-de-blasio.

6. Joselin Linder, "Teddy Roosevelt Started the Museum of Natural History in His Bedroom," *New York Post*, https://nypost.com/2016/04/17/how-teddy-roosevelt-started-the-museum-of-natural-history-in-his-living-room/.

7. Michael Patrick Cullinane, "Why Teddy Roosevelt Is Popular on Both Sides of the Political Aisle," *Smithsonian*, April 23, 2018, https://www.smithsonianmag.com/history/why-teddy-roosevelt-is-popular-on-both-sides-political-aisle-180968870/.

8. Daniel Ruddy, *Theodore the Great: Conservative Crusader* (Washington, D.C.: Regnery History, 2016), xiv.

9. Theodore Roosevelt, "Birth Control—from the Positive Side," Metropolitan, October 1918.

10. Moseh Wander, "The Naval War of 1812: TR's Forgotten Masterpiece," *National Review*, April 28, 2018, https://www.nationalreview.com/2018/04/theodore-roosevelt-naval-history-war-of-1812-still-relevant/.

11. Theodore Roosevelt, *The Strenuous Life* (Birmingham, Alabama: Palladium Press, 2016), 14.

12. Theodore Roosevelt, *Letters and Speeches*, ed. by Louis Auchincloss (New York: Library of America, 2004), 778–98.

13. Eugene Volkh, "UC Teaching Faculty Members Not to Criticize Race-based Affirmative Action, Call America 'Melting Pot,' and More," *Washington Post*, June 16, 2015,https://www.washingtonpost.com/news/volokh-conspiracy/wp/2015/06/16/uc-teaching-faculty-members-not-to-criticize-race-based-affirmative-action-call-america-melting-pot-and-more/.

14. Roosevelt, *Letters and Speeches*, 374–76.

15. Ibid., 16–17.

16. Ibid., 347.

17. Theodore Roosevelt, "Address at the Lincoln Dinner of the Republican Club of the City of New York," February 13, 1905, Theodore-Roosevelt.com, http://www.theodore-roosevelt.com/images/research/txtspeeches/117.txt.

18. Ibid.

19. Roosevelt, *Letters and Speeches*, 244.

20. Ibid., 244–45.

21. Ibid., 465.

22. H. W. Brands, *T.R.: The Last Romantic* (Norwalk, Connecticut: Easton Press, 2001), 182–83.

23. Daniel Ruddy, *Theodore the Great: Conservative Crusader* (Washington, D.C.: Regnery History, 2016), 136.

24. Brands, *T.R.: The Last Romantic. Norwalk,* (CT: Easton Press, 2001), 263–64.

25. Theodore Roosevelt, *The Rough Riders* (New York: Charles Scribner's Sons, 1899), 19.

26. Roosevelt, *The Rough Riders,* 19–22.

27. Stephen Kinzer, *True Flag: Theodore Roosevelt, Mark Twain, and the Birth of American Empire* (S. I. Griffin, 2018), 43.

28. Roosevelt, *Letters and Speeches,* 175–77.

29. Cheryl Miller, "Americanism," What So Proudly We Hail, April 30, 2013, https://www.whatsoproudlywehail.org/curriculum/the-american-calendar/americanism.

30. Miller, "Americanism."

31. Roosevelt, *Letters and Speeches,* 405–6.

32. John Jay, "Concerning Dangers from Foreign Force and Influence for the Independent Journal," The Federalist Papers No. 2, The Avalon Project, http://avalon.law.yale.edu/18th_century/fed02.asp.

33. Roosevelt, *Letters and Speeches,* 750–51.

34. Ibid., 750.

35. Theodore Roosevelt, "Don't Spread Patriotism Too Thin," http://www.theodore-roosevelt.com/images/research/treditorials/m2.pdf.

36. Roosevelt, *Letters and Speeches,* 52–53.

37. Ibid., 52.

38. Ibid., 52–53.

39. Theodore Roosevelt, "The Man in the Arena," Roosevelt Almanac, June 03, 2012, http://www.theodore-roosevelt.com/trsorbonnespeech.html.

40. "Barack Obama's Berlin Speech—Full Text," *Guardian,* June 19, 2013, https://www.theguardian.com/world/2013/jun/19/barack-obama-berlin-speech-full-text.

41. Kathleen M. Dalton, *Theodore Roosevelt: A Strenuous Life* (New York: Vintage Books, 2004), 127–28.

42. Theodore Roosevelt, "True Americanism," Forum, April 1894, http://www-personal.umich.edu/~mlassite/discussions261/tr1.html.

43. Ibid.

44. Molly Prince, "Upcoming Neil Armstrong Movie Won't Show US Flag Being Put on the Moon," The Daily Signal, August 31, 2018, https://www.dailysignal.com/2018/08/31/upcoming-neil-armstrong-movie-wont-show-us-flag-being-put-on-the-moon/.

45. Brad Slager, "Why Hollywood Censors Your Summer Blockbusters," The Federalist, June 16, 2015, http://thefederalist.com/2015/06/16/why-hollywood-censors-your-summer-blockbusters/.

46. Jarrett Stepman, "Disrespect for National Anthem Damages NFL as Unifying American Passion," The Daily Signal, September 12, 2017, https://www.dailysignal.com/2017/09/11/disrespect-national-anthem-damages-nfl-unifying-american-passion/.

47. Mary Dejevsky, "Why Do We Treat American Nationalism as a Harmless Pageant?," *Independent*, March 16, 2016, https://www.independent.co.uk/voices/why-do-we-treat-american-nationalism-as-a-harmless-pageant-its-nothing-of-the-sort-a6934881.html.

Chapter 7: The War on the American Century

1. A. J. Baime, *The Arsenal of Democracy: FDR, Detroit, and an Epic Quest to Arm an America at War* (Boston: Mariner Books, Houghton Mifflin Harcourt, 2015), 285.

2. Julie Zauzmer, "Holocaust Study: Two-Thirds of Millennials Don't Know What Auschwitz Is," *Washington Post*, April 12, 2018, https://www.washingtonpost.com/news/acts-of-faith/wp/2018/04/12/two-thirds-of-millennials-dont-know-what-auschwitz-is-according-to-study-of-fading-holocaust-knowledge/?utm_term=.2f689553972b.

3. Philip Wegmann and J. Scott Applewhite," Democrats Can't Make Up Their Mind on Antifa," *Washington Examiner*, January 04, 2018, https://

www.washingtonexaminer.com/democrats-cant-make-up-their-mind-on-antifa.

4. Doug P., "Amazing! AntiFa/D-Day Hero Comparisons Caught on FAST in the Media," Twitchy, August 16, 2017, https://twitchy.com/dougp-3137/2017/08/16/amazing-antifad-day-hero-comparisons-caught-on-fast-in-the-media/.

5. Peter Beinart, "The Rise of the Violent Left," *The Atlantic*, August 06, 2017, https://www.theatlantic.com/magazine/archive/2017/09/the-rise-of-the-violent-left/534192/.

6. Steven Watts, *The People's Tycoon: Henry Ford and the American Century* (New York: Vintage Books, 2006), 396–97.

7. Catesby Leigh, "3 Reasons The Eisenhower Memorial Design Is a Disgrace to America," The Federalist, October 12, 2017, http://thefederalist.com/2017/10/12/3-reasons-dwight-eisenhower-memorial-design-disgrace-america/).

8. Lauren La Rose, "Canadian-American Architect Frank Gehry 'Very Worried' about Donald Trump," iPolitics, December 04, 2016, https://ipolitics.ca/2016/12/03/canadian-american-architect-frank-gehry-very-worried-about-donald-trump/.

9. Walter A. McDougall, *Freedom Just around the Corner: A New American History, 1585–1828* (New York: Harper Collins, 2004), xi.

10. Fred Miller, "Aristotle's Political Theory," Stanford Encyclopedia of Philosophy, November 07, 2017, https://plato.stanford.edu/entries/aristotle-politics/.

11. Watts, *The People's Tycoon*, 8–9.

12. "Greenfield Village Buildings," The Henry Ford, https://www.thehenryford.org/collections-and-research/digital-collections/sets/7501.

13. Watts, *The People's Tycoon*, xi.

14. Richard Snow, "The Wonderful, Horrible Life of Henry Ford," The Daily Beast, May 14, 2013, https://www.thedailybeast.com/the-wonderful-horrible-life-of-henry-ford.

15. Richard Snow, "The Father of All Patent Trolls," *Forbes*, July 30, 2013, https://www.forbes.com/sites/forbesleadershipforum/2013/07/30/the-father-of-all-patent-trolls/.

16. Watts, *The People's Tycoon*, 141.

17. Richard Snow, *I Invented the Modern Age: The Rise of Henry Ford* (New York: Scribner, 2014), 217.

18. Snow, *I Invented the Modern Age*, 223.

19. A. James Gregor, *The Ideology of Fascism: The Rationale of Totalitarianism* (New York: Free Press, 1969), 172–76.

20. "Ford Signs Agreement with Soviet Union," History.com, May 31, 2019, https://www.history.com/this-day-in-history/ford-signs-agreement-with-soviet-union.

21. Jay Franklin, 1940 (New York: Viking Press, 1940), 216–17.

22. Watts, *The People's Tycoon*, 438.

23. Ibid., 439.

24. John Marini, "Roosevelt's or Reagan's America? A Time for Choosing," Imprimis, August 31, 2018, https://imprimis.hillsdale.edu/roosevelts-or-reagans-america-a-time-for-choosing/).

25. Henry Morganthau Diary, May 9, 1939, microform at the Franklin D. Roosevelt Library.

26. Burton W. Folsom, *New Deal or Raw Deal? How FDR's Economic Legacy Has Damaged America* (New York: Threshold Editions, 2009), 248–49.

27. Ibid., 245–52.

28. John Quincy Adams, "July 4, 1821: Speech to the U.S. House of Representatives on Foreign Policy," Miller Center, February 23, 2017, https://millercenter.org/the-presidency/presidential-speeches/july-4-1821-speech-us-house-representatives-foreign-policy.

29. Ibid.

30. Baime, *The Arsenal of Democracy*, xi.

31. Arthur Herman, *Freedom's Forge: How American Business Produced Victory in World War II* (New York: Random House Trade Paperbacks, 2013), 218.

32. The Development and Growth of General Motors General Motors, https://www.gmheritagecenter.com/docs/gm-heritage-archive/historical-brochures/Corporate_GM_History/Development_Growth_of_GM.pdf.

33. Herman, *Freedom's Forge*, 115.

34. Ibid., 91.

35. Ibid., 334–35.

36. Baime, *The Arsenal of Democracy*, 257.

37. Joel Stone, "Detroit: The Arsenal of Democracy," Detroit Historical Society, https://wwii.detroithistorical.org/sites/default/files/pdfs/AoD_Paperv2.pdf.

38. Baime, *The Arsenal of Democracy*, xvii.

39. Walter Russel Mead, *Special Providence: American Foreign Policy and How It Changed the World* (New York: Routledge, 2009), 252–53.

40. Winston Churchill, "Dieu Protégé la France," The Churchill Society London, October 21, 1940, http://www.churchill-society-london.org.uk/LaFrance.html.

41. Paul Johnson, *Eisenhower: A Life* (Waterville, Maine: Thorndike Press, 2015), 1–5.

42. Max Hastings, *Overlord: D-day and the Battle for Normandy* (London: Pan Books, 2015), 28–29.

43. "General Dwight D. Eisenhower (Ike) D-Day Message: Order of the Day: 6 June 1944," Kansas Heritage, http://www.kansasheritage.org/abilene/ikespeech.html.

44. Winston Churchill, *Great Republic—a History of America* (Orion Publishing, 2015), 370.

45. Scott Simon, "The Speech Eisenhower Never Gave on the Normandy Invasion," NPR, June 8, 2013, https://www.npr.org/2013/06/08/189535104/the-speech-eisenhower-never-gave-on-the-normandy-invasion.

46. A. J. Baime, "How Detroit Won World War I," History.com, https://www.history.com/how-detroit-won-world-war-ii.

47. Victor Davis Hanson, *The Second World Wars: How the First Global Conflict Was Fought and Won* (New York: Basic Books, 2017), 513–14.

48. Iris Chang, *The Rape of Nanking: The Forgotten Holocaust of World War II* (New York: Basic Books, 2015), 6.

49. Gavan Daws, *Prisoners of the Japanese: POWs of World War II in the Pacific* (Carlton North, Victoria: Scribe, 2008), 18–19.

50. Gar Alperovitz, "The War Was Won before Hiroshima—and the Generals Who Dropped the Bomb Knew It," *The Nation*, August 5, 2015, https://www.thenation.com/article/why-the-us-really-bombed-hiroshima/.

51. "Diary Shows Eisenhower Had Misgivings about A-bomb Attacks," *Japan Times*, https://www.japantimes.co.jp/news/2015/08/05/national/history/diary-shows-eisenhower-misgivings-bomb-attacks/#.W4FuC5NKhE4.

52. Victor Davis Hanson, "The Bombs of August," *National Review*, August 23, 2018, https://www.nationalreview.com/2018/08/president-truman-atomic-bombing-of-japan-better-option/).

53. Samuel Eliot Morison, *The Rising Sun in the Pacific* (London: Little, Brown and Company, 1950), 125.

54. Paul Johnson, *Eisenhower: A Life* (Waterville, Maine: Thorndike Press, 2015), 177–78.

55. Lee Edwards, "Pursuing Freedom and Democracy: Lessons from the Fall of the Berlin Wall," The Heritage Foundation, https://www.heritage.org/global-politics/report/pursuing-freedom-and-democracy-lessons-the-fall-the-berlin-wall.

56. Cabot Phillips, "VIDEO: Millennials Say America Was 'Never That Great,'" *Campus Reform*, August 21, 2018, www.campusreform.org/?ID=11237.

57. "In U.S., Record-Low 47% Extremely Proud to Be Americans," Gallup, July 2, 2018, news.gallup.com/poll/236420/record-low-extremely-proud-americans.aspx.

58. Ronald Reagan, "Farewell Address to the Nation," The American
Presidency Project, January 11, 1989, https://www.presidency.ucsb.edu/
documents/farewell-address-the-nation.

59. Stef W. Kight, "The U.S. Is Back to Being a Nation of Immigrants," *Axios*,
August 30, 2018, www.axios.com/us-nation-of-immigrants-24723a19-
892a-4a7d-8298-f48c563f1526.html.

60. McDougall, *Freedom Just around the Corner*, xii–xiii.

Index